WAKE UP
to your
(W)HOLE LIFE

NOW is the time!

Created by Alaya Chadwick
Co-written with Lisa Scally

**Written for the benefit of self, other, and the world.
We are one.**

5/4/18

Remember you are precious and your Value is a given!

Love A

ISBN: 978-0-615-24749-6

Published by (W)hole Point Press

At the end of the games we played as children,
we would call ourselves back to "home" by singing out:

"All-y, All-y In Come Free!"

"Come out, come out wherever you are."

Now is the time to wake up, stop hiding,
and step into your own (W)hole Life!

Words From Someone Who's Been There

By Bob Stone

Simply put:
Here is the problem we address in this book.
Here is how we solve that problem with you.
Here is what makes us different from everyone else.

The problem is that life has a way of catching us off guard. Our world turns upside-down and our understanding of life can be shattered in a second. We become disoriented and feel like we are falling into the unknown. We do our best to avoid these scary, painful, lonely, and frustrating experiences. Whether subtle and almost invisible or dramatic, these are the experiences at the root of our suffering. Unfortunately by preparing ourselves to avoid the harsh realities of life, we simply end up numbing ourselves to our lives.

The Solution: The Wisdom basics in this book, solve the problem of coping with life's unbearable experiences by recognizing that we cannot cling to ideas of safety, like we would cling to a life raft in a storm. This book offers step-by-step skills, training, and insight that teach us how to stand on holy ground, strengthen our relationships with all that is, and to build an "ark" that will sustain us.

What makes this book different from other self-help or spiritual journey books is that the author does not simply write about abstract ideas. Her writings and her workshops share the practical wisdom gained from examining her own pain and buried grief. She makes visible the curious and often hidden elements of our inner worlds that determine how we experience life and the stories we tell ourselves.

Only through examining our own particular experiences and stories can we express in a logical way the "truth" of our lives. This book provides the tools to examine our experiences, our thoughts, our feelings, and ourselves in a way that transforms our view of the world and our ability to thrive in difficult times. The essence of The Wisdom WAY is the redemptive and healing power of speaking our darkest secrets, facing our deepest fears, and moving us to personal transformation.

We promise that if you invest a few hours reading you will learn to move with your unique body, to think with an open mind, to feel with a loving heart, to be a wise spirit, and you will experience your life with a new and extraordinary sense of aliveness and awareness.

Bob Stone a Vietnam Veteran, father of a grown daughter, and a Unitarian Universalist. For twenty years Bob earned a living as a procurement and subcontracts administrator. Bob has a visionary ability to integrate the impressions, words, and wisdom of complex emotional and spiritual issues.

What Others Are Saying About This Book

With wisdom, compassion, grace and soul, Alaya Chadwick weaves us a tapestry upon which we can journey for the purpose of, finally, reclaiming our wholeness and aliveness. We've thought that's what we were going to get as we spent hours and dollars with therapists, mainstream or off the beaten path.

Alaya confirms what we've long feared: it's a near impossible journey to complete with only a partial understanding of how one integrates psyche and soul. Yet here, in the hands of this storyteller, therapist-minister extraordinaire, we find what we've longed for.

Alaya gifts us with a guide that begins with the very holes we hide from self and others and constructs and completes a walkway that bravely leads us to our brand new and astounding home. Thank you, Alaya.

Sunny Shulkin, LCSW, BCD, *Master Trainer of Imago Relationship Therapy where she teaches Harville Hendrix, Ph.D.'s* Getting the Love You Want *couples workshop since 2000. Co-author with Pat Love of the book:* How to ruin a perfectly good relationship, *Sunny has been in practice in Bala Cynwyd, Pennsylvania for twenty-six years.*

Alaya's newest book offers readers an opportunity to discover the beliefs and attitudes (emotional holes) that have kept them from feeling fully alive and able to enjoy their everyday experiences. She offers readers a step-by-step practical yet inspiring method for reclaiming our own true self and waking up to our own 'strategic responses to life happening.' I was impressed with the detailed discussion of her process and the easy but extremely useful way she takes us all with her on this healing journey. I know that readers will enjoy this wonderful book as much as I have. It may even change your entire life perspective!

Meredith Young-Sowers, D.Div. *Director, the Stillpoint School of Integrative Life Healing. Author of* Agartha, the Angelic Messenger Cards, Wisdom Bowls and Spirit Heals

Weaving psychology and spirituality together, this book accompanies you along your own path toward your own unique (W)holeness – you being the fully alive and real you. The way is revealed in simple language and respectful compassion. I thank Alaya deeply for this loving map to us all. I LOVE IT. You will too.

Joyce Buckner, Ph.D, *Author of* Making Real Love Happen, *Master Imago Therapist, and Guest on the Oprah Show*

In her generous sharing of the pain and pitfalls on her own journey toward peace of mind, Alaya Chadwick outlines a more direct route to feelings of wholeness. You'll find the road shorter and less arduous if you honor the 'potholes' by consciously choosing to reshape or transcend them rather than by steering around them.

Mark W, Shulkin MD *Clinical Asst. Professor of Psychiatry, Drexel University College of Medicine; Clinical Instructor Emeritus, International Institute of Imago Relationship Therapy. Distinguished Life Fellow of the American Psychiatric Association.*

In our modern world where self-help techniques abound, the single determining factor as to a particular program's effectiveness lies in the answer to the question, "Does it work?" After years of traditional therapy that left me at a dead-end and stuck where I started, I found the (W)hole Point model to be a pragmatic and powerful process for successful personal transformation. I found my own experience with Chadwick's (w)hole work to be so positive and successful that I would warn others not to try it unless they really wanted their lives to be elementally different and substantively better.

Rev. Claudia A. Moore, MSW, B.Div, *Certified in the Wisdom WAY method, Reiki Master.*

When I first began working with the (w)hole point model I had no idea that I had a strategy for survival. I was amazed at the brilliance behind my strategy. As I used the model, I began to see that my meaning making was my survival strategy. I started to see myself and my past as a perfect path to my present life. I experienced feelings of hope, surprise and awe. In sharing this concept with close friends I have watched their perception of themselves and their situations change from one of victim to creator. The (w)hole point model offers a profound opportunity to appreciate yourself and your current life.

Patricia Miske BSEE, MBA *Technology Marketing specialist Certified in the Wisdom WAY method, Graduate of The (W)hole Point Institute, LLC*

In *Wake Up to Your (W)hole Life,* Alaya lovingly guides fellow seekers to fully and purposefully engage their own (w)holes using The Wisdom WAY map. Through the application of this practical and profound tool, you will experience a Portal that opens to the (W)hole Truth of your living as a Radiant Pulsating Being of Light. If the psychological and spiritual question, "Who do you say you are?" intrigues you, get this life-changing book and walk the path to "come home to BE!"

David J. DePalma, Ph.D, *Director HeartVoice and Author of* Remembering Your HeartVoice: The Guidebook.

A summary endorsement from Martha Harrell M.S.N., Ph.D.

Very seldom does a person come along with the unique gifts which Alaya Chadwick brings to this work. She is able to put hands and feet on extremely complex concepts in a way which connects them to the living reality of everyday life. This no small feat makes ancient wisdom accessible to a person opening to the experience of inner reality for the first time. With virtually no experience in psychotherapy or spiritual study, one can step onto this path and be well along the way to life-changing understanding in an amazingly short time.

Alaya is a guide extraordinaire for a person wishing to live a free and relevant life and go beyond just the consciousness of the individual. Times have changed quickly in the past decade. This model is an answer to the emerging culture of today which requires a more proactive response than the quiet reflective mode of psychotherapy. She and the Wisdom Way process are exactly what is needed to begin an awakening on a large scale.

Accessibility and simplicity of application make it an indispensable tool for assessing oneself in these volatile times. Alaya's highest accomplishment is to simplify things down to their bones. Her model reaches to the cause of our psychological and spiritual troubles, rather than their effects. To simplify something down to its bones is to reach the place where the opposites of our experience become complimentary, no longer fighting on the battleground of our emotions.

Bone and flesh exist together to form the foundation of a person. Bones hold the shape; tissue the movement. The Wisdom Way reaches back into the center of a personality to find the obstacles to the movement in each particular life. As it unwinds the story woven around the bone, it finds each person is a unique brushstroke of the divine, painted in living flesh, situated between heaven and earth.

The Wisdom Way is a map which guides you to take back your life from the dictatorial control of an outmoded defense system once constructed to save this very life which now strangles it. You find ways to break out of self-imposed limits that contaminate every interaction with yourself and the significant others in your life.

Claiming an "authentic and sustainable authority" is your birthright. Alaya Chadwick has devised a strategy to take back authority from our devious and critical judge and use this power to create a real relationship to our true and actual self.

Alaya lays bare one of life's great truths; at heart we are a paradox. As young children we are forced to turn against ourselves in order to save our emotional lives and sometimes our very sanity. We use blame and rejection to create a system that splits us into warring opposites. Most of the time, at great expense, this split makes life possible. But at a later, less helpless time, if the adult of that child doesn't want to live imprisoned in her desperate, but brilliant strategy, it becomes necessary to reject the very thing that once saved one's life.

The wonder and power of the Wisdom WAY's map to freedom is that it recognizes the dilemma of the human condition. With compassion and laughter Alaya helps us walk between these conflicting yet ultimately complimentary opposites. She helps us recognize the ingenuity, courage and creativity we use to save our lives. She helps us discover the freedom to be who we actually are. And, she does this with love, humor and play, allowing everyone to come to the feast table to celebrate the return home of all our parts.

The brilliancy of this path is that once you learn to use the map, the way home is lovingly put into your own hands. You are empowered to collapse all your own (w)holes whenever you need or want to. This system is particularly relevant today when the deadly environment of polarization with neighbor against neighbor threatens to destroy the known world. This system offers empowerment from within, uncovering a wholeness which can calm the agitated waters that threaten to engulf us all, not just the enemy "over there."

In the twenty-first century there is no longer an 'over there.' Home includes all of us, both inside and outside, over there and right here. A new day is dawning and the Wisdom WAY map is a bridge to link us to the promise of that dawning.

Martha Harrell M.S.N., Ph.D., *Licensed Training Jungian Psychoanalyst, Initiated Shaman (Andean), Continuum Teacher, Biodynamic Cranio-sacral Therapist and contributing author in* Transforming Terror: Reclaiming the World Soul

Dedication

Each word is written in service for the benefit of all: self, other, and the world. Placed upon these pages, a moment at a time, these words only come alive in and with the particular presence of you, dear reader.

The words and pictures you will find between the covers of this book are offered with my heart-felt gratitude for the opportunity to share with you what I have discovered about the mysterious wonders of Life Holes.

A hole is the metaphor used throughout this book to reveal the bare bones of our shattered (W)holeness **and** our path back to consciousness or (W)holeness. In essence, each time you read the word (W)holeness, a profound wisdom awakens within you. Called forth from deep inside your cells and your psyche, the truth of your (W)holeness is invited to move into greater and greater awareness.

I am honored to be in your presence and it is my greatest wish that The (W)hole Point Wisdom **WAY** inspires you to "Walk Awake saying **YES**" to every expression of life that you are – holes and all.

Dedicated to the (W)HOLE of US: you and me … us

Acknowledgments

It takes a village to birth a book!
Let me introduce you to my village.

My Mentor of 30+ years :

Martha Harrell – "M," my Primal Truth Seer, my Master Teacher, my Life-Long Mentor, and Mother of my soul, it is beyond words. Thank you for my life. Thank you for being Synthesizer of complexities. Thank you for your integrity and generosity of spirit and mind. Thank you for being THE bald naked truth presence for me over and over again. Thank you for birthing my soul anew and thus this book's wisdom. Thank you for your grace-filled presence.

Thank you to those of Martha's lineage: *Dr. Jonathan Goldberg* – a Wisdom Presence; *Carl Jung* – and all those who have gone before.

The midwives of The (W)hole Point Wisdom WAY model:

I wish to express my deepest gratitude and appreciation to all of my intimates who live their own magnificent radiance and who have encouraged me to live mine. These are the folks who have been in the delivery room with me as the words you are now reading slowly crystallized into being. In particular, I wish to thank:

Dorie Cameron – a Compassionate Presence - without whom this book would not be… holding hope and vision despite all appearance. A Teacher, Sister, and Friend to me.

Karen Kuhl – a Truth Speaker & Healer – who is a living wisdom presence for all around her.

DeeDee LaCrosse – a Healing Presence – whose words and being embrace all those she touches.

Suzie Moss – a Courageous Radiant Being – a person who lives the greatest gift of all: Friendship.

Judy Lewis – a Healer of depth and wisdom, a woman of grace & courage – always a steady embrace.

Claudia Moore – a Midwife of Radiance & Healing – a woman who heals by her commitment to truth.

Janice Welch – Angel of Sanctuary – a gift from heaven, a teacher of life's raw truths: leader to us all.

My precious teachers: the ones who went first:

Dave DePalma – a man of Solid Integrity – who saw through my fear and believed.

Harville Hendrix – a man who dared to look intimacy straight in the eye and then live it for us all.

Sunny & Mark Shulkin – a PAIR of people – who taught me that everyone's world is "right" for them.

Meredith Young-Sowers – a woman who believed in me the moment it really mattered: she said YES.

The Original Teachers of The Wisdom of The (W)hole Point Wisdom WAY:

Thank you for your openness to a new way of being, your courage to live it for yourselves and then sharing my joy of bringing it to the (W)hole World – one student at a time. You are great playmates!

Anne Suddy – the Ripple of Transparent Presence – a woman of courageous tenacity and healing authority.

Lisa Scally – the Light in the Darkness – a beacon of hope and possibility when all else falls away.

Steve Burison – the Heart of the Rock's Foundation – a hero of soul and heart, a man of bold abundance.

The Second Generation of Teachers:

Thank you for your presence. You showed me that The (W)hole Point Wisdom WAY really works – over and over again. It isn't about me; it is about a map that offers hope, clarity, and empowered choice.

Marianne DiBlasi – a special light in the world, dancing in her naked and ordinary presence.

Steven Scally – a bright presence of love, holding the light for all to see and find their way home to be.

Lizzy Derecktor – a bold splash of wisdom, singing her grand expressions without apology.

Rochelle Maustellar – a deep, quiet, flowing presence of wisdom and grace.

Jean Macdonald – a bright presence of gentle stories and bold wisdom.

My Parents:

Thank you for all the (w)holes you helped me create and all the (W)holeness you empowered me to discover and thus reveal the wonder of WHO I am! I love you, still.

> *"Bunny" Runyon Craven Cameron*
> *Howard T. Craven, M.D.*
> *Steele C. Cameron*

My Clients, Students, and Apprentices:

All of you who have honored me by sharing your journeys, your (w)holes, and your radiant (W)holeness. You are all my dearest and most precious teachers!

The Readers before you:

Thank you for your time, your attention to detail, your critiques, and your steadfast efforts. I especially want to thank *Myron Miske, Dee LaCrosse, Anne Suddy*, and *Amanda Johnson* for your insightful comments. Thank you to *Kevin Micalizzi, Linda Doty, Suzie Moss, Rick Felty, Diane Fuller, Cindy Carroll, Bob Welch*, and *Patty Miske*.

To The Wizard:

Charlie, thank you for your steadiness as I printed out reams of words and for never asking the question, "When will it be done?." The Edgartown@MailRoom has encouraged and supported me, for years, through all my writing efforts. Finally, these words are home, at last!

The "Ripple" and a Soul Sister:

Anne Suddy, thank you for standing in your full and powerful presence, on behalf of us all. Thank you for teaching us, that while shame and blame do cripple us all in some way, that the true glory & wonder of life is when this all falls away and we find ourselves dancing in play and celebration. Thank you for your precious Twinkle. Your steady presence and open hearted willingness to go into the darkest of places has touched more hearts than you could ever count- mine most of all. I am humbled in your potent presence. "Hey Anne, thank you for saying YES-again and again."

The "Big-Hearted Light Brother" to us all:
Steve Burison, thank you for being the one to teach us, all, the meaning of "What ever it takes." You have dared to be the first in so many ways: The first man to complete the certifications, The first man to mentor another man through The Apprentice Radiance Teacher program, The first man to shed his own tears on behalf of so many men, right in the middle of a (W)hole Shop. And, yes, the first man to bring his own father into this Wisdom WAY work and thus begin the lineage of The Light Brothers. Thank you for your open-hearted courage and naked human vulnerability. Your presence truly does matter to us all.

A special blessing to "POP": The Most Valuable Player (MVP) and grandfather to us all and "MOP," a walking "Welcome Home" presence. Thank you for giving birth to this precious man.

My editor & co-writer & Soul Sister:
Lisa Scally, thank you, dear soul-sister and friend and editor. I firmly believe that without your computer wizardry, your extraordinary attention to detail, your capacity to organize wildly disparate sections of this book into a coherent (W)hole, and most all of your big heart, this book would not exist. Thank you for your capacity to live this work in your life in such a way that has helped you craft words that capture the true heart and soul of The Wisdom WAY. Thank you for your dedication, your daring, and your (W)hole-Hearted Presence. Most of all, thank you for turning around and embracing the wonder of you. I couldn't have done it without you. Yes, your presence really does matter - "For no reason and for every reason."

And most especially my dear husband, John Richard Chadwick:
John, thank you for believing in me when I had doubts. Thank you for all you do and all you did that has supported the birth of this book. Thank you for being my husband and my friend. Thank you for being the first person, whose (w)holes I spun. Thank you for being the ONLY man in ALL the first (W)hole Shops of every level! Most of all, thank you for teaching me that I am lovable, (w)holes and all! Without you, I would never have dared to begin this 10-year long process! Thank you for being you. Your courage, your patience and your presence is and has been the foundation upon which this work rests. I love you dear Man of my Soul. Thank you, again, for being you.

Table of Contents

Greetings to You, Dear Reader

I decided to write this book for two reasons: You and Me.

My greatest joy is witnessing the relief and light of hope that comes into the eyes of those with whom I have shared The (W)hole Point Wisdom map.

Each time I would reveal The Wisdom WAY to someone – friends and family in the beginning and then students and clients – I would see a precious light sparkle in their eyes, a light that wasn't there a moment before. I call this light, "**Radiance.**" I want to offer this to you.

I would hear them say things like, "Finally – I make sense to me! I had thought I was stuck forever." "How surprising – what felt so overwhelming a moment ago is now manageable." "Now I know *how* to love myself! I have wanted to, longed to, hoped to, but I never could seem to take the concepts and make them come alive in my life." "Yes, now I see – it really is all up to me! And I can do it now, one precious (w)hole at a time." "I wish someone had told me this years ago!"

I wrote this book for *YOU*. Know that I celebrate, in advance, the Light of Radiance shining in your eyes as you, too, reveal yourself as (W)hole.

These are my promises to you:

By the end of this book,

- You will know The Wisdom WAY map of (W)holeness.
- You will know the basics for applying it to yourself, your relationships, and your spiritual awakening.
- You will be able to appreciate just how creative you have been throughout your life.
- And best of all, you will have the how-to's for loving yourself and loving your (W)hole life NOW!

I wrote this book for *ME*, for the joy of sharing Light. The promise I made to myself when I came to understand the potency of The Wisdom WAY was to share it. By writing this book, I am fulfilling this promise.

Blessings and Gratitude,
Alaya
Autumn 2008

Preface

My goal is to give you, the reader, a set of tools to allow you to become who you really are. This method of unlocking your inner self I call "**The (W)hole Point Wisdom WAY.**" This model is more than simply another empowerment tool; it is also a method, a map, and a means for purposeful, particular, and sustainable transformation.

This profound and yet simple map applies to anyone anywhere – individuals, families, communities, and even companies. This map reveals an essential pathway imbedded within the process of awakening to our own (W)holeness. Exploring the intersection between psychology and spirituality, The (W)hole Point Wisdom WAY is both radical and unique. It's radical because it extends an invitation for full participation in (W)holeness to both our human psyches and our essential spirituality – neither one excluded nor judged. It is unique in that it moves quickly in offering an applicable, practical, and sustainable approach to living our (W)holeness.

This is not a book about a theory alone, but rather, it is primarily a "Hands & Feet" or a "How-To" guide to awaken the (W)holeness that is already within you!

How The (W)hole Point Wisdom WAY is unique: The "Hands & Feet" of empowerment.

This approach offers a practical way to meld all of your psychology and all your unique spirituality into embodied (W)holeness or Oneness.

Psychological or spiritual practices alone only carry any of us so far. Held apart from one another, each is less than the (W)hole of ourselves. Have you ever attended self-development seminars which left you feeling that there must be more or feeling like "it's the teacher's way, but it's not my way?" Have you ever attended a lecture or read a book that spoke deeply to your heart about loving your-self, only to feel a sense of frustration that you didn't quite know *how* to implement these good ideas? Well, I have too.

Up until I discovered the secret of (w)holes, I was blindly feeling my way through the dark. All parts of this skeleton or Wisdom map were elements I had studied here, there, and yon. However, up until I discovered the map nothing put all the understandings together. I felt unable to use what I knew when I was standing at the kitchen sink, when I felt in the pits, or head first in a (w)hole.

I had affirmed, chanted, examined, and analyzed. Sure, it was all worth it, and each of these practices have been helpful and valuable. But before The Wisdom WAY floated up into my awareness, I would struggle mightily when the stuff that hurt happened. Which tool should I use? Is this the time to meditate or chant? Or I would wonder what is going on with me that I am in this messy place again. Does this sound at all familiar to you?

The absolute gift of The (W)hole Point Wisdom WAY is this: It works when you're standing in front of a sink full of dishes. It works as you are walking into a large corporate meeting. It works with your intimate partner. It is usable regardless of your background, your issues, or your emotions. Once you get the hang of it, you can apply it on the run or take time to draw it all out. If you know the map, you have the tools to live your (W)holeness one (w)hole at a time. If you are reading this book, you have a hunger to be all you are, not just read about how you should be this way or that way.

In addition, The Wisdom WAY is unique in that it is designed to empower each person to awaken to their own unique (W)holeness through the integration of **psyche and soul**. One without the other is less than (W)holeness. By definition, (W)holeness must include all ele-ments of one's being. The integration of our human psychology with our soul presence via a practical map and methodical approach that is based upon our own particular wisdom (no one else's), is distinctive indeed. The key is **how** to embody this process of unveiling our (W)holeness to ourselves not merely as a concept, but for real.

How to do this has been the stumbling block for many of us. Encouragement from friends, family, and society to embrace our fullest expression is not lacking. We hear this from all directions. What has been sorely missing has been what I call the "Hands & Feet" or the "How-to's" for awakening to our own (W)holeness. It's easy to find lots of books describing the psychological elements of this, and there are even more books offering spiritual practices

3

to support (W)holeness. However, the "how-to's" of melding the psyche and soul are merely hinted at or are available only through inference.

The Wisdom WAY offers a viewpoint which integrates these two elements into an awakening process, without dictating to you a rigid or stereotypical framework. Your answers and your individual process of awakening are empowered, guided, and supported through the (W)hole Point Wisdom WAY model. As you move through this book, you will be offered opportunities to apply what you are learning directly to your own life. Practical and immediate, The Wisdom WAY can be easily transferred from any situation involving one human being to an entire organization and to the interactions between organizations. I have called it "The Wisdom WAY" because it is based on your wisdom and experiences, not anyone else's. You are your own expert. This essential framework of empowerment lets you apply your own life experiences and follow your own wisdom to discover the truth that is waiting to be awakened within you.

One of my greatest joys is the process of translating complex life experiences – my own and those of my clients – into pragmatic simple processes which awaken and empower (W)holeness. May The Wisdom WAY serve you as it has served – and continues to serve – me and many others who have embraced this process of empowered awakening. This is a book that makes sense of the confusion by showing you how to sort and sift through all you know and all you have experienced to make sense of you!

- I offer this book to you who want something that "pulls it all together."
- I offer this book to you who are feeling lost in the maze of healing therapies, self-development options, and integrative modalities.
- I offer this book to you who are seeking something that works once and for all and can be done easily on your own, at your own pace.
- I offer this to you who want to get on with your lives and stop going around and around the same old stuff.
- I offer this book to you who know what you are missing and are choosing to be (W)hole, now.
- I offer this book to all human pioneers of abundance, creativity, and aliveness, who are interested in the "Hands & Feet" of realized potentiality: awakened, empowered, and embodied (W)holeness.

This is not a book claiming to be an expert of you. Rather, this is a book that is all about **revealing you to yourself**.

This book provides the "How-to's" for awakening your own particular (W)holeness, NOW.

A Bit About Me

Everything I will be sharing with you in this book has been birthed first in my own life. It seems only appropriate to provide you with an overview of some of my own journey to date.

Nearly my entire life has been spent in the study of the psyche for the purpose of healing and (W)holeness. As a therapist, I have listened for approximately 55,000 hours to my greatest teachers – my clients and students. These hours are my greatest professional credential.

To date, I have spent over twenty-eight years as a psychotherapist and healer, completing two master's degrees – a three-year Masters in Divinity degree from Yale Divinity School, with an emphasis on pastoral counseling; and a Masters in Social Work degree from the University of Connecticut, School of Social Work, with an emphasis on clinical social work. I held an associate teaching position for three years at the Clinical Neuroscience Research Unit at Yale, where I taught family therapy to the nursing staff and the psychiatric residents. I am a certified Imago Relationship Therapist, a teaching Reiki Master of the Usui Tradition, as well as having been the founder and director of three separate private psychotherapy practices in three different states. Currently, I reside in New Hampshire on sixty-five acres of land which my husband, John Richard, and I have dedicated to transformation, renewal, and healing. We have named this land "Sanctuary."

I am an ordained minister, as well as a Licensed Clinical Social Worker in the state of New Hampshire. I am a Board Certified Diplomate, a member of the National Association of Social Work and a member of the Social Work and Spirituality Association. I am a graduate of The Stillpoint School of Integrative Life Healing (a year-long program) and am a Certified Intuitive Healer (CIH). Currently, I am also the director and founder of Alternatives in Counseling and Personal Development (ACPD), my private psychotherapy practice. I am, most recently, the founder and director of The (W)hole Point Institute, LLC (WPI), an organization created to offer intensive seminars, called (W)hole Shops, in the (W)hole Point transformational empowerment system. I am the creator of the (W)hole Point Wisdom WAY model.

On a more personal note, just like you, I am a person on my own unique path. What we all have in common is our human self and our soul self. We are all the same in our essence and in our experiences. What makes each of us unique is how we express this sameness called "being alive." Our particular life paths are distinct, and yet, we all have a universal story in which we are "filling in the blanks." What I am sharing with you in this book is a weaving together of all my personal life experiences and my professional expertise, as well as all my academic studies. As you read on, I invite you to think of me as standing beside you, for we are all in this (W)hole universe together. We are unique, we are the same, and we are One! This is the paradox held within The Wisdom WAY.

It is my own life experiences that first led me to plunge into the depths, and ultimately emerge with The (W)hole Point perspective. Here is a condensed version of some of my life experiences, for which I am deeply grateful. Yes, even the painful ones!

I am a survivor of three parental deaths – two biological parents and my step-father. I have been divorced. I have experienced rejections, losses, failures, and successes in schools, in jobs, and in friendships. I have been alone, and in relationships. I have experienced date rape. I have moved and changed jobs. I have worked in corporate situations, and in the business of healing. I have loved myself, and hated myself. I am now married to an amazing man. I do not have children. I love our two cats, and I love to teach and to witness folks seeing their own brilliance. My greatest joy is to be a witness of the radiance waking up inside of another person and myself.

My search for understanding began at the age of eight. This was the age when my father chose to die. Yes, he committed suicide. At the moment he made his choice, I made mine. I began a quest, formulated and implemented beneath my conscious awareness. This "mission" became the orienting focus of my life.

This quest was not spoken aloud; however, it was deeply entwined into my being. This quest led me through professional and personal explorations until I revealed to myself The (W)hole Point Wisdom WAY model. My life is now about BEING me rather than SEEKING for who I am supposed to be, or how I am supposed to be, or worse, for permission to be me. It is this wisdom I am choosing to share with you.

So, in addition to all of my formal education and professional background, I also have over forty-five years of seeking, searching, reading, loving, crying, laughing, analyzing, studying, failing, being totally frustrated, being in analysis, attending hundreds of workshops and seminars, journeying to study with spiritual teachers and masters, practicing yoga, fasting, embracing and enduring intense psychotherapy, grieving, celebrating, and risking my life over and over again, to finally see what was before my face the entire time: the (W)holeness within ME!

Looking back on it all, I can say it was worth it a thousand times over! I am now ready, willing, and able to share what I have come to understand about this with you. My choice is to offer the (W)hole Truth to you so you, too, will be where you want to be and can *celebrate yourself* now, not later. It does not require great study and effort; all that you really need to know is the essential framework to sort through all of the wisdom you have gathered about yourself up to this point. I call this a practice of sorting and sifting.

I entered into psychotherapy from the motivation of personal pain. As I continued on, I became more and more fascinated by the complexity and brilliance of the psyche and the soul. I often say to my clients, "A therapist can only take you as far as he/she (the therapist) has gone himself/herself." My personal work has included Jungian analysis, sand tray therapy, shamanic soul retrieval, dream analysis, Reiki, Ennersense, Deeksha, theological studies, experiential spiritual seminars, alchemical ritual studies, and Imago therapy, while simultaneously participating in nearly a life-time of integrative psycho-spiritual analysis. My personal process is still an ongoing backdrop to my life's work of teaching and mentoring. It is my greatest gift to myself. It is true to say the dark side of life's experiences, the places where we hurt and ache for clarity, are the realms in which I have spent much of both my personal and professional lives. Ultimately, these dark places revealed to me the doorway of empowered (W)holeness. Available to everyone, awakened (W)holeness is merely a few steps of awareness away for everyone and doesn't require all the thousands of hours I happen to have invested. This is great news; you can awaken your inner radiance, NOW. If I had known what I am sharing with you in this book, I would have spent far less time on "self-development," and lots more time playing and enjoying life.

This book is a result of an integration of my life's experience, my professional evolution, and my persistent curiosity. The hidden skeleton or bare bones of healing became clear to me in the year of the new millennium (2000). It was as if it floated up into my conscious mind in a gentle and wild experience of recognition. It wasn't new at all, and yet it was entirely new; surprisingly simple, and yet, deeply profound.

The (W)hole Point Wisdom WAY is a simple pragmatic map and compass for awakening and empowering your particular personal (W)holeness. This is not just another theory. It is a practical, usable, doable process that empowers you right from the very beginning. What you do from that point on is, of course, entirely up to you.

This book is very personal to me. I first recognized the Wisdom WAY map within myself, and it has since been recognized as essential wisdom by clients and students alike. It is at their urging that I have taken pen to paper.

A Basic Belief of Mine

I believe everyone is doing the absolute very best they know how, with what they know and understand. Everyone's life choices make sense if you understand their inner heart logic.

This logic exists in all of us; however, most of us never even know it is present or how to look at it, assess its effectiveness, and alter it. This logic of the heart took shape in our early years and most of the time is unknown to us.

It is a logic of feelings and reactions rather than of purely cognitive reasoning. However, it also contains a logic of the mind as well! All of us participate in this inner life logic. Additionally, it "runs" behind the scenes of our lives like an automatic program. Essentially, we are blind to the most fundamental elements that run our lives. Until this heart logic is revealed to us, we are in the dark about ourselves!

We are living our lives based on an inner logic which in effect withholds our own (W)hole-ness from us, while encourages us to quest (i.e., self-develop ourselves) in an attempt to heal what we perceive as "our brokenness." All this is resting upon a "secret kept from us" by us! No wonder we have all gone around and around the same old issues! We didn't know about the inner heart logic.

How This Book Began

My clients and students asked me a question: "How do I stop going around and around the same old stuff and just LIVE?"

A dear friend of mine and a healer in her own right named me as an expert of the "Hands & Feet" of life's complexities. I have gained an ability to comprehend complex psychological and spiritual processes and then translate them into simple elements that everyday people – like you and me – can get their hands around to use them to move forward with their lives. I am deeply committed to providing access to wisdom that people can apply while doing the dishes, driving to work, and moving through life in all its varied forms. This is what I mean by "Hands & Feet" – practical, usable, do-able, sustainable, simple (W)holeness in the midst of life.

The heart and soul of this book is an illumination of the "Hands & Feet" of awakening your own (W)holeness.

For quite some time, my clientele have been primarily couples and individual adults who are well skilled in the journey of self-exploration. Most come to me quite expert at delineat-ing all the places in which they are "dysfunctional." They come to me having revealed a great longing to themselves, to lay the quest aside and come alive as themselves. They have begun to discover that something is still missing.

Often they come in saying, "I am sick and tired of going around the same old stuff. I am ready to move on. Show me how." What they are asking is to be shown the skeleton or map and to be given the compass so they can live their lives fully, NOW. One of my (W)hole Point Institute teachers said it this way, *"I had nearly self-developed myself to death."* (Well said, dear Marianne!) The good news is that there is a point to all of this – The (W)hole Point! And there is an end to the questing! There is awaking into our Radiant (W)holeness as we are!

Currently I teach the skeleton of (W)holeness and reveal the bare bones of empowered awakening to my apprentices, clients, and students. Inevitably, they move into being the receivers of their own (W)holeness. In effect, they meet themselves as they are walking their own path of (W)holeness. This is a radical shift from simply seeking to name and eradicate types of "dysfunctionality." What is unique is that students of the Wisdom WAY learn how to sort through the chaos of their life's experiences and respond in an immediate, transformational way. They find their own particular answers to the question, "How do I stop going around the same old issues?" The Wisdom WAY is not about me! It is all about YOU!

The (W)hole Point Model: An Orientation

This book isn't merely a set of words; it is an experience and an invitation. Extended to individuals, families, corporations, and nations, the invitation is the same. It is for you to come home to your (W)hole self, to wake up to your entire experience of being alive, to "walk awake" each moment, whether you are making breakfast or leading a meeting or making a sales call – to know deeply that your presence matters to the (W)hole.

Around the globe, waves of (W)holeness-awareness are rising. These waves are the increasing recognition that we may no longer think of ourselves as pieces, sections, and separate parts of a planet. We can no longer continue to think of ourselves as separate from the others. We can no longer live from a shattered viewpoint – internally or externally.

(W)holeness of viewpoint offers peace instead of war. Rather than segments of humanity at war with others, there is a mutual engagement for a common cause – global health and (W)holeness. This hunger or yearning for inner and outer harmony is evidenced globally. Around the world, folks are seeking and searching for a way to find peace and to be at peace with themselves, for it is only when the wars inside of us cease will the wars outside have a chance to come to an end. This is not a new concept. In many forms it has been told that what is within is evidenced by the outer world. Now is the time for something more than concepts.

We are now called to know ourselves as one great (W)hole expression of life – with many forms. Whether as an individual or nation or organization, we are all now riding the ripples of a great shift in our interior and exterior landscapes. Yet, how does one even begin to make this shift practically and in every day life?

If you are scanning these words, you are likely one of those who has heard or perhaps felt a call. Just as when we were children and we would play the game of hide and seek, at the end of the game we would hear the call "All-y all-y In Come free." This call is now rippling around the globe for us all to come home to our own (W)holeness, to remember who we all are: one (W)hole planet and each of us a part of the (W)hole.

This hunger to remember ourselves in our entirety is evident everywhere. We can observe it in the massive number of self-development approaches we can find on the Internet or in every book store. The difficulty is that much of what is available is either offered in a somewhat theoretical way or is too particular to apply to our own life.

This book is different. The truth is we cannot follow another person's footsteps, for we are all exceptional and distinct expressions of life, living our unique life situations. Simply put: You are the expert of you – no one else. (W)holeness is re-awakened in particular ways for each person. How do we weave our uniqueness with our sameness? How might we make sense of our own path while also embracing our universal human journey?

What if there was a map that was universal and allowed for your unique precious life expression? What if there was a map that could be applied in all the different aspects of your life, empowering without imposing a "cookie cutter" reductionism to your life questions and quandaries? What if there was a compass which would lead you on a journey of weaving your psyche and your soul into an awakened (W)holeness now? What if there was a map that allowed you to bring all your wisdom, previous learning and uniqueness together into an integrated (W)hole package? What if all the tools and knowledge you needed, apart from the compass, were already yours?

Offered in these pages are the "Hands & Feet," the "How-to's" of (W)holeness. I like to think of it as the bare bones of an empowered (W)hole life. Once this approach is clear, you may apply it in response to whatever situation you encounter. Knowing *how* to use your personal and particular life experiences to take you home to youself is the key. What we are all expert on is our own experience in the moment. How another has moved into or revealed their (W)holeness is interesting but serves us only by inference. This is a book that will take you on your own path to your own (W)holeness using your own personal situation and life history. Your psyche and your soul are both necessary. (W)holeness with parts missing isn't (W)hole. Psychology and spirituality must be woven together into a living (W)holeness for it to be real and alive as you being you. That is the point of this book.

Let me start by telling you a great secret. The secret is that the map to (W)holeness is hidden inside of you! It is inside of every life moment in which you are engaged. It is in your psyche, in your cells – yes, every one of them – and in your thoughts and feelings. It is part of every corporate structure, and it is part of every nation's creed. It is the "bones" of every living and constructed form. It is everywhere. It has simply been hidden – in plain view.

If you know the bare bones of (W)holeness, not as a theory but as a practical, applicable means to expressing your greatest potentials, then you are in charge of who you are, and you can decide just how alive you want to be! When you know this map, your path is revealed to you in particular, one step at a time. You not only remember who you really are right now, but you also can live your (W)holeness right now. You can choose to be all you are meant to be and not just be pieces at war with one another. Longing for something or searching for something is sometimes more comfortable than being given a way to live it now, because when we live it now, we are face-to-face with the bald naked truth: Are we willing to do whatever it takes to come alive fully? Do we really believe what we have read or heard in self-development seminars – "Love yourself," "Wake up to your own wonder," "Change for the better" – or would we prefer to continue the quest of learning all the different possibilities for change, while never actually coming alive? Concepts of self-love, for example, are useful only if they can be lived for real!

I invite you to risk losing **who you think you are** for the ever greater (W)holeness you are meant to be. This opportunity is not for the faint of heart! It will take courage beyond anything you have ever dreamed. And yet, it will offer you that which so many are seeking: (W)holeness – awakened, revealed, empowered, and embodied as YOU.

If you are interested in only a cognitive process, now is the time to put this book down. If, however, you are ready to take this journey with me, read on.

Word Play: Terms and Definitions Used in This Book

The concepts presented in this book pivot around one term: "(W)hole"

This is an obvious play on the words "hole" and "whole." Not so obvious is the transformational power of the processes outlined in this book which essentially reveals "holes" – our fears, insecurities, and dark places – as doorways of "wholeness," an expression of our true selves: confident, secure, at peace with ourselves and with our surroundings.

In this book …　　　　**(W)hole = wholeness**

　　　　　　　　　　　(w)hole = hole

Notice when there is a capital "W." It points to wholeness and the state of being whole. The capital "W" is in a parentheses to remind us that we are always evolving, rather than being, "finished" products. The little "w" is also in a parentheses to remind us that there is always more to discover about ourselves. Bearing this in mind, let's look at the term "(W)hole Truth," which is what this book is about.

"(W)hole Truth" is an expression which has a direct and indirect impact upon the individual seeing and hearing the term. This effect occurs because of the way the words themselves are written. The letters as a whole are taken in on many levels simultaneously, while also stimulating internal shifts and changes since the words don't settle into one meaning. For example, how would you answer these questions?

- What is the difference between "Whole" and "(W)hole?"
- What are their meanings?
- What is the significance of the difference? Of the "( )?"
- How does the term "(W)hole" feel inside of you?
- What about "Whole" or "Hole" – can you FEEL the difference?

Notice that these questions and the feelings they evoke are stimulated by the form of the words themselves. The power of word play is engaged because both the psyche and soul are dancing as one (W)hole as they digest and experience all the layers of the invitation. The psyche, or the psychological viewpoint of a person, can perceive the term in many ways, while the soul, or spiritual life force, flows with it in various directions – all at the same time.

Word play is an invitation to all parts of our being: our human selves, our psychological facets, our mental elements as well as our Soul Self. Throughout this book you are being invited at multiple levels to wake up to more of **who** you are. The wonder of this is that you don't have to put forth much effort for this to happen. Word play has an alchemical effect, sinking deeply into the unconscious, inviting self-unveiling, and surprising revelations.

This image of a hole is the metaphor used to reveal the bare bones of our shattered (W)holeness **and** our path to awakened (W)holeness. In essence, each time you read the word (W)holeness, a profound wisdom awakens within you. Called forth from deep inside your cells and your psyche, the truth of your (W)holeness is invited to move into greater and greater awareness. This effect references the impact upon the psyche and the soul whenever this term is encountered. A movement is initiated or stimulated between and in both the psyche and soul of the person which requires no conscious effort.

To clarify: by the word "**psyche**" I am referring to all the elements of a person's psychology, including historical life events, the myriad of responses, feelings of yesterday, today, and even about what might happen tomorrow. With the word "**soul**" I am pointing to the elements of spirit, that which enlivens the physicality of our human bodies – the mystery of life in each of us. When psyche and soul meld into (W)holeness, turmoil and struggles melt away. The human-ness of us is no longer shattered into bits and pieces, thus our spirit is now fully present to experience life itself, thus supporting the (W)hole person.

Long ago we were all born (W)hole, but we were unconscious of this (W)holeness. We were not aware of it. At some point in time our (W)holeness shattered into bits and pieces because life started to hurt too much. We began to flee from life, and from our original (W)holeness. We fled by pushing away or running away from life experiences. I call this our **Shattering**.

For our purposes, the use of the word "**(w)hole**" is an invitation to recognize how we feel when we hit those tough patches in our lives. When a life moment happens and we **feel** like we've fallen into a big, black hole, we are actually being offered an invitation to awaken (into wholeness). This is a secret lost to many of us because the experience of being in a "hole" hurts so much.

What's surprising to many folks is that the point of all of our experiences in life's "black holes" is to access our (W)holeness. In fact, our particular route to revealing our inner selves is found in each and every (w)hole we stumble into. Once the secret of (w)holes is revealed and felt, individuals, families, and corporations quickly begin to apply it to their distinct situations.

This book is written in a style to invite the (W)hole image of you to be reflected and revealed back to you. Reading this book will call forth a direct encounter with yourself – your (w)holes and your (W)holeness. This book is an invitation, an initiation, and a revelation of (W)holeness, which is called by your name.

It is my explicit purpose to extend a direct and personal invitation to you to step into and live your (W)hole life right now!

After all, **The (W)hole Point of the (W)hole Truth is YOU!**

An Invitation to Live Your (W)hole Life

There are many books that can tell you the theories of (W)holeness – psychologically and spiritually. Topics discussed include the impacts on health, corporate success, and individual relationships. However, knowing something from an intellectual place, though very important, will not carry anyone to the place of living the learning in one's particular life situation. Knowing something conceptually is helpful, and yet again, it will not empower you with the "How to do its" in your daily life. Frankly, I have felt secretly ashamed that I couldn't implement the concepts of self-love and inner peace. I would at times think, "What is wrong with me? I agree with this concept. I understand it, but I just can't seem to bring it into my daily world."

Revealing yourself to yourself requires more than cognition; it requires a depth of emotional and spiritual melding. The tools required for empowered (W)holeness are already yours: your feelings, your thoughts, your body, your history, and your desire to reveal your (W)hole self! These tools pivot upon your capacity and willingness to **feel** feelings. Feelings are like doorways to the ever-expanding vistas of our being.

Feelings matter! Being able to feel our lives allows us to be present in our lives and awaken to our own spiritual nature. Feelings are the vibrations of emotions and are necessary for a cognitive truth to reach deep inside of us to awaken our cells, our psyches, and our lives. When we feel a life moment touch us, there is a deep physical, cellular level, system-wide effect. In fact, there are numerous studies being done now that show this connection. Emotions, "life in motion," or "felt-life pulsating as us," are what we experience when we open up and allow life to touch us.

Notice how life feels differently when you are in inner conflict as opposed to when you are experiencing inner peace. The outer situation may be the same, but the interior spaces are different. Feelings are the colors of being alive. Our capacity to feel has significant impact upon our life experiences. Feeling responses can lead us to open up more or shut down or even flee from those we say we love. If we feel a deep emotional pain, we can create shutdowns inside of us. Doesn't this make sense? Yes, life can hurt so much that sometimes we don't want to feel **that** way again. We will do whatever we imagine will stop and prevent that pain from happening again!

This is one of the reasons so many of us get stuck. We just can't seem to move past a situation, issue, or feeling. Thinking about life is far less challenging than feeling life as it moves through us in its entirety. Frankly, in some way, we all have shut down from experiencing the (W)hole of life because life has hurt us – in big and little ways.

The (W)hole Truth is that there isn't one of us who hasn't been hurt many times in life. We have all felt big and little "heart pains."

We may find ourselves far more comfortable with theoretical ideas and cognitive suggestions, rather than feelings and emotions. We may find ourselves limited in some way or another to disallow the entire felt experience of life. Full embodied presence – that is, being awake and feeling each moment as it moves through us – is a big thing to swallow for most of us. In secret, we have bound or limited the flow of life experiences so we have control over how life happens, when it happens, and how it may feel. Yet, we still long to be at peace and at ease with all of ourselves and with life. This longing doesn't disappear because it is our natural condition. However, despite the longing, we continue hiding from parts of ourselves and from feeling life itself. This is the secret we keep from ourselves while we continue to seek after the (W)hole abundant life. We are going in two opposing directions at the same time! No wonder we feel stuck! No wonder we feel ourselves going around and around the same old issues. This is a great, big-deal secret we keep from ourselves!

As a result of this secret, we can stay away from the bald naked truth, that we are all in some way afraid of our (W)hole aliveness, of being **that** bold and alive. For years I have said to clients that, "We often run from the doorway while longing to go through that same doorway." How we run and how far we run from "life-in-motion in every moment" (emotions) is distinct to each of us. However, the fact that we all have pushed away feelings that hurt too much and life moments that overwhelmed us and dreams that seemed beyond us is a truth that none of us can sidestep. The very feelings we flee from are the keys to the (W)holeness or abundance we long for.

Other people's feelings or solutions or definitions will not gain us access to ourselves. We must find our own way.

Feelings and sensations occur when life is touching us deeply. The bare bones truth is that in each of us, in each family and, yes, in each nation, there is a secret fear. We fear **our** full life force and **their** full life force flowing freely. Fear of this wild, free flow of life is what drives conflict, violence, and a planet that is now endangered by its very own inhabitants. We are afraid of the very experiences we are seeking: (W)holeness, peace, harmony, abundance

– whatever name you might apply to "that much life." This is not a new thought. However, it is the seed-point where the wisdom of the (W)hole Point model of empowerment begins.

The Secret of The Wisdom WAY

When feelings, comprehension, and revelation come together as one (W)hole realization – empowered transformation must occur. This is the essential potency of The (W)hole Point Wisdom WAY model. There is no place to hide from your (W)hole Truth, your (W)hole Self, and your (W)hole Life. Even if you choose to back away, this, too, cannot be hidden from you. Another way to say this is that once you say YES to your (W)hole Life, you will find that there is no place to hide from the experience of being loved for no reason. This is what stimulates the radiance shining from the eyes of those with whom I have shared this. How do you imagine life would feel to you if you felt and knew you were "loved for no reason?"

The (W)hole Point Wisdom WAY model offers you a clear path to access your particular felt brokenness and a way to embrace, for real, your life force and to do this in a way which is authentic and particular to you.

Just as when one is driving, having a map is helpful. If you were to drive from New York State to California without a map and a compass, you would wander around for quite a while before finding the correct turns and straight-aways. This truth also applies to coming into awareness and embracing our own (W)holeness.

This book will provide a map, and offer you a compass to revealing your own (W)holeness. The degree to which you choose to open your heart, your mind, and your soul to your (W)hole Truth is the degree to which you will once again come to know and live the (W)holeness of you – consciously. The good news is that this is your decision! The great news is that once you begin to welcome yourself home to yourself, there is a cascade of life force energy! The best news of all is that you have all you need within you for this to happen to you!

Being aware of your power to choose and knowing how to choose (W)holeness places the power of your life squarely back in your hands!

Be on notice that reading this book will change how you see everything, how you experience everything, and how you live your life, that is, if you choose to open your heart to the (W)hole Truth of YOU.

Chapter 1: (w)holes are Everywhere ...

Let me introduce you further to this idea of (w)holes. I am intentionally using this play on words to refer to 'life holes," those emotional spaces and places where we feel we've fallen into the pits. (W)holes are the dark pits, the scary, sad, hurting places, the life messes into which we all fall at some time or other in our lives. Most of the time we spend lots of time and energy desperately trying to get out of the (w)hole, while the only true way out is to go **into** the (w)hole. The truth of (w)holes is that your (W)holeness is the gift found in every "pit" you fall into. Your (W)hole Truth has been hiding in plain sight each time you struggled with "those same old issues." In fact, we are destined to continually repeat those "same old issues" until we find a way to fully "process" the (w)hole – the WAY is what this book is about.

No one is exempt from (w)holes. Some of us seem to fall into more (w)holes than others. Some of us seem to fall into darker (w)holes than others. Some of us seem to fall into (w)holes so often that it feels like all of life is one big, gigantic (w)hole. The (W)hole Truth is that we all are very experienced with life's dark places, or (w)holes. This is inevitable. (W)holes are inescapable.

The tangle we all face is, what does one do with a (w)hole? Our usual response is to scramble and climb out as fast as we can and hope we don't fall into that dark place again. Here is a (w)hole truth: ***You most certainly will fall in again, since the only (w)hole you cannot fall into is one that is collapsed.*** What's the payoff? Freedom to live your life your way.

Let's begin with the essential "tools" for recognizing and collapsing (w)holes.

The "No Rules" Rules for (w)hole Play

When I teach the Wisdom WAY to groups, I like to start off with the rules. Everyone always wants to know what the rules are, right? This gives folks a chance to settle in and understand what is expected of them. Even though we are not sitting face to face, I still think you might like to know what the "rules" are for doing this work. Janice, the Office Angel at Sanctuary, is the one who named these the **"No Rules" Rules** because when you look at them, they really aren't strict and rigid rules. First, these are **invitations** that you offer to yourself in the form of a question: Will you decide to use this Rule? How about that one? They also are reminders about how to be with yourself as you reveal yourself to yourself: "Remember, apply this rule now." In addition, these are great "rules" or "guidelines" for living your (W)hole life. In particular, these are the **"No Rules" rules** that apply as you begin your (w)hole play.

Rule #1: There is no way to fail. There's no test you have to pass. There are no pop quizzes. In fact, just by breathing you are succeeding at being you in this moment. Trust me, it's impossible to fail at being how you are in any one moment. You are just being you. By believing there is no way to fail, there is an opportunity for you to learn *your* way as opposed to being told how to learn this material someone else's way. (W)holeness is uniquely ours!

Rule #2: You are the expert of you. No one knows you like you know yourself. Therefore, no one is an expert on you but you. This is true no matter how many people try to tell you about you. Only you know how you feel, what you think, and what your preferences are. In the most subtle of ways we give our power away by allowing someone else to speak for us. Just for fun, reacquaint yourself with what your voice sounds like, speaking your truth your way, whatever that looks like. You may confuse yourself sometimes. You may blind yourself sometimes. But finally, you are the only one with the answers about you! This is very good news. It means you have all you need within yourself.

Rule #3: Be curious without judgment. Ask questions of yourself, and be sure to drop all self judgments. Judgments stand in the way of our seeing the answers clearly. We have all the answers inside of us; however, when we make judgments against ourselves, we block our sight. These judgments are assessments of "right," "wrong," "good," "bad," "have to," "shouldn't," etc. When we make these internal evaluations, we imprison our own curiosity and impede our fullest expression of (W)holeness. Judgments against ourself or someone else cloud our vision and hide the truth. So, drop the judgments and just be curious. It is especially helpful NOT to ask the question, "Why?" and keep all the others: "How?" "What?" "When?" "Where?" "Who?" You will learn more about this later. Curiosity without judgment is like having a mind of a beginner – open to whatever shows up! Judgment has the effect of censoring what is allowed into our awareness. The reason we have been a mystery to ourselves is because we haven't allowed full access to all of ourselves, hence we have felt more broken than (W)hole.

Rule #4: Enjoy. This process is for you, just for you. Enjoy it as you will. Joy isn't just about a "happy, happy" feeling. Joy is an inner space that allows us to appreciate the creation and creator we are. Joy is a way of being with ourselves gently. Sometimes in the beginning this can be a bit challenging; however, since you can't fail, just stay curious and notice your "not-in-joy-ness" as well as moments of enjoying. All else will ripen from there. To be in joy is to strengthen our heart's capacity to enjoy who we are! So, begin now – by enjoying your openness to something new!

Rule #5: Have fun! When has anyone ever said that having fun was a rule? Life (w)holes can be pretty serious stuff, so let's make sure we have some fun along the way. This "rule" is to encourage you to not take yourself and your experiences too seriously – even when they are very "serious" concerns – because when we tighten up, we slow ourselves down and sometimes even become stuck. As we move through this book, you will be taught some ways to "lighten up" so you can wake up to your (W)holeness.

Rule #6: Be gentle with yourself; slow down. There is no need to hurry. Don't expect yourself to reveal all of your (W)holeness right away. There is no need to push yourself to exhaustion. Slow, gentle ripening is far more effective and sustainable than tearing and pulling and pushing to "get somewhere." Besides, you have already tried this approach! It is exhausting. You deserve gentle care, and who best to start giving it to you than you? Gentleness is all about knowing that you have always been doing the very best you could do with what you understood and knew. This is true no matter how messy things may appear or feel to be in the moment.

There you have it – all the rules you need for following and implementing the Wisdom WAY and for living life from now forward on your own behalf. Here's an invitation: Take a piece of paper or an index card, and write down the "No Rules" Rules so that you'll have them in an easily accessible form. If you want, for the fun of it, circle the rule that is your favorite and the one that is most challenging for you. At the end of reading this book, look at your "No Rules" Rules list, and see if your choices have changed.

Where and How to Begin…

You simply start where you are, and by that I mean start with what is bothersome to you right now, in this very moment. Be particular, for there is power in the particular. What issues have you found yourself going around and around on? Where in your life situation, in your company's situation, in your relationships are you dissatisfied? What hurts? What do you find yourself judging in yourself? This is where to start. Be very specific.

A (w)hole Play Opportunity for You

As you move through this book, you will find these boxes which indicate an opportunity for you to apply what you have learned to your own life, which is the point! As you work through each of these steps, you will be given instructions regarding where and how to record each Wisdom WAY element you have sorted. All you need is some blank paper and a pen or pencil.

What you will be creating for yourself is the Wisdom WAY map onto which you will be adding your particular expertise about yourself. You will be doing this one step at a time. By the end of this process you will have the entire anatomy of a (w)hole as well as a framework based on sorting through your life experiences. The effect is that you arrive at an empowered position where you get to choose how to live your life! You may want to keep your worksheet with you, and perhaps put the page number of the (w)hole play opportunity for your reference. Add the date.

For this opportunity …

Take just a few moments and jot down all of the issues in your life that you find troubling or bothersome. Maybe it's your job or your relationships. Maybe it's your car or a financial situation. Maybe it's your weight or your diet or your health. Don't spend a lot of effort doing this. Simply write down whatever pops into your awareness right now.

Include feelings, thoughts, fears, judgments, frustrations, etc. Include the things you are unhappy about in your life. Just list your concerns without censoring them.

After you have your list of concerns, issues, and feelings, put it aside and continue reading. We will come back to this later.

Compassion Expansion

As I said, no one can tell you more about you than you. However, there is often so much to tell that trying to make sense of it or to sort through it all seems impossible. This is where the magic of the Wisdom WAY begins to shine through. It provides a framework for you to show yourself, quite clearly, all you know about you. Change begins with understanding what you know already. Once you have an understanding of what brought you to this moment, then you are in a position to make different life choices from a platform of truth. This platform is initially a felt experience of self-validation

The wonderful truth is that when we can show ourselves how illogical or "bad" choices really have an interior felt logic or "heart logic" of their own, there is a softening that allows our (W)holeness to surface into our awareness. This is not about creating (W)holeness; it is about revealing our (W)holeness to ourselves consciously. By recognizing the logic behind our life choices – not just theoretically but truly in our hearts – we shift into embracing our own (W)holeness, and this opens the doorway to change.

The Wisdom WAY is all about creating an inner softening which allows our (W)holeness to rise from within. We don't need to create our (W)holeness, it's a given! What we do need to do is make space for it!

For example, let us say that you find yourself yelling when you are actually secretly scared. You may have even kept this a secret from yourself – you don't know why you're yelling, just that you are yelling! You may then judge yourself for doing the very thing you hate doing. However, if we looked closer, we may see that you yell now when you are afraid because it helps to hide a vulnerability that wasn't allowed in your family when you were younger. You just "knew" that boys "never got scared," so you hid "being afraid," and still do. When we understand what and why something is happening, we gain compassion.

When we understand ourselves, we begin to have compassion for ourselves. **Compassion expansion** is the effect of softening towards oneself. When we are soft and pliable, we can accept who we are and can then change our behavior, if we choose to do so. This is not a new idea; in fact, once you understand this skeleton or map, you will see that it has within it the elements of many various modalities. It is a skeleton. Many have fleshed it out differently. The secret is if you know the bare bones of (W)holeness, you can take advantage of all the different ideas about (W)hole Life living.

However, what makes the Wisdom WAY different is that the basic schematic of (W)holeness is exposed. It is no longer hidden or buried within a theoretical overlay. Anyone is able to directly access it, in their own personal and particular way, an actual moment of (W)holeness recognition. Now, I realize that I am writing about something you are yet to be shown; however, it is helpful to have this orientation at this particular time.

What you are going to learn is how to decipher the mystery of yourself one step at a time, by uncovering your personal story, wounds, longings, fears, and your solutions to avoiding the parts of life that hurt too much to bear. In this manner you will reveal your own psyche, your own heart-felt anatomy, to yourself. This has the effect of compassion expansion, which softens and allows your being to become malleable. (W)holeness is about softening into greater expressions of life. Knowing our own heart anatomy empowers us to let all of our life force flow without restraint! This is the (W)hole Point.

The skeleton automatically creates a sorting process through the elements crucial to your own (W)holeness. You do not need to know or decide what is important or less important. The activities of (w)hole play are sorting and sifting. You are guided by a universal map or skeleton. The contents that are sorted and sifted and revealed are yours alone! As your own expert, you reveal yourself as (W)hole at the pace you choose and to the depth you dare to go. This map empowers you to follow the bread crumbs of your own dark places, or (w)holes, to your (W)holeness.

You simply follow your own (w)holes to the (W)hole Truth of you.

Chapter 2: What I Wish I Had Known ...

To review, what is a (w)hole? For our purposes a (w)hole is a painful place we "fall into." A (w)hole is a space between one side and another, or one object and another, or one expression of yourself and its opposite. A (w)hole is a space in-between. A (w)hole is a hole or space between parts of ourselves.

> *"I just don't get it! I am willing to do the work. I have attended lots of self-development workshops. I have read book after book about my particular issues. I have been in some sort of therapy on and off for years with a number of well-trained therapists, and I have learned a great deal about myself. But over and over again, I am stuck in this same place, feeling like I'm right back where I started!"*

Have you ever said this? I sure did.

If you're just beginning your self-exploration, are you wondering if this is the book that will really help you amidst the hundreds that are out there? Of course you are! My answer to you is, "Read this one first, and then see if you need the others." Once the framework or skeleton of understanding yourself is clear, the particular way you decide to flesh things out is up to you.

Without this framework, we are left with only two positions: being in the (w)hole or hoping to avoid (w)holes. In many circles, this is called "**Being on the journey**." Many people today speak of being on journeys to discover themselves, to recover the joy of being alive, or to simply free themselves from that which has become a painful experience of being alive.

However, it often morphs into a circular movement around and around the same issues, without any actual direction, only a hope of "one day." Most of us on the self-awareness path use a "shotgun" approach based on "I heard this is helpful" or "They are recommending this now."

We often begin full of hope that this way or that way will finally free us from circling around the same thing over and over again. The problem is that after a time most of us find ourselves right back to the same issues we started with. It's frustrating. It's maddening. It's so totally aggravating that some of us give up – or give up for a while anyway – and then we try again. Some of us just don't even bother trying at all. What does this tell us? It tells us that there is something missing in our approach. (W)holeness isn't a journey. (W)holeness is all about unveiling and revealing the (W)hole Truth of ourselves. The truth is that there is no place to journey to and no destination to arrive at and no "right" way to be. At the same time we find ourselves acting, being, and feeling stuck in the dark. Again! So what is going on?

What we do know is that whatever is going on is actually happening deep within our being. It is driven by profound motivations that defy our own conscious adult choices, and all our blind efforts to "get better," are not very effective. In fact, it can be quite exhausting. We know that something is missing, or we would have resolved the "issue" already – never to revisit it again.

When we feel depressed, down, and sad, we may describe this experience by saying, "Oh, I am in a pit. I have fallen into a big black hole." "I am in the pits today." At this point we are clear that what we want is some speedy assistance with climbing up and out of the (w)hole. Then somehow, some time later on, we inevitably end up falling right back into that (w)hole again. Perhaps there will be different details, but the feelings will be very, very familiar. This is the story of all (w)holes. We cannot escape them without fleeing from our own life force! We cannot avoid them without cutting ourselves off from life experiences! We can't make them go away no matter how hard we try! The "issues" keep showing up!

Sound familiar? So what exactly is this thing, this (w)hole that we seem to keep falling into?

There is a famous autobiography written by Portia Nelson, called *There is a hole in my sidewalk: Autobiography in five short chapters*. Perhaps you are familiar with this, as it is often quoted in seminars and self-development programs. It goes like this:

Chapter One: I walk down the street. There is a deep hole in the sidewalk. I fall in. I am lost. I am helpless. It isn't my fault. It takes forever to find a way out.

Chapter Two: I walk down the same street. There is a deep hole in the sidewalk. I see it is there. I still fall in … it's a habit … but my eyes are open. I know where I am. It is my fault. I get out immediately.

Chapter Three: I walk down the street. There is a deep hole in the sidewalk. I pretend that I don't see it. I fall in again. I can't believe I am in this same place. But it isn't my fault. It still takes a long time to get out.

Chapter Four: I walk down the same street. There is a deep hole in the sidewalk. I walk around it.

Chapter Five: I walk down another street.

Of course, we can all see that there is great wisdom to be found in her five chapters. There is wisdom about self-responsibility, choices, and acknowledging what is unchangeable. However, her essential solution leaves a person with fewer and fewer paths to walk down, since ultimately one will find a pothole on any sidewalk. We would end up living a very small life.

The core assumption made by Ms. Nelson is that we are stuck with these holes and that all any of us can do is either avoid them, avoid the situations in which they show up, explore the issues until we are tired of doing this, or just give up and suffer "better" as we fall in over and over again. If we want something different, then something different must happen. The Chinese definition of insanity is: **To keep doing the same thing over and over again while expecting different results**. Ms. Nelson's autobiography suggests one solution – avoid the (w)holes. The Wisdom WAY suggests an alternative that preserves all possible pathways. The choice is yours to make.

If each time you find yourself falling into a hole and you solve the pain by simply choosing another street or avoiding that situation, eventually you would find very few places left to walk. You would end up living a very small life.

There is no way to avoid (w)holes!

Even if you have examined every one of the (w)holes you are aware of, named, defined, and fixed the identified issues, I promise that you will still find yourself falling into the same deep pit at some time in the future. The only way to eliminate a hole is to collapse it and be (W)hole! Until then, you are simply managing the inevitable condition of being full of (w)holes. This is a condition we all have! We are (w)holy human beings!

Unpleasant moments happen in life; it's a fact that can't be changed. This is because there are all sorts of people bumping up against each other. Accidents happen. Death, illness, and pain touch all of us at some time or another. This is life happening.

Each one of us has our own story, our own history, which has led us to exactly this moment, to exactly who we are and how we experience life right now. Our story is unique to each of us. Sprinkled throughout our stories are places of pain, anger, or hurt which we have experienced over the course of our lifetime. One might say that the (w)holes that Ms. Nelson is refering to are the repeated experiences of touching these same places of pain or hurt or anger over and over again. I call these "**life (w)holes.**" These life (w)holes operate like "open sores." They still hurt enough to dictate the choices we make now. When we fall into a "dark place," we are, in effect, head first in a (w)hole, which is a space or a void in the interior places within our sense of self.

We know that we have fallen into that place when we recognize the same old story and feel the same old pain. It feels familiar deep inside of us. I've listened to my clients say, "Here I am again! What is the point to all this self-exploration if I keep falling into this same place?" Here is a (W)hole Truth: Each of us will find that our personal stories lead us right back to the edge of our (w)holes, right back where the (W)hole mess started. After listening to people as they wrestle with their dark places and having spent years excavating my own, I came to realize the obvious secret. It had been before me the entire time. What is it that we have been missing? What is the one thing we have not been told? What is the one option not mentioned in the autobiography of Ms. Nelson?

The Secret of (w)holes

The missing piece is our relationship to the (w)hole. What we have not been told is to **change our relationship to (w)holes!** It is as simple as that. Ms. Nelson sees (w)holes as obstacles, as pit-falls, as experiences to avoid. The difficulty is we can't avoid them. Life is full of (w)holes. Instead, the WAY is to change our relationship to the (w)holes themselves, to let ourselves know a great mystery: (w)holes are doorways, pathways, invitations to our own Holy (W)holeness! We can't awaken to our (W)holeness without walking through the door!

In order to change our relationship to (w)holes, the actual **anatomy of a life (w)hole** must first be revealed. Let's take a look at exactly what a life (w)hole is.

Let us start at the beginning. We can see physical holes all the time – a pothole, keyhole, porthole, peep hole, nail hole, sink hole, knot hole, bullet hole, worm hole – just to name a few. In actuality a (w)hole is a space between two objects or edges. Let us take you and this book you are reading. There is you…a space…and this book.

There are also (w)holes that are internal or felt (w)holes. These are the life (w)holes inside of us. These are spaces of pain, hurt, and anger inside of us. These are the black pits we fall into when we feel "in the pits."

When I am referring to a life (w)hole, I am referring to a place in our hearts or feeling-selves that hurts whenever it is touched. Some examples of (w)holes might be the "I hate being single" (w)hole, the "I am a child of an alcoholic" (w)hole, the "Please like me" (w)hole, or the "Fear of Failure" (w)hole. A life (w)hole is where we hurt and struggle but can't seem to figure out how to stop the pain from happening. There is no human being who doesn't have (w)holes or unhelpful patterns of response.

Typically, what we do is create a protective shield or "defense" against what hurts. These defenses or heart-fences are designed unconsciously to accomplish one thing: stop the emotional/physical pain. In ego-based psychology a fundamental approach is to defuse these defenses to enable folks to self-reflect. The difficulty with these patterns of defense is that they commonly are the root of the very behaviors we would like to change, and they sidestep the hidden brilliance of our creation. Therefore, the ways in which we are protecting ourselves from the life pain are the very source of our "unwanted" life responses. Eliminating a defense without first understanding and appreciating it does not empower you. The shift I am pointing to is to move into living your life from inside out rather than designing yourself from the outside in. This is a very rich arena to explore because it points to the intersection of psychology and spirituality.

We are Holy beings, full of (w)holes wandering around "looking for" our (W)holeness.

We are all full of (w)holes because we all have places that trip us up or trigger reactions. Our uniqueness is also reflected in our sameness. We all have (w)holes, and yet, each of us experiences our (w)holes in our own particular way. **Having** (w)holes is **not** the problem. It is our **relationship** with these (w)holes that creates the difficulties.

Changing our relationship to (w)holes is totally in our hands. This is very good news. It means that you do not have to be victim to any (w)hole you fall into or are pushed into or discover! Let's look closer – and in slow motion – at what happens when we fall into a life (w)hole.

When we fall into a (w)hole, what is occurring is we feel the same pain or hurt we felt yesterday or ages ago. There are countless books out there on how to manage this pain, what the different causes of the pain might be, how to have a different attitude towards current and historical painful events, how to identify all the ways that we are dysfunctional in our reactions, and why (i.e., Adult Children of Alcoholics, Survivors of Abuse, Adult Children of Divorce, and so on). They all have multiple strategies for helping manage these particular difficulties. All of these references are rich in wisdom and helpful understandings. What they do **not** tell you is the secret of (w)holes – there is much more to (w)holes than is readily apparent.

You may have attended one or more self-growth and self-discovery experiences or you may have been someone who resisted any idea of help until now. Either way, most of us somewhere deep inside believe something is broken in us, something is wrong with us. We believe in a "bad essence" inside of us which we each name differently. We quest to find a way to "fix" ourselves. What I know from personal experience is this simply doesn't work. The "fixes" at best are only temporary. They cannot be maintained or sustained. They only keep us going around and around the same old issues – going nowhere. I guarantee that by following the approaches that presume you are broken, you will not get beyond the past, regardless of how many excellent books, seminars, teachers, therapists, healers, family, or friends you turn to.

There are three reasons for this. These reasons will reveal three truths to you.

First, you are not broken. You are feeling the pain of a (w)hole. You are not the problem! The (w)hole isn't the problem, even when it feels awful. Falling into a (w)hole when you don't understand what is happening is the problem. How you **respond** to a (w)hole is what really matters. Your relationship to the (w)hole is what makes all the difference! Most of us haven't been taught what (w)holes are, how to relate to them, and how to collapse them. As a result all our (w)holes remain dark spaces to avoid! It's like having a flat tire and fixing it by changing the oil. The tire will still be flat.

Second, unless you know the point of a life (w)hole, you will end up lost. You are not blind. You are simply just sitting in the dark. It is a question of turning on the lights! I could say it this way: unless you know where you are going, you won't know how to get there, you won't know what arriving even means or feels like, and you surely won't know when you get there. Without a map to reveal your particular process and the entire (W)holeness path, you will be lost in the dark. It isn't your fault; **we all need light to see our way**.

Third, your path to embracing and activating your (W)holeness is unique to you, so following anyone else's path simply won't bring you to the joy of being you. **Only your path will take you to YOU.**

When I first meet with a person, I ask them, "Tell me about yourself." They usually rattle off a list of their issues and dysfunctions – quite quickly, too. They frequently know all about what is "wrong" with them, and they are quite frustrated that they cannot find a way to keep from falling into the same old pit again. "No matter what I do, I keep finding myself in this (w)hole!" As the saying goes, "If I had a penny for every time ...." Fill in the blank.

Stop and consider how many self-help books you have read, heard about on television, or have gotten from friends. Stop and consider how much time, money, and effort you have invested into identifying the cause of your difficulties. I know how you feel. I've been there!

One day as I was listening to another client ask me "So, what is the point of all of this, all these (w)holes? – I just keep falling into them. I am sick and tired of these (w)holes," I stopped and really considered the question in its simplest form.

Everyone on the self-growth/development quest can attest to the fact that we've become experts in these old feelings. However, this expertise does not automatically translate into the illumination of the (w)hole itself. Just as a pothole in a road remains a hole, even if we get proficient at driving around it or over it or simply drive a different road, the pothole remains. This is also true of life (w)holes. Life (w)holes do not resolve themselves nor do they stop stealing our lives unless we collapse them. This is another way of saying we bring the two sides of the (w)hole together! The effect is that there is no longer a (w)hole or felt-space to fall into! It was that simple thought that opened the door for me to the (W)hole Truth. Think about it a moment. Doesn't this make sense?

Have you ever been told how to collapse a (w)hole? I'll bet you have read all about the life (w)holes you have fallen into, learned to name the feelings you have when you fall into them, and can even name the cause for the dysfunctional responses you have had in the past. But have you ever been told how to collapse the doggone thing once and for all?

Before we go on, let's clarify a key point about collapsing a (w)hole. Filling up a life (w)hole is not the same as collapsing it. Studying and analyzing a life (w)hole is not the same as collapsing it. Chanting affirmations while circling a life (w)hole will not collapse it. Reading another theory of self-development, empowerment, or chicken soup "for whatever" will not collapse it. We cannot collapse a (w)hole by thinking our way out. We cannot collapse a (w)hole by comforting ourselves while sitting in the dark. Life (w)holes remain no matter how much we study them, define them, or understand them. They will remain until we collapse them. However, once we have collapsed a (w)hole, we can't fall back into that exact same dark space because there is no space in which to fall.

To reveal how to collapse a (w)hole, a closer look at the anatomy is required.

(w)hole Anatomy

Our (w)holes are not just openings with a bottom and edges! They are actually compressed spirals. They are not just "bins" or "containers" or wounds we are stuck with forever. If you were to open up a life (w)hole, you would see your personal path to (W)holeness – **your** (W)holeness. If you were to do a cross-sectional anatomical study of life (w)holes, you would discover there is a spiral that looks much like the Slinky™ toy. When a Slinky™ is compressed, it appears to have solid surfaces. When you extend the Slinky™, you discover a spiral path. Life (w)holes are different from Slinkys™ because at the bottom of a life (w)hole, there is a doorway I call a portal.

So, imagine, if you would, a Slinky™ extended so that one end of it comes to a point, much like a spinning top rests on a point. At the bottom point is a "doorway" we can only access at the bottom of the (w)hole. The bottom of a life (w)hole is the place most of us flee from! Only by walking through this portal can you reveal what has been lost in the dark of that (w)hole.

Any (w)hole you fall into has a spiral path built in automatically to take you to the portal or doorway at the bottom of the (w)hole. This spiral path is made up of your expertise about YOU! This is your Wisdom WAY. It is particular and unique to you. We all have created in every (w)hole, without realizing it, a pathway of (W)holeness for ourselves. Each and every (w)hole has a (W)holeness path you alone may walk. My path isn't your path, and your path isn't my path. The (W)hole Point Wisdom WAY model is the skeletal anatomy that allows for you to "fill in the blanks" and "flesh out" your own private and personal stepping stones of (W)holeness revealed.

Consider this image again. (W)holes are like a compressed Slinky™ toy, appearing to simply be a (w)hole with wire sides. If you were to imagine a wire coil that is opened and stretched as far as it could go, you would begin to see parts of the anatomy of a life (w)hole. These parts of all life (w)holes are: an opening, a spiral path, and a doorway or portal at the bottom end of the spiral. Radiance, (W)holeness, the (W)hole Point of every (w)hole, is found at the bottom of this spiral path on the other side of the portal.

The top of the (w)hole is a wide open space between the edges, and the spiral path increasingly narrows, down to a point where the doorway of (W)holeness is found. **We have all been running in the wrong direction – frantically trying to climb upward, out of our (w)holes instead of to the doorway of (W)holeness.**

So, now what? The first step is to know how to follow the spiral path of each (w)hole, not to run from it, desperately climb out of it, or cover it up. The point of a (w)hole is to go into it, explore it, and follow it where it leads you, to the real, authentic (W)hole awakened you.

The great news is that when a (w)hole is collapsed, we cannot fall into it again because, quite simply, there is no place to fall. This is cause for great celebration, for now we are finally free to be alive as who we are rather than chase after the "right way" to be or trying to avoid being who we are or hating our life or suffering from it. The freedom to be who we really are, fully and without apology, is a miracle I have witnessed over and over again.

Ever the pragmatist, upon realizing this secret about (w)holes, I was most interested in the application of this new understanding. Many questions formed in my mind; however, the most central one was, how would one go about collapsing a (w)hole? In all my years of education and hours of listening, I had never heard the idea of the practice of (w)hole collapsing or healing a (w)hole!

The basic anatomy of a Life (w)hole:

Some Original Moments and Experiences

When I realized the (W)hole Point of (w)holes was to collapse them, not climb out of them, run away from them, or avoid them but to experience them by going into them, I developed a map of sorts to empower myself, my clients, and later my students so we could all collapse our own (w)holes.

I have to admit I had been stuck within the traditional boundaries of healing that assumed that (w)holes were a "given." The best that could be hoped for was a mature resolution and management of the facts of life with the greatest degree of compassion towards oneself as possible. Now, I can see how blind I had been. Even though I had experienced many moments of relief in my own growth work, there was always the presumption of (w)holes as a given, rather than (w)holes as an invitation to (W)holeness. Once I had made this shift in focus, my entire internal position as a psychotherapist or counselor shifted and so, too, did the experience of my clients.

I soon discovered that my clients and students were moving at light speed through the very issues that had held them stuck for years. Clients were now coming into my office to tell me how they had collapsed a (w)hole on their own, even some (w)holes which had plagued them for years. At first, I was a bit taken aback at the potency of this simple, yet profound, process. Then I realized that authentic empowerment was actually the (W)hole Point of my profession and the actual effect of this model. I became quite excited to witness the blossoming of my clients and myself. Yes, you bet I was applying this to my own life too! After all, we are all Holy Beings. I was captivated not only by the efficacy and rapidity of this new process, but also at how people were independently choosing to move deeply and fearlessly into places they had been too resistant to even acknowledge, much less boldly embrace. It was, and still is, so exciting. The process was not dependent upon me! The degree of empowerment and transformation was totally in the hands of the one spiraling (exploring) their (w)holes. I found myself sitting back and watching the excitement, the radiance light up the darkness!

I was being given the opportunity to witness my clients becoming truly alive. Since then I have witnessed this with families, couples, and yes, even corporations who have taken the Wisdom WAY model and applied it to their own stuck places or (w)holes. Now, I am able to say with great conviction, "Trust the map – your (w)holes will reveal your (W)holeness."

Rather than being dependent upon me, folks were quickly able to use this framework themselves. Although my presence was still helpful, they were pioneering and embracing their own (W)holeness with an open and eager curiosity. Each of them set their own pace, chose the particular (w)hole that called to them in any one moment, and carried their own responsibility for their own awakening. It was quite an exciting time for my clients and for me. My belief and conviction in the Wisdom WAY continued to deepen as my students continued to actively move beyond the past and into the now, being alive as themselves – (W)holeness awakening one (w)hole at a time! This was no theory. It was happening before my eyes.

Finally, it wasn't the pace or even the breadth of the applicability of the model; it was the depth and permanence of change and empowerment within people that was so precious to witness. Before my eyes, clients and students alike were awakening, empowering, and embodying (W)holeness in a conscious integration. Nothing about the model contradicted traditional therapy or any spiritual wisdom traditions with which I was familiar. In fact, the model was empowering individuals to become their own mentors! Rather than having to let go of all I had studied over my professional life, I found myself weaving it all around the basic Wisdom WAY model. I felt increasingly able to empower students to be their own source, not conceptually but for real!

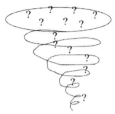

Actively choosing how to move and where to move within this map, these people were falling in love with the wonder of who they were discovering themselves to be. (W)hole work, or (w)hole play as some call it, is about falling back in love with yourself consciously. By discovering in a felt way that we are not broken, we can all fall back in love with who we are. The only thing that had been missing was knowing the secret of (w)holes.

Now in the simplicity of (w)holes, I found a way to love myself – one (w)hole at a time. The universal message of love now had "Hands & Feet" that could walk into my life situation or a client's and awaken the possibility of (W)holeness. It offers folks a simpler, easier, more connected way to live.

I offer profound gratitude to all of my clients and students – and to myself – for not giving up, no matter how many (w)holes we all fell into until the (W)hole Point Wisdom WAY revealed itself.

Chapter 3: A Universal Story

Universal means that it is true for everyone from every walk of life, to whatever (w)hole or (w)holes you are in, to all ages and faiths and cultures. The Wisdom WAY map and method is usable, do-able, immediately accessible, easily learned, and practical for anyone. It doesn't require years of study or dreadful disciplines. It doesn't shame you, blame you, or chastise you. There is no judgment or assessment about your (w)holes or yourself or your reactions to your (w)holes. The simple truth is that we **all** have (w)holes, and we **all** fall into them over and over again. We are all Holy. These (w)holes are the felt experiences where the life seems to drain away, the vitality is missing, and there is a dimming of enthusiasm. Every single one of these (w)hole experiences has a message.

(W)hole experiences simply tell us you and I are normal human beings who are waking up to the (W)hole Truth of ourselves. The (W)hole Point Wisdom WAY is a path of celebration – which begins right where you already are – in a (w)hole. You already know all you need to know to get started because you are the expert of your own (w)holes and your own story. Your story refers to all your history, your beliefs, and your inner orientations to life. The Wisdom WAY is not about my telling you the answers, but rather it's about **my** revealing the map of (W)holeness and **your** using all of your intimate self-knowledge to simply follow the bread crumbs you left for yourself on your own pathway.

Here is a (W)hole Truth hidden in plain view: Every (w)hole we fall into is actually an **invitation** rising up from within us. Every (w)hole is an invitation to look, to see the (W)hole Truth, and to be the (W)hole of ourselves. Of course, we can say "No, I don't want to today."

YOU get to decide what your relationship with a life (w)hole will be! This is your free will choice each time you fall into a (w)hole!

If you decide, "No, not today," the (w)hole will wait for you – it will not go away or disappear. Neither will (w)holes force you to accept the invitation. All life (w)holes are insistent invitations to embrace the life force at the bottom of the (w)hole. You choose when: now or later. I hope that you choose NOW!

The awakening cannot be stopped once it has begun; in fact, it can be quite addictive. I have found clients and students become very excited about awakening their own aliveness, about being empowered to be (W)hole rather than working to "fix" their brokenness. Once a person has felt his first experience of a (w)hole collapsing, he simply wants more – more (W)holeness, more aliveness, more freedom to be! The motivation is from within rather than from without. Awakening (W)holeness is captivating, potent, and powerful!

In the Beginning

Truth, discovery, and change are found within our life (w)holes. However, (w)holes are not the point; they are a place to begin. From the beginning we access our (w)holes through our feelings rather than our thoughts; however, since our minds are also precious, we want to include them as well. Any time we exclude an aspect of our experience, we are, in effect, making a (w)hole or a space between parts of ourselves. **The (W)hole Point method touches our hearts with truth and comforts our minds with logic.** The inclusiveness (i.e., "All parts of us are welcomed and included") combined with the universality of this method of (W)holeness is the source of the effectiveness of this approach. To put it succinctly, there is no place to hide from the glorious process of revealing your (W)hole self to yourself. There is no place to hide from being you because being YOU is the (W)hole Point.

When I describe this orientation to students, I often say, "It is the skeleton inside of transformation. Once you know the skeleton, you can flesh it out however you choose and then embrace your (W)holeness." We look different to one another on the outside because of how our unique bodies are shaped; however, our flesh hangs on the same basic skeletal frame inside each of us. The skeletal frame of the Wisdom WAY does not tell you any answers; it invites you to reveal your own answers, your own heart's logic, and your own life alignment to yourself. Then, once revealed, you are positioned to be able to make choices and changes at a cellular, spiritual, and psychological level of your being. This is the "Hands & Feet" of empowerment.

The Wisdom WAY is a framework or skeleton hidden inside almost all of the various modalities of self-discovery, healing, and awakening you'll find out there. How amazing it is to see through to the skeleton! It is like having X-ray vision on behalf of oneself! My clients and students are often shocked by the simplicity of the skeleton and its presence in movies, books, workshops, seminars, relationships of all kinds – almost anywhere you look for it. It has always been there; we just weren't ready or able to see it. Soon you, too, will be able to see (w)holes and (W)holeness everywhere, but most importantly you'll see them in yourself.

I have written this in the form of a book; however, it may also function as a personal workbook as you read along. I have done this because people seem to want to engage rather quickly with their own personal (w)holes. The "hands & feet" of (w)hole healing might be likened to a toolbox filled with questions (tools) that allow you to reveal, recognize, and re-embrace your own (W)holeness, if you choose. Finally, the power is totally in your hands, no longer dependent upon the "helper."

Begin where you are, in a (w)hole. It is where we all begin this awakening, in the places that hurt or create discomfort in our lives.

As you begin to see the simplicity of the skeleton and the complexity with which we have disguised it, be gentle with yourself. Each of us has been trying to make sense of our own experiences and make the pain go away and never happen again. It is my firm conviction that as we clear the darkness from our own lives, we clear the darkness from each other and our (W)hole planet. Our light is present; it has just been obscured by the darkness of our (w)holes.

As we move through the chapters, we will explore each part of the Wisdom WAY separately. I invite you to remember that you are the expert of yourself. Some have found it helpful to have some paper or a journal to write down personal information. Do this if you so choose. At the end of each section will be a page with the next step diagramed for you to see visually. I suggest that you copy the image onto a blank sheet of paper and fill it in with your personal particulars. In this manner you will not only move through a cognitive recognition of the (W)hole Truth, you will simultaneously move through a felt embrace of your (W)holeness a bit at a time. The intention is to elicit a logical, cognitive, and felt experience of your (w)hole.

At this point, I have been building a foundation upon which to demonstrate and draw the Wisdom WAY map. We have not yet covered the implementation actions. There are just a few more foundational facets to cover before diving into your precious (w)holes.

Sorting, Sifting and Revealing

There is one more element I would like to introduce to you before we plunge directly into the WAY of spiraling your (w)holes. Over the course of my professional life, I have become convinced that every person is simply doing the very best they know how with what they understand. It is not that we are broken and in need of being fixed. The difficulty is actually found in an amazing and surprising truth – we are mysteries to our own selves. We become tangled up in the mystery of ourselves and move in all sorts of directions to relieve what hurts, but we have no idea of the "end game." It's no wonder we find ourselves tangled up even in the middle of using all the self-help stuff we have gathered about us. We have kept many secrets from ourselves about ourselves, even the secret that there are secrets! One of the biggest secrets concerns the strategies we use to control life that run beneath the surface of our awareness.

These strategies we have created, unbeknownst to ourselves, dictate and rule our lives, our reactions, and our decisions. We may intend to react in a particular manner as the person we are today, only to find ourselves responding as the person we were years ago. What is happening is we are confused about who we are in that moment. Our histories, our wishes, our intentions, our choices, our fears, and our secret strategies all collide in that moment, and we react in surprising ways. Before we can choose differently, we must sort out all the parts of ourselves enough to have a clarity of choice.

This crucial step involves unraveling the mystery of ourselves. It is much like clearing away clutter in a closet or a file bin. When we clear away the clutter, there is a spaciousness, and new possibilities unfold. This activity allows us to reveal ourselves to ourselves.

In (w)hole play, we clear inner clutter through the practice of **sorting**. To sort simply means to identify and place items into categories. Sorting is a way to take a look at ourselves without being overwhelmed and confused. It also allows us to see the hidden heart logic upon which we have built our own identity.

Sorting is an ancient alchemical process. Woven throughout many folks tales and primal stories, the activity of sorting points to the empowerment inherent in separating similar elements into "piles" to gain a transformative perspective of the entire entity. A common theme is for a person to be asked to sort an impossibly huge number of differing items, and if he fails in the task, there is a great penalty. Only through special assistance is the impossible task completed. Sorting requires not just our minds, although they are necessary components. Sorting calls our (W)hole being to participate. To sort a feeling from a thought from an event from a reactivity, for example, invites all of our selves to engage. This is part of the power of sorting. For it to be effective, all of us is invited to show up. It is true that in the beginning, we are less skilled in sorting than after a bit of practice. This is only natural. What matters is to begin the process!

Another reason sorting has such a potency to it is that it begins an empowerment process from within the person who is entangled. Sorting through an impossible number of elements requires support beyond our efforts. The special assistance in the case of the Wisdom WAY model is the "map" itself. This allows for experiences, thoughts, strategies, fears, and feelings all to be sorted into categories so that the actual points of choice become evident. Rather than flailing around hoping to hit the right thing, clients are now able to see where there were choices made, how they made them, and what actually happened in their feelings and minds and bodies. Once this is revealed, there is a spaciousness to consider what is in alignment with their current life preferences.

Woven throughout The (W)hole Point Wisdom WAY is this fundamental act of sorting. Whenever you get frustrated, aggravated, or deeply hurt, let those feelings tell you that it is time to do some sorting. Sorting is based in the (w)hole play "No Rules" Rules laid out earlier and written on your index card. So, you already have the beginning point for sorting.

In general, sorting tends to be confused with self-blaming and criticism. This is not sorting. Usually, what folks ask themselves sounds like this: "What is wrong with me? I am reacting the same way I did ten years ago, and it isn't what I want to do." " Why do I keep making this same dumb mistake?" This is the type of phrase someone might use if they have found themselves in the same (w)hole once again. This is NOT sorting. This is self brutalizing and is, in fact, based on a false assumption. It presumes a flawed state of being rather than a (W)hole being, which gets all of us into a great deal of trouble.

Here is the difficulty: The way these self-accusing questions are framed does not lead anywhere but to shame or self-judgment because it presumes a flaw rather than a brilliance of being. Inevitably, a client or student will come to me with lists full of "What is wrong with me," and it is these very lists that are filled with a clutter of unsorted information, thus clouding the essential (W)holeness of their being. There is simply no chance to reveal your own radiant presence when the internal spaces are cluttered with the unsorted chaos of history, feelings, thoughts, and fears.

Sorting is the activity of sifting through our internal clutter and separating out yesterday from today and thoughts from feelings. In a life (w)hole, there are all of these elements all jumbled together in a heap! No wonder we feel lost in the dark! (Be sure to notice the Appendix page on Sorting and Sifting.)

The truth is we all get stuck with and in front of a huge mound of unsorted stuff. The only solution is to sort and sift through what is still valuable today and what you are done with. Sorting begins to establish space for free choice. Only then can we authentically live the freedom of our power to choose and regain access to our free will consciously. (W)holeness is found and felt after sorting. One cannot skip over the action of sorting. Sorting reveals parts of ourselves to ourselves. It is the place to begin.

Sorting is a powerful step towards unveiling our (W)holeness.

All of our past experiences – our history – dictates our life until we reveal the mystery of who we really are. This is the cause for the flood of self-growth, transformational books, videos, seminars, workshops, and retreats. We sense the imprisonment of our history, and yet we were unaware of the key that unlocks the door and leads the way out of the (W)hole mess. Along with some of you, I, too, spent many, many years trying to "figure out" my life. Then I realized: "If all I did was look backwards, how was I to live in the moment?" I had simply felt frustrated on behalf of both myself and my clients. There was something more to this story of becoming conscious, but it seemed to hover just out of my grasp. Sorting is not the same thing as "figuring me out."

Please do not misunderstand what I am saying. I am a great proponent of self-examination and reflection, of psychological work and its value. I have great respect for the power of psychological wounds and their resulting pain and confusions. I truly believe that a person who is experiencing pain or who is suffering, benefits greatly from looking at their life with the intent to change and free themselves. I deeply value in-depth analysis and exploration of the psyche; after all, it is through that journey I came to this simple model of (W)holeness. I sorted through much clutter to arrive at this clarity.

My contention remains that unless someone has done a particular type of sorting, all the self-examination in the world will not collapse any (w)hole, nor will it create true freedom of decision. The sorting I am suggesting is not complicated; however, it does require a steady persistent curiosity, since we are sifting through elements of ourselves we believe we have already examined ad nauseam. We have examined each element and then placed it back in the mound of stuff. The pile remains, and nothing has changed. This is not sorting.

Sorting to Reveal the Wondrous Truth

Therapies of various types are designed to help us sift through all our historical material to free us from the past. The trouble is that often by the time a person decides to seriously engage in this inner work, the mound is huge. My clients used to say, "I just don't know where to start." "I thought we talked about that last week." "You mean there is more to look at?" Now, I hear, "That's it! I get it! No wonder I've done this for so long!" These people have moved into living their (W)holeness rather than living from inside the same old (w)hole, buried up to their eyeballs in a mound of unsorted history. However, sorting history is the first, and frankly, smallest step of awakening to our own (W)holeness.

Sorting out our past from today and sorting out our feelings from our thoughts requires separate bins for each element. Just as if you were placing shoes in one box and hats in another box, we are going to separate out the wisdom elements from one another so we can view the (W)hole picture.

Our journey from unconscious (W)holeness to (w)holes to awakened (W)holeness is the (W)hole Point, and the first step is sorting. To sort we must identify the "bins" or categories into which we will place the different elements.

Across our lifetime, we each experience a basic universal process called living. I call this the **Universal Story**. Sorting our particular thoughts, feelings, and histories, into universal categories allows for the paradox of our uniqueness as particular people and our sameness as human beings. As we sort, our life (w)holes begin to transform, and our relationship to these (w)holes becomes one of appreciation rather than judgment.

The first sorting step is to identify the difference between our history and what is commonly called "our wounds." In order to be able to look at any (w)hole into which we fall, first we must sort through the elements of that (w)hole. As we do this, our spiral path of (W)holeness is revealed, in particular. In the next sections of this book, I will be taking you through each of the elements of a (w)hole, ultimately revealing the entire anatomy of a (w)hole. As we do this, we are sorting.

All (w)holes have a universal anatomy made up of **elements**. These elements are:

The Horrible Truth
The Curb
The OUCH
Our Meaning Maker
The Allowed Me
The Space Between
The Not Allowed Me
Our Feeling Spiral
The Portal.

As we review each of these elements, you will see how they are all linked together in one (W)hole interior orientation, designed by you, to protect you from experiences in life that hurt. Once we have a personal map of a particular (w)hole completed, then we are in a position to step into our (W)holeness. Where do we start? We begin at the beginning – when we were born.

Chapter 4: Waking up to the Beginning of (w)hole Formation

The Universal Story is what we all experience. It is what we call living life. None of this will sound new to you; in fact, it will sound rather simple. However, do not let the simplicity deceive you, for contained within it is the key to the door of awaking, embracing, and being your (W)hole Self.

The beginning of the Universal Story sounds like this. We are all born (W)hole – complete, magnificent, and unconscious. We are newborns. We have no conscious idea of how wonderful and how truly magnificent we are. We just are! We sleep, we eat, we poop, we pee, we have sensations of life. We are unable to self-reflect. We are not born designing, evaluating, considering, adjusting, or censoring ourselves to please those around us until it becomes a matter of survival to do so. Then, at that point, we begin to use any and all capacities to re-design ourselves to survive the context into which we are born.

Self-censoring is not our true nor our original purpose or way of being. We were just being who and what we were. When we were sad, we cried. When we were hungry, we screamed for food. When we were happy and felt safe, we giggled.

Then experiences happened. The easy, gentle, cared for, embraced state of infancy was interrupted by experiences that were painful in some way. These moments wounded us. This happened to all of us. This is life happening. It is no one's fault. The Wisdom WAY model is not about blame; it is about the (W)hole Truth. We are born (W)hole and unconscious, and then "stuff" that hurt, confused, shamed, or frightened us occurred. This was and is true for all of us.

For some of us, the events that hurt happen sooner rather than later, but it does happen for all of us. For some of us the tough or painful moments are less dramatic, and for others they are much more traumatic. Perhaps it is obvious pain; perhaps it is subtle, but rest assured discomfort will occur. The name I apply to this discomfort is the **Horrible Truth (HT)**. Simply put, things happen, and we hurt. What are these Horrible Truths? Only you know!

And Then the Horrible Truth Happens

We recognize our Horrible Truths because they feel horrible to us. They are facts in our lives that still have a felt presence to them. These "factual events" hurt, and the pain seems to stick around. While some experiences hurt and then the feeling-memory falls away, leaving little trace of its existence, other things feel horrible to us and stick like splinters in our hearts. It is these experiences that feel horrible and stick to us that are named the Horrible Truth. The Horrible Truths are not the feelings; they are events that hurt us. Each of us has our own unique list of Horrible Truths, and yes, each of us does have a list of Horrible Truths. Many of us are quite skilled at identifying our particular Horrible Truths, and it is the first bin into which we sort and place our history.

The basic definition of the **Horrible Truth** is: "Experiences – big and little – that we felt were horrible to us." This is a place where many of us who have spent lots of time in self-development seminars feel quite comfortable and are adept at naming. These are the events, facts, and behaviors that others did or didn't do, said or didn't say, that felt horrible to us. The Horrible Truths are behaviors, events, words, reactions, or actions of other people, that occurred and were so very painful, so horrible for us, that we would do anything to avoid feeling that pain again. Each of us determines what we feel is horrible because it's how we feel about it that is important, not what others feel about it.

Some people have objected to my use of the word "horrible." However, at the moment of these experiences, I could think of no better word. I chose the word "horrible" to capture the pain of the moment of the felt experience. It does not mean it must be a dramatic, dreadful event in itself. However, for YOU it was a deep, painful, horrible experience. The key point of the Horrible Truth is that it felt awful. These "Horrible" experiences may be many small repetitions of something challenging; they may be little small moments on the playground or in the classroom, or, they may be one time big dramatic moments. There are no "wrong" Horrible Truths – only yours!

Some examples of Horrible Truths include:

Parents divorced

Family moved
A new teacher came to class
A best friend went to a different school
The bully on the playground was mean
They laughed at me
A baby sister came home to stay
Dad re-married
Mom hits and yells
Mom/Dad is an alcoholic

By themselves, you can see they are simply neutral events. But in our own personal history, they had a big impact upon us – so much so that we would call them "horrible." Sorting through our Horrible Truths is also about separating "us" from "them." Horrible Truths happened to us.

Experiences, which we consider horrible, are due to actions others have taken and which then impacted us. Sorting "us" from "them" opens up space for us to consider what and who we really have control over in our lives. Identifying what was horrible for us as separate from what they did or didn't do or said or didn't say, begins to reduce our tendency to feel victimized by our history. That does not mean it didn't hurt!

It is important to understand that what one person may consider a Horrible Truth, another may not even notice that it occurred. Each of us has the power, right from birth, to determine what will be considered a horrible experience. We are born with a felt power to name and notice what feels bad, dreadful, painful, and horrible. This ability is not conscious, it is not verbalized, and it is not dependent upon cognitive thought. Our capacity to feel and react is on a limbic or cellular level. Pain causes us to recoil and to cry and to get away. Just as some people have a higher physical pain tolerance or a lower one, so too, some people have a higher tolerance or a lower one for emotional pain. In addition, we live in different cultures, societies, and families, all of which also shape our sense of what we might believe to be a horrible event. We are all unique and distinct. At the same time, we are all the same in that we all have experiences so hurtful, shocking, or shaming, that we would call them horrible.

One of the points of empowerment in the Wisdom WAY model is that you and you alone are the expert and authority about you. Sometimes others try to tell us what is horrible. However, only if we believe it was horrible, only if we feel it is horrible do we have to agree with that assessment! This is important. Sorting what we felt was horrible from what others are trying to tell us "ought" to be the Horrible Truth, is crucial. Our (W)holeness is only authentic when it is based on our truth, not on anyone else's.

Events alone, no matter how dramatic they may be, are not automatically a Horrible Truth. The experience must be linked to our personal reaction to that life moment. The decision to call something an HT isn't usually in our awareness, rather this assessment happens at a limbic or gut level. "We just know!" We know that this is "horrible!" No one can make this feeling decision for us, and no one can tell us our feeling decision is wrong!

Let's look very closely at how truth experiences become Horrible Truths for us.

Truths become Horrible Truths when we experience them as being so painful that we conclude to ourselves (usually secretly and without conscious words), "Never again do I want to feel that pain!" "Never again will I feel that horrible!" "I will do whatever I have to do to not feel that and to keep that from ever happening again!" Whatever you experienced that felt horrible in this way to you is your Horrible Truth.

For example, let us say a child has been in a car crash and remembers only the hug of her mom afterwards. The child suffered no harm physically. This child hasn't logged this experience as horrible even if she can still distinctly recall it as an adult. Alternatively, let us say another child has been in a car crash, again escaping all harm, but this experience logs in his psyche as horrible because both mom and dad screamed at him for crying after the wreck. Neither child was hurt; the same type of event happened to both of them, but only one child might call it horrible. Meanwhile, let us say a third child had the same car crash experience and was also yelled at, but she didn't log it limbically as horrible because "my parents always screamed – it seemed normal." Can you see the differences? No one can tell you your Horrible Truth but you. The only thing that you can count on is that each of us has our own list of Horrible Truths.

There is a "Lisa Litmus Test" for the Horrible Truth. Lisa, a senior faculty member of the (W)hole Point Institute, an editor of this book, and a teacher of the Wisdom WAY, developed this "test" to help people sort out their Horrible Truths from just Truths. If you are having difficulty determining what events may or may not have become Horrible Truths for you, consider these questions. Remember, questions are how we sort.

- Would you say the event felt horrible? Was it deeply painful to your heart?
- Did the event make you feel horrible about yourself? Did it make you feel like there was something wrong with you, perhaps in some way you were to blame for this thing happening?
- Did you feel deep down inside that you just had to find a way to make sure this event never, ever happened again to you?
- Is this an experience where you can easily call up the feelings attached to it years later?

If you can answer "yes" to all four questions, you have surely found a Horrible Truth for yourself. If you can answer "yes" to two of the four questions, you may be close to identifying a Horrible Truth, and it is worth looking more deeply again at your actual description of the event. Remember, the first Horrible Truths happen when we are very young. So the way we think and feel about the event, behavior, responses, and reactions of the others is not from the viewpoint of an adult.

Consider this example: someone whom you loved dearly passed away when you were a small child. Yes, the event was horrible and painful (Question one is a "yes"). You miss them and feel sad they aren't around. Maybe, even yes, it made you feel horrible about yourself or inside yourself. Maybe you didn't say something to that person you wished you had, or maybe you didn't do something for that person when you had the chance (So Question two could be a "yes"). Then maybe you realize that while this event is horrible, there's nothing you can do to stop those you love from dying (Question three is a "no"). And finally, you can think about it, but the raw feelings of that moment don't flood into you (Question four is a "no"). In this case, what has happened is just a painful, sad event. It's not a "true" Horrible Truth.

If, on the other hand, we look at this again and answer "yes" to the first two questions (like we did before), but for the third question, maybe deep down inside we realize that we decided (at a level deep in our guts, not in words cognitively) never to love another person that much again because it's just too painful when they die, then the answer to the third question is "yes." And further, let us say every time we think about that person, a wave of guilt and shame washes over us. Question four is now a "yes." A painful, sad event has now become a Horrible Truth. Can you see the difference? Can you feel the difference?

Sorting our particular Horrible Truths out from our entire history begins to make some space inside of us for further sorting. The next step is to look at the event which occurred today, which seemed to "push us into" our (w)hole. This is called **Identifying the Curb**.

Identifying the Curb

The Curb is the edge of a (w)hole. Imagine that the Curb is raised up a bit to get your attention. It is what trips you up in that particular moment. Often Curbs are very simple events; however, we have a big or deep reaction to them. This is how you recognize a (w)hole. Curb events are contemporary or current events that happen today.

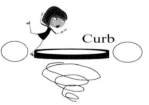

The Curb is an important element of any (w)hole. It is whatever just happened (or didn't happen) that left you feeling "in the pits." The simplest description is the most helpful. The Curb is not the same thing as the Horrible Truth, although they feel similar. The Curb is about today, what happens today to trigger your (w)hole. This is different from the Horrible Truth, which is all about long ago history. However, the Curb is linked to the HT through what I call **Memory Lane**.

Horrible Truth

Curb

For many of us, we simply cannot remember right away the Horrible Truths of our childhood, so the Curb is the next best place to go. For some folks, the Curb can seem like the Horrible Truth. It certainly feels like one. However, it is today's reminder of what happened long ago. Even though the connection may not be obvious to you, you can be sure that it is there! So let us look at an example to show the difference.

There is a young woman, I'll call her Susan, who works in an office as a legal secretary. One day she sends out an announcement memo to all the employees at the firm, announcing the appointment of a new law partner. A day or so after this announcement has been distributed, another secretary, Donna, comments to her in passing that the name of the new law partner was misspelled in the memo. Donna did not say this maliciously and even tried to joke with Susan about how long and complicated the spelling of this person's name was. But all Susan could feel was that she was suddenly in a dark pit. She had made a typing mistake, and it had tripped her into a (w)hole. The typing mistake was the Curb that tripped her in. Upon reflection, Susan discovered that her Horrible Truth was that her Father said, "You're a disappointment," when she got a C on her report card. Can you feel the link between the today event and yesterdays' hurt? This is "Memory Lane."

When Susan learned of her typing mistake, she felt the same intense sense of failure and unworthiness that she felt all those years ago when she was eight years old and her dad called her a disappointment. Today she felt like a failure to her boss. Back then, she felt like a failure to her dad. When we fall into a (w)hole, the feelings are "like back then" and are far more intense than the current event would seem to warrant. When we react in a way that is above and beyond what one might expect given the situation, we have fallen into a (w)hole by tripping on a Curb. The (w)holes are created when we are little; it is only later that we can begin to recognize that our reactions seem more severe than is warranted for an adult. What is happening is that two time zones are present simultaneously – yesterday and today.

This is one of the reasons people sometimes feel "confused" or "crazy" or "mixed up inside." When there are two time frames operating simultaneously within us and our emotions are calling for a response – it is confusing. Does the small child of yesterday respond or does the adult of today? When we are in our (w)holes, the time frames and our responses blur, resulting in surprising re-activities.

Again, sorting the Curbs from the Horrible Truths begins the awakening of empowered (W)holeness. We begin to reveal to ourselves that we truly do make sense! Curbs are "reminding us" of a place still hurting inside our hearts. Curbs are not the issue. Curbs just show us that there is something more to sort through.

Can you see how closely the Curb and the Horrible Truth are related? Can you see how tripping on a (today's) Curb might trigger a trip down Memory Lane to where the HT lives? HINT: When we find ourselves overreacting to an event today, it really helps to be curious about it. By being curious, we can usually find our way back to our Horrible Truths. Simply ask yourself questions such as, "What does this remind me of from when I was little?" "What am I feeling right now, and when have I felt this way before?" "What is the earliest time I remember feeling these same feelings?" "What about this Curb feels familiar?"

Stay curious without judging yourself, and you'll soon unravel a bit more of the mystery of you. As mentioned earlier in the guidelines, staying curious without being judgmental is essential because it's our judgments that keep us in the dark and keep us from seeing clearly. We also know we're in a (w)hole when we find ourselves being very judgmental and unable to explore with open-hearted curiosity. In order to do this sorting effectively, it is crucial that you do not engage in any judgment about what you are feeling or about the "size" of the Curb that pushed you into the (w)hole or your reactions. Every (w)hole is filled with surprises; judgment against yourself will blind you to the revelations you are now actively inviting.

Before we move on from the Horrible Truth, let's look more closely at how (w)hole creation is our response to a Horrible Truth experience. Yes, it is true that (w)holes are a result of the Horrible Truths, but the Horrible Truth itself does not offer a doorway to (W)holeness. This is a point of great confusion for many! It is the reason that looking to our history alone does not bring freedom or greater aliveness – there is no portal to (W)holeness for today in the events of yesterday. Paradoxically, our Horrible Truth experiences motivated us to create every one of our life (w)holes, which we now repeatedly fall into over and over again.

A (w)hole Play Opportunity for You

Start where YOU are! In preparation for sorting through your Horrible Truths, you are offered this (w)hole Play opportunity to look at your paper where you listed all of your current concerns and issues. Now, take a few moments to write down all of the Curbs you can think of that correspond to those issues. Be as inclusive as you dare, for the (w)hole Truth of your life is hidden in this "mound" of life stuff. Now is the time to stop and really be with your self!

If you wish, you can draw a circle (or (w)hole) on your paper with a thick outline around it to indicate the Curb. Write down your Curbs next to it.

After you have your list of Curbs, put it aside and continue reading. We will come back to this again later.

More about the Horrible Truth

Our first HT moments happened to all of us when we were kids. As you begin to consider your own Horrible Truths, keep in mind that it helps to think from a kid's perspective – the thought process is more of a gut reaction than a logical thought process. A Horrible Truth requires that in some way it felt horrible to us, and we have the conviction (usually secretly held within our being) that we can prevent the experience or feeling from ever occurring again. ***Prevention of a re-occurrence of the Horrible Truth is the motivation behind the creation of all (w)holes.***

How precious all our self-exploration becomes as we open the doors hidden behind the Horrible Truths. As a great proponent of self-reflection, I applaud all of us who have been intensely engaged in our journey! Dedication to being all you are is the fuel behind both the creation of our life (w)holes as well as the motivation to step into (W)holeness. After all, the point of all our "self-development" or "self-discovery" work has been to become (W)hole. The silly wonderful secret about (W)holeness is we don't need to become (W)hole; we already are! It is just that all the bits and pieces and parts of our entire self are scattered all about. Rather we are now inviting ourselves to collapse the spaces between all our parts. And to do this we must first sort out all the different elements of our (W)holeness. Any expertise we have developed at naming our Horrible Truths in a clear, simple way is quite useful.

Horrible Truths have secret gifts to offer when we are able to name them in a bald naked way. This is because our Horrible Truths have served as fundamental life-motivators deep within our beings. The clarity you have about your Horrible Truths will serve you well as you move into the recognition of how you created brilliant strategies to prevent any repeated occurrences. Typically, we all have long stories about our Horrible Truths, and those of us on the self-development path have often honed our storytelling to a fine art. The difficulty is that the HT alone will not free us to be fully alive.

Each of us in our own way has been at war with the Horrible Truths. For most of us, we can readily identify what isn't working and what is wrong with us. Self-hate, self-judgment, self-belittlement are art forms in the realm called "self-discovery." It is done under the guise of "being honest with ourselves." This is not honesty; it is self-judgment and self-blame which results from a confusion between a Horrible Truth and the strategy you have creatively developed to ward off any further experiences of that particular type. Remember, just because one HT has happened doesn't mean life stopped happening; more Horrible Truths kept coming into our world as an infant, a toddler, an adolescent, and even into our adult years.

How do any of us move to a place of celebrating who we are when we are engaged in so much self-evaluation and belittling of the majesty of ourselves? How do we gain clarity when we are secretly and subtly at war within ourselves working to prevent any reoccurrences of The Horrible Truths? How do we shift into living our (W)holeness while we are flailing around inside the darkness fearing a possible repeat of this, that, or the other HT moment?

There are tools and strategies we can learn, but these do not access and heal what is happening in the core of our being. They do not collapse the (w)holes; they just teach us to manage them. We are told that we really are wonderful, and we just need to know this. We are encouraged to believe in ourselves. We are supported by the many available self-help groups, so we know we are not the only ones with that particular Horrible Truth. We often engage in affirmations, visualizations and other practices. Please do not misunderstand me – I know and understand that all of these are powerful and useful tools. But honestly, who can really believe or feel any of the "good stuff" when inside we are feeling "icky" about ourselves?

I really tried to convince myself that I loved myself no matter how "icky" any moment felt. My clients and students have tried. But in all honesty we were simply working very hard to contain what we were feeling, fearing, and believing, and then covering up the (w)holes and the pain with the proper appearances. I surely didn't **know** in my heart that I was okay, much less great, when I sat squarely in the dark (w)holes. I surely didn't believe all the affirmations I so religiously chanted. I wanted to. I longed to. I hoped to. I worked really hard to arrive there one day. I really loved learning all the various approaches, and it wasn't that there weren't positive effects. There were! But really deep down, there was still something missing, something beyond what I was offering my clients and what I was using on my own behalf.

So often we have all heard some version of "You're OK, you're fine just the way you are," while on the inside we were screaming, "I'M NOT OK." And inside we feel shame for not understanding ourselves and for feeling this way again! It all becomes a vicious circle. Essentially we end up circling around the Horrible Truth experiences, hoping that this approach or that will change what happened! The truth is that they don't and they won't.

Simply put: Life doesn't feel so great sometimes. This is true for all of us. We didn't make that up. Life hurts, and we began to manage the pain. I applaud all of us for being creative enough to respond with ingenious management strategies to stop, block, prevent, or simply not feel the Horrible Truths inside all of us.

Healing and Horrible Truths: Here are more tips for being very clear about what your Horrible Truths are, and are not:

• (W)hole healing does not happen by changing the HT. The Horrible Truth is a fact of an experience which has already occurred and cannot be changed, ever.

• (W)holeness will not be a truth for you if you get caught up in fighting against the HT or trying to change the fact of the HT.

Horrible Truth Sorting Guidelines

- Horrible Truths are **from yesterday**, the past.

- Horrible Truths are **events, behaviors, words, experiences that happened and felt "horrible" to you.**

- Horrible Truths **are not about blame**. They are simple "news bulletin" descriptions of what occurred to us, around us, and in our presence when we were little, and they felt horrible to us. HT's are stated as neutral descriptions of the events. To be able to name your own HT's is the beginning of your own authority to know, name, and reveal yourself to yourself. Listing your own Horrible Truths is not about blaming others, for this would leave you disempowered. Blaming is a tempting path to take sometimes, so no judgment of yourself even if you notice a bit of blaming feelings rise up. Let them be there, and continue to make your HT sorting list.

- Horrible Truths are always **about what *others* did or said** (or didn't do and didn't say). As you can see, the Horrible Truth is external or outside of us, beyond our control. Horrible Truths are not about something we did, and they are not even necessarily about us personally. Rather they are about *what others* expressed in our presence, whether it was directed towards us or not.

- Horrible Truths can be **patterns of events, behaviors, feelings, or responses** that were painful to us. For example, "Every Sunday mom and dad dressed us up for church. At church they would talk all about how family members love each other and how lucky all children with nice parents were. Then after church we would come home, and my parents would yell at us. It was totally confusing! I never understood what was happening." This is an example of one person's HT. It was the pattern and juxtaposition of events that was most painful. Sometimes HT's are patterns rather than one-time events.

- Horrible Truths usually, but not always, **involve the important people in our lives** – mom, dad, grandparents, teachers, friends, aunts, uncles, step-parents, siblings – and occasionally even strangers in our lives. A key element is that the person or persons involved have a big impact upon our own inner experience. What they do, say, or don't say mattered greatly to us.

- Horrible Truths are a **litany of the bad memories** we have growing up. This is always a good place to start. Most of us can begin there. It is often what has been called the beginnings of self-awareness: Being able to name what hurt from back then. I call it making a list of the Horrible Truths; name your HT's from birth forward. This helps to ensure that the oldest HT's are noted down.

- **Horrible Truth statements are not about us. In fact, it is most helpful to state them without including the words "I" or "me" in the statement.**

- Horrible Truths are best sorted as **neutral descriptions** of the event or behavior even when we have big feelings about them. These feelings are sorted in another way. So, let your feelings be, and just list your HT as neutral descriptions or news bulletins.

Further Horrible Truth Discussion and Exploration

One of the traps that can occur for folks is that the Horrible Truths and our response to them get mixed in together. As part of the sorting process, it is particularly helpful to refer to yourself in the third person if and only if you must put yourself in the HT at all.

Keeping ourselves out of the Horrible Truth is our first step of empowerment. As long as we keep ourselves in the description of our Horrible Truth experiences, we stay in a victim role of "this is what they did to me." By removing ourselves from the statement and keeping it simply about them, we can then close the lid on the Horrible Truth, since history is a done deal (i.e., "They did this."). Consider the Horrible Truth like a square box with a lid on it. We can open it up, place our HT events in it, and then close the lid. The past is the past. If we write our Horrible Truth with us in the description, we are holding ourselves in the past, and we are confusing us with them!

True empowerment begins by sorting "them" from "us."

Sometimes the idea of keeping the HT neutral is difficult to accept, so let me make this a bit clearer. The observed facts of what has occurred are neutral. Upon coming upon a dead animal, one could say, "There is a dead animal." This is a neutral statement without an emotional charge. Conversely, another person in the same situation might say, "Oh no, how terrible." Yet another person might say, "At least it isn't a person." The event or fact is neutral until an emotional charge, value, or preference is added to the equation. It is the participant who determines the emotional meaning or significance of the fact before them, not the fact or event itself. This is a very important distinction to make as we prepare to look at our own Horrible Truths.

In the beginning we are sorting (separating) the HT events from our feeling responses. In the beginning we are sorting "me" from "them." When you are listing your HT's, always list the events without including your personal feeling responses. A key way to make sure you have captured a Horrible Truth is to be sure the words you use to name it hint at the pain the event caused you. If you can still feel just a touch of that hurt today, or even that you notice yourself wanting to avoid even mentioning it, you can assume you have located a Horrible Truth.

Do your best to keep your words at the vocabulary level of a child rather than that of an adult. This helps to make the feel of the Horrible Truth more obvious. Remember, lots of these HT's happened to us as children, so it helps us to access the language of children as we begin to identify our particular HT's. We are going right to the heart of the matter, so to speak. In the Wisdom WAY model, identifying elements of a (w)hole from a child's viewpoint helps to unveil these hidden feelings without getting lost in an emotional overwhelm.

Adults can overwhelm themselves by long wordy descriptions, while our inner child might use one or two words to say it all! Notice that these Horrible Truth examples have a feeling experience embedded in them. So, let us consider some HT examples:

- Father or mother died.
- Parents yelled and fought.
- Mom never had time to play.
- Sister was much smarter in school.
- A "new brother or sister" was brought home.
- Parents got divorced.
- Dad was in the military service. Family moved every year
- Father or mother were drinking all the time.
- A stranger raped the child.
- The Sunday school teacher said, "Sinners go to hell" and "You are a sinner for sure!"
- Dad said that "Sending girls to school was a waste of money."
- The family rule was "Children should be seen and not heard."
- They said, "It was God's will that sister got sick and died."
- They (the adults) kept changing the rules.
- Mom laughed when child fell down riding the bike the first time and said "How clumsy."
- The teacher said the child would be a failure at life when the child didn't spell 'house' correctly. All the kids laughed!
- The substitute gym teacher yelled at the kid for not knowing the rules for softball.
- Family laughed whenever the child cried.
- Mom said, "You will never amount to anything."
- Father suddenly stopped hugging.
- Second grade teacher called the kid stupid and slow.
- Other kids laughed at the kid when he tried to talk and stuttered.
- Father said, "Stop crying – boys who are men don't show feelings!"

Many of us have learned all about our Horrible Truths from self-discovery books, therapy, television talk shows, or workshops in which we have participated. We can name them, describe them, and feel the feelings about them. Many of us are very adept at this first step. Good for us. This is the crucial foundational work that allows us to move deeply into empowered (W)holeness as we come to know the secrets of all Life (W)holes.

Sorting begins with being curious about the link between the Curb and the Horrible Truth. So if you are more comfortable beginning with a Curb (a today event), so be it. If you are more comfortable beginning with a Horrible Truth (yesterday's event), so be it. It doesn't matter where we begin, only that we begin somewhere. Our (w)holes are based on inertia. Motion is the first step to any (w)hole play.

Here are just a very few of my own Horrible Truths:

- Grandmother died.
- Stepfather made the child (me) eat all the vegetables on the plate.
- Teacher embarrassed student for not knowing how to take dictation.
- Father killed himself.
- Mother re-married.
- Sister went to a different school when family moved.
- Mom miscarried at home.
- Family moved in the middle of the school year.
- They made fun of the way the kid dressed.

Your list of Horrible Truths may feel infinite. I assure you that quickly your HT list will become smaller and smaller as it becomes more particular. In the beginning let it be as big as it is. Many Horrible Truths will seem to fall away as we become adept at moving through the map. This is because the most ancient Horrible Truths are what later HT's rest upon. As your interior (W)holeness awakens, there is a cascade of (W)holeness that seems to carry folks to their essential or core Horrible Truths. There is more about this later – for the moment, just celebrate that you are succeeding by just boldly and bluntly listing your HT's. All you are asked to do right now is sort.

Remember, what is a Horrible Truth for one of us isn't a Horrible Truth for another because we are all unique. What makes an event or fact a Horrible Truth for you is how it **felt** to you. It isn't for anyone else to decide. This point is very, very important! The same fact or event or exchange may not strike one person as horrible, while for another person, the same moment may feel devastating. There is no one like us in the (W)hole world, and this is the reason each of us must take on the job of naming our own personal Horrible Truths for ourselves. We cannot copy anyone else's path to (W)holeness, and the path begins with the HT – **your** Horrible Truths.

The fundamental skill you are already using and which is the bedrock of the Wisdom WAY is **curiosity without judgment**. To dare to be curious, wide open to whatever one discovers while dropping all self-judgments, expectations, and blame, is one of the most powerful actions you can take on your own behalf. As you consider what you would put on your Horrible Truth list, do it from an orientation of curiosity without judgment. Implied in this is that there is no way to fail. After all, you are the expert of you.

Curiosity without judgment may sound simple and perhaps even easy, and yet it is one of the greatest challenges for all of us. To be able to look at **anything** inside of us and outside of us without judgment or reaction, calls us to admit to ourselves our spiritual arrogance! Judgment is the activity of assigning "good" or "bad" as evaluations to what we are looking at or feeling or thinking. Hidden in this is a presumption that we know what is better for another person, that we know how the world "should" be, that we know what is the "correct" way, and that we are "better than" anyone else. Earlier, I mentioned Compassion Expansion. The actual daily practice or the "Hands & Feet" of Compassion Expansion is to approach any experience from a position of curiosity without judgment.

In the Wisdom WAY, you are invited to apply curiosity without judgment to your own life! How radical! For most of us, being "kind," "gentle," and "open" to others is far easier than applying this same approach to ourselves. So here is the way to begin to move into self-love. Begin by developing the art of curiosity without judgment. Each time you notice a judgment of "good" or "bad" about something inside yourself or another, pause and invite yourself to name what you are seeing **without** any judgment. You will notice the world begins to change.

The art of **curiosity without judgment** is directly related to listing your Horrible Truths. As you list them, make every effort to remove judgment and simply describe the event as you would for a newspaper article. For example, one might read in a newspaper headline "Body found in street" or "Child left on doorstep of church" or "Prince and Princess married at sunrise." Notice there is no judgment embedded in the descriptions. Just the facts.

If you can't think of or remember things from being a kid, just make a list of the Horrible Truths from as early back as you can remember. If you are not sure what to put down, think back as far as you can to the most embarrassing or hurtful or "secret from everyone" moments, and then write the facts. Trust me here – more memories will surface as you go through this process. Remember the rule – there is no way to fail, there are no right or wrong answers. Just stay curious and drop all your judgments, including the one that says, "I did this all before." Yes, most likely you have named much of your history, but this time, it is only the beginning. Wherever you are is perfect. Start with what you know!

A (w)hole Play Opportunity for You

Take a moment now, if you wish, and on the top right-hand corner of your blank paper, write three or four short phrases that describe your Horrible Truths. Then you may draw a box around the list. We call this the "Horrible Truth Box." As I mentioned earlier, this "box" has a lid on it, for the purpose of closing the box and moving on to the elements where YOU are empowered. The secret of the HT is that you had NO say about what

THEY did! Consequently, all we can do is look at it and name it from the point of view of being curious without judgment. You may create a box if you wish, just as you see in the image.

Remember, we are all born (W)hole and unaware of ourselves. We are born with a big fat heart, deeply sensitive to life experiences. Then stuff happens. When it hurts and feels horrible to us, we name it a Horrible Truth. If you are unclear about what your Horrible Truth(s) might be, you may use your list of Curbs. List those feelings associated with your Curbs, and then ask yourself when was the earliest time you can remember feeling this same way. Beginning today to touch yesterday is just fine!

Horrible Truth

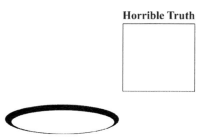

If you are clear about your Horrible Truths but are uncertain about how they are related to today, simply begin by listing your HT's and then notice how you felt when those events happened. Once you are clear here, you can ask yourself, "When in the present have I felt this same way?" You see? Beginning in yesterday to touch today is just fine too!

This is the process of sorting "US" from "THEM," and "TODAY" from "YESTERDAY." Where you start doesn't matter – just start in the way that is easiest for you.

Begin your HT list now:

Consider the ages zero to twenty years old. Simply hit the highlights and jot down the HT's you name for yourself in the upper right corner of your paper. You don't need to make an exhaustive list; this is just to get you moving. And don't worry about making it perfect, you can always go back and add to or change your notes at any time as we move ahead.

Again, remember, the big Horrible Truths usually happened when we were little, so start young and work forward. Just jot them all down. It doesn't matter how many you write. Many or a few is fine! This is the beginning of the sorting process.

It is especially helpful to **keep the HT as simple** as possible. Do your best to avoid putting yourself in the event. Remember, the **HT is about others** – what they said to you, what they did to you, and even what they didn't do or say to you. Write it like a news bulletin.

The harder it is for you to do this, the more significant this HT is in your life. Finally, do your best to write it as a kid would rather than the adult you are! "Left alone" feels very different than "Abandoned."

So, relax, take a deep breath, and try your hand at listing a Horrible Truth or two on your paper. Do not try to list them all in the box. If you have a big list, make a separate paper for all your HT ideas and then pick the top two or three.

If you have an idea of what the Curb is (the today event that feels the same as the HT event) for any of the HT's, write it on the edge of the oval, where a Curb is in the image.

Congratulations – this is the very first step in empowering your (W)hole life!

Even though you may know all about your Horrible Truths, this knowledge has not prevented you from falling into the same (w)hole again and again and again. Knowing your HT's will not change a thing. The Horrible Truths are *not* where healing happens or where (w)holes collapse or where empowerment happens. HT's are just where lots of us begin. Our Horrible Truths are often what we are most familiar with – so we start with what we know. Ultimately, once you know the entire (W)hole map, you will spend next to no time at all with your HT!

At this point you are just learning, so be gentle with yourself and continue reading.

Two Awareness Invitations

First, naming the HT is a beginning step, *not* the solution or a quick fix. This is an important distinction. Secondly, there is a danger of mixing up blame with healing and thinking that assigning blame is what healing is about. Blaming and healing are not the same. Blame is not empowering, nor is it empowerment!

Often clients have been quite stunned to realize that they have been engaged in blame when they were under the impression that they were engaged in a healing process. They have come to me feeling frustrated and disappointed that they were still stuck in the muck. The important point is that now you are considering exploring the point of true power – your feelings. Yes, the important people in your life did things or said things that hurt horribly. Knowing this and acknowledging this is the first step, and it in itself does not affect healing or stimulate any lasting change. Blaming the people who gave us life and touched our lives, choosing to stay stuck in the past by playing out the same reaction to the Horrible Truth, or bemoaning our fate or life circumstances, will not change our life. It will definitely not free our life force. If we stop at the HT exploration, more precious moments of our lives are squandered. Be aware of these two dangerous and very seductive detours. The key is just to list the HT's as facts, and then move on.

This is a very important point to understand, so let me say it again. Our Horrible Truths are just that – facts or events or expressions of other people which we have feelings about. There is no need to apologize for it or explain why it was. The Horrible Truth is just what was; it is just the facts!

Many people get mixed up here because much of the self-help materials available to us seem to focus on just the Horrible Truths and then offer suggestions for managing or handling the leftover feelings. Often my students and clients want to spend lots of time going over and over the dreadful details of what went wrong in their lives. They come to me believing this is where the action is and this is what will move them into (W)holeness. Yes, of course it is important; however, once we know what happened and we really look it "in the eyes," then it is time to move on, because you have wonderful places to go.

Chapter 5: Waking Up to What a (w)hole Feels Like

What We Know so Far

Below is a summary image of what we have revealed so far: We are born (W)hole and unconscious and then "stuff" happens. This "stuff" is called the Horrible Truth. These events hit our hearts, and we feel how "horrible" they are for us. The "X" on the big heart is a way to say, "Ouch, that hurt!"

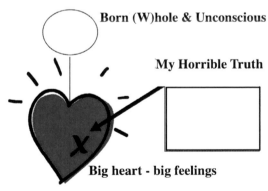

The Wisdom skeleton is already being revealed. For consistency and for other reasons, we encourage you to always locate the sorted elements on the same place on your paper. The reasons will become clearer later. The image above is the beginning of the Wisdom map. It always looks the same, because each of us is living the same Universal Story.

Paradoxically, the Wisdom map, always looks different because what we each write in the Horrible Truth Box will be different. The Horrible Truth box is only and always about the OTHER. At this point you have sorted "ME" from "THEM." What they did is inside the box, and how you felt is outside the box. You can imagine yourself sitting in the heart, looking at the HT box.

Now, let's move on to our feelings.

Feelings: Where the Real Power Shows Up

The Horrible Truth is what we keep trying to get past, heal from, move beyond, or get over. Our reactions to a Horrible Truth and how we felt in the moment we experienced an HT is a key to our (W)holeness. The Horrible Truth is what most of us know a great deal about. It is the series of facts, events, and moments that so deeply wounded us they continue to show up in our lives. Now be careful. This isn't about blame. This is simply about what actually happened to us when we were little.

It is what happens next that makes all the difference. What happened, no matter how horrible, isn't as important as what you did with it! It is here we begin to enter into the arena of where our power has been secretly active on our behalf. In essence, we all make meanings about and out of the Horrible Truth. We grant significance and place emotional values upon the events we have experienced. Here is the Horrible Truth formula, with which you are now familiar:

Historical Event + your "horrified" Feeling Response = a "Horrible Truth Experience"

The next Wisdom element to sort is your **Feeling Response**. Again, you are the expert about how you felt at the time. Usually we have many feelings; remember, we are not limited to just one feeling. However, there is the "first" or our most primal feeling response to the Horrible Truth. I call this The **OUCH!**

The OUCH is associated with the HT and is the core feeling response we had to the HT event. You will feel the OUCH associated with a HT when you name it. The OUCH feeling (whatever you might name it to be, i.e., hurt, sad, shamed, embarrassed, etc.) is what makes an event, a fact, a truth, feel horrible.

Event-fact + your "OUCH" feeling = a "Horrible Truth Experience"

I use a "kid word" to describe this felt moment because we were kids when the HT happened! Again, to the degree you can keep your language "young" is the degree you are touching your own (W)hole life. Often this is a challenge for adults, and they can feel judgmental or silly. This is OK. Just do it anyway. There is power hidden here!

Now, let's first recognize the good news about feelings. If we didn't have such big, huge, magnificent hearts, we wouldn't be able to feel much of anything. Being (W)holly alive means being able to and willing to and wanting to feel deeply what is occurring in the moment. Aliveness is all about feelings. For all of us, when the HT happened, we stopped letting ourselves feel certain things. It just hurt too much. In that moment we also inadvertently reduced the amount of life force that could flow through us! So the good news is that by naming your Horrible Truth moments, you are also showing yourself that you had and still have the capacity to feel deeply. You were born feeling life directly and deeply!

This is important because it is the beginning of remembering and revealing the wonderful truth of you. Feelings are where the power, the action, and the potency of our presence grow from and out of which true transformation can occur. Feelings are the power or juice hidden in your life (w)holes and which actually fuel and nurture your (W)holeness. We create (w)holes to NOT feel. We collapse (w)holes TO feel and be (W)hole and Alive!

Feelings are the charge we attach to HT's. The "first" feeling is called the **OUCH**.

Remember the Universal Story? We are born (W)hole and unconscious, stuff happens (HT), and we feel its impact on us. Feelings are what we attach to and what attaches us to the Horrible Truths. Feelings are what give depth and substance to the bare facts.

We might have felt hurt or sad or mad or ashamed or embarrassed or frightened or confused or angry or incompetent or whatever we felt when that event occurred. The one thing you can count on is every HT moment has at least one, usually more, emotional experiences associated to it, or it would not be a Horrible Truth. We felt horrible. It felt horrible. Our feelings are the feeling facts or OUCH of the HT. The OUCH of the HT is the essential, most raw naked feeling you can name as it is related to the HT.

Preferably, the OUCH of a particular HT is named using kid-language rather than adult verbiage. For example, "hurt" is more preferable than "aggravated;" "scared" is better than "terrorized;" "crushed" is easier to feel than "dominated." The OUCH is a prime motivator for adjusting or shifting our behavior. If you do something and the big people hit your hand, you feel the hit, the physical pain, and the emotional OUCH. One is sensation, and one is emotion – both can be part of the OUCH experience. To avoid it, you stop the behavior; you adjust yourself. However, there is much more to the story than that. Let's look more closely at feelings.

Feelings, our feelings, are the way we motivate ourselves and how we apply significance to something. For example, "I like coffee ice cream" is a thought. What I **feel** about coffee ice cream is the memory of my Dad and Mom treating me to ice cream as a kid. My taste and sensation of coffee ice cream is the flavor and the temperature and the texture. These, too, have a value or judgment assigned to them by me. I judge and decide internally that these are all pleasurable in some way and are, therefore, "good" and desirable to repeat. Granting significance or making meaning occurs from our own inner felt experience.

What Are Emotions?

This may seem like a very simple and obvious question; however, it isn't. As infants we simply feel. We do not think about our feelings first. We just have sensations and react. At the heart of any emotion we are having, even now, is a sensation in our bodies. It is only after a sensation experience when a meaning, a name, or a value can be assigned. Consciously or not, we assign a value and a name to each sensation. We have all learned to do this. In one way we essentially distance ourselves from the sensation by applying a name to it; however, this is the impact of language. Since we still use words to communicate to ourselves and to each other, it is simply important to recognize that both sensation and emotion are present in what we call **a Feeling.** Notice that the process of assigning a meaning or a value is a thought or judgment, while a feeling sensation is an in-the-moment experience that doesn't have any words attached to it.

Our next sorting process is to become clear about the difference between a feeling and a thought. Often when I ask a new client, "What are you feeling now," they respond with something on the order of, "I feel that I am a failure." "I feel like a jerk." Do you notice what has happened here? A thought and a feeling became mixed up. Any time the words "I feel" are followed by the word "**that**," or "**like,**" a confusion has occurred. A feeling has been confused with a thought. As we are sorting through things, it is very helpful to know when you are naming a feeling and when you are naming a thought. "That" is not a feeling word.

A list of feeling words in the appendix can help you sort through your feelings. Here are a few basic feelings to get you started:

- Hurt
- Mad
- Sad
- Scared
- Small
- Uncertain
- Embarrassed

Having a list of feelings to start with is particularly helpful to those of us who have, until now, denied many, if not all or most, of our feelings. **Denial** is a complex word for "keeping ourselves in the dark" or "pretending" with ourselves and/or others. The fact is we all feel, whether we let ourselves be aware of it or not. Sometimes, feelings can be scary to admit, so we just keep them secret from ourselves. We pretend that we aren't terrified of our own feelings. When we are scared of embracing a part of ourselves, we automatically believe less in ourselves, thus we are less powerful than we truly are! Our goal is to reveal ourselves to ourselves so we can move into our own fully-empowered selves. The question we now come to is, will we let ourselves know what we are feeling?

Life (w)holes are often (but not always) about not letting ourselves know our feelings or feel our feelings.

Now, where do we feel our emotions? Where do we feel life touch us? We feel it and let it touch us in our hearts and in our bodies. We experience life in and from our hearts. Our heads don't have feeling or sensation experiences, but the rest of us does experience life directly. We do not *feel* in our heads; rather, we have thoughts and beliefs in our heads about what we are experiencing. Sometimes our awareness of our feelings is in the form of body sensations and emotions, and at other times, it's in the form of body sensations, alone. The (W)hole Truth is that whenever we are having an emotion, we are also having body sensations whether we are aware of them or not. What occurs in our minds are thoughts, ideas, constructions of meanings, and conclusions. These are thoughts, not feelings. Feelings are energy sensations that move through our bodies. Throughout the remainder of this book, whenever I use the word "**feelings**," please allow yourself to recall that this means both emotions and sensations.

Understanding and knowing the difference between "**head smart**" and "**heart smart**" is crucial if you are serious about awakening and empowering your own (W)holeness. A more technical term for heart smart is "**emotional intelligence**" (from the book *Emotional Intelligence* by Daniel Goleman). This distinction is important to know if we want to collapse (w)holes rather than to continually fall into them, with the result of spending our life in the dark. Now that you are aware of the difference between feelings and thoughts, it is time to locate a (w)hole!

To Collapse a (w)hole, We Must Feel it First

To collapse a (w)hole, we have to find a (w)hole. To find a (w)hole requires attending to our feelings. We have to admit that we have feelings – big feelings, little feelings, and everything in between. (W)holes, the black pits we fall into, are located in our hearts or "feeling centers." When we fall into a (w)hole and feel "in the pits," we may put this into words by saying, "My heart hurts." Our (w)holes are located in our hearts where we experience that moment. When we fall into a (w)hole, we know this because we *feel* "lousy," "crappy," "mad," "sad" – we feel something that isn't desirable. We recognize that we are in a (w)hole when we *feel* in the "pits." The clue that we are in a (w)hole is in our felt experience – **our feelings are the clue.** Most folks know immediately what I mean by "being in a (w)hole" or "falling into a pit." It is a common and familiar experience.

All of our hearts are full of (w)holes, and every (w)hole is Holy. This is true for all of us. Here is where the mystery of what is happening begins to become clear. The motivation behind all (w)hole creations is a flight from a feeling experience. And our feelings are the first clue that we are in a (w)hole. What is happening is that we are feeling an emotion that we decided a long time ago to NOT feel! In fact, falling into the "pit" is falling face first into our feelings.

Remember that you are the expert about your own feeling experience. You know how YOU feel when you are in a "bad way" or "a pit" or in a (w)hole. No one needs to say more. You are the expert of you!

(W)hole empowerment is a felt process, not a thought or a conclusion.

Authentic, last-a-lifetime aliveness is from inside our guts out. It cannot be forced, pushed, or contrived. Alive empowered (W)holeness is about gut-aliveness that simply overflows into every moment and interchange of your life.

(W)hole play or Intentional Spiraling is what is gradually being revealed through this book. You already know many of the basics: "Curiosity without judgment," sorting "Me" from "Them," and feelings are different than thoughts.

What Makes (w)hole Play, Play?

What is (W)hole Play? **(w)hole Play is the practice of collapsing a life (w)hole**.

It is based upon the practice of curiosity (without judgment). (w)hole Play has the effect of collapsing a (w)hole or space in our heart which is between what I can feel and what I don't dare feel! A (w)hole is a space between who we are trying to be and all the other expressions of ourselves. When we fall into a (w)hole, we fall into this space or void.

When a (w)hole is collapsed, there isn't any place to fall since there is no (w)hole. This becomes "play" when you begin to experience the (W)hole Truth that every (w)hole is brimming with your life force. Empowerment is all about giving your permission for your life sensations to flow freely.

If you were driving down a road and the car fell into a pothole, the car would bounce and jar you and your passengers. If you were driving down that same road and the pothole was "collapsed" so that there was no hole to fall into, it would be a smooth ride. This is the point of every (w)hole; it is a call for attention so the (w)hole can be collapsed, and your ride through life will be smoother and gentler and far more vital. Empowerment is all about attending to the signals that you just discovered another (w)hole and thus, another bit of your life energy.

To summarize:
- **Feelings are precious,** for they tell us where the pot (w)holes are in our hearts!

- **Our minds and thoughts are precious,** for they help us comprehend the anatomy of a (w)hole.
- **Our bodies are precious,** for they are the way we know and experience (W)holeness.
- **Our spirits are precious,** for they are our vitality or (W)holeness in its most original form.

No aspect of who we are can be left out! (W)hole awakening or Intentional Spiraling is a process that engages the (W)hole person. Our minds, hearts, bodies, and spirits are all part of the Wisdom WAY process. It is also true to say that our hearts (feelings) are especially crucial since (w)holes are located by feelings and are in our hearts. Our minds, our hearts, our bodies, and our spirits are all necessary as we walk the path of (W)holeness.

It is **not** helpful to focus *only* on the mind or *only* on the heart or *only* on the spirit. We are all one (W)hole being, and the path we are walking is to come to know this in every cell of our bodies and in every thought and feeling. Often clients or students have explored in depth one aspect or another but haven't found a way to integrate all of them into one entire form. The Wisdom WAY model does just that. It requires all parts of us to be engaged, and yet there is no pressure to force this upon us. The sorting process itself has this effect. Sorting thoughts from feelings is essential. What makes this so?

We cannot do (w)hole work with only our hearts. We need our heads to support us in getting to where we are going. Thinking is just as important as feeling. However, the trouble many of us have is that the difference between the two has been lost. All too often in today's society, thinking has been given preference over feeling. Those with great minds are praised, revered, and rewarded. Those with great hearts are dismissed, and devalued; they are considered "less than" or weak and emotional. This is, again, a sorting process. It is about having our heads do what they were meant to do – to help us sort things – and allowing our hearts to do what they were meant to do – to feel things.

Any time you notice that you are judging a particular form of expression of yours or any time you notice you are naming a part of you as "bad" or "wrong," chances are you are confusing feelings with the process of applying a meaning or a thought to an experience. In effect, when we do this we are engaged in making a meaning about a feeling.

Sorting Feelings From Thoughts

Here is a way to practice being curious about feelings and thoughts so as to begin a deeper sorting practice. It is important to keep our **hearts feeling** and our **heads thinking**. By doing this we are minimizing confusions that can pop up in the sorting process. Just keep your eyes and ears out for the floating "**that**" (i.e., I feel **that**…) and the floating "**like**" (i.e., I feel **like**). These are signals that tell you that you have accidentally moved from a feeling to a thought.

After recognizing the confusion, simply choose to express either a thought or a feeling. "I feel" is followed by feeling words, i.e., hurt, mad, sad, scared, or resentful; while "I think" or

"I feel that" is followed by a belief, idea, or opinion. For example: "I feel that you are being mean to me." (This is a thought disguised as a feeling.) "I think you are touching my heart with joy." (This is a feeling experience disguised as a thought.) Although it sounds easy to distinguish between the two, trust me when I say that after hours of listening and working with seasoned "self-developmenters," I am still helping folks sort feelings from thoughts.

The Secret Behind Thought-Feeling Confusion

What creates such befuddlement? It might be worthwhile to consider the reason we tend to allow these two elements to become confused in particular situations. There are a number of basic reasons, but at the heart of them all is a sneaky belief, a belief that we most likely have never considered before now. At an unconscious and unaware level, we may be believing and even hoping that, "If I stay confused and keep confusing my thoughts and feelings, then I won't really be able to sort through all this, I won't have to feel all that old icky stuff again, and I won't have to take up the responsibility for my life." To take up responsibility for one's life means to feel and experience one's life. This requires learning to distinguish between a thought and a feeling. This is not easy to do because we have unconsciously confused thoughts and feelings. Keeping thoughts and feelings confused keeps us in the dark and often in a pseudo-safety, or so we hope. While this can be a very strong "defense mechanism" or "safety mechanism," the truth is the opposite. The more internal chaos and confusion we have, the greater danger we face of more (w)holes and more painful experiences.

Staying bewildered by not sorting only serves to keep us stuck in familiar places. Change is scary! We've all experienced moments when we were afraid of change, and despite all we might say, change, even for the better, is scary. Make sure not to judge yourself even about your hesitancy to change. Just be bald and naked with yourself, and admit it. Then try something new. Say, "Good for me. I noticed that I'm resisting making a change." Be curious, in a gentle way, about your inner workings,

I have spent this much time and many words on the difference between thoughts and feelings because awakening to your (W)holeness is a felt journey. There is no way around feelings! If you begin the path confused about the tools or reference points, you will inevitably become disoriented.

So what is the point? The point is that to move beyond the past, we must **choose** to engage our hearts and our heads and our bodies and spirits. All of our parts are necessary for (W)holeness because (W)holeness is just that: **all** parts of us together. In my opinion, part of what stagnates awakening (W)holeness is that various techniques access only portions of ourselves, rather than engaging all of the facets of our being.

A (w)hole Point: the Paradox of Our (w)holes

(W)holeness cannot be revealed partially, for by definition a part isn't the (W)hole. Yet it is the ripening and sorting of our parts that leads us to (W)holeness.

We could say it this way: We gradually reveal ourselves as "more (W)hole," a (w)hole at a time, until we know ourselves as (W)hole. This is a paradox! Life is all about learning more of ourselves while being (W)hole the entire time.

It is inevitable that we will fall into (w)holes over and over again because we inadvertently leave parts of us out. When a part of us is left behind or left out, there is a space or a void or a (w)hole. When we leave out a part of ourselves, we automatically create a space or a (w)hole within our (W)holeness, while we are simultaneously wishing for conscious (W)holeness in all we do. Can you see how we compromise our (W)holeness while at the same time are not aware of how we sabotage ourselves?

In the past when a Horrible Truth happened, it hurt us so much that without our awareness (usually), we decided to do whatever it would take for this to never, ever happen again! We reacted with an instinctive, felt determination to prevent that pain from occurring again. Good for us! We know what we want – not to hurt (feel) like that again. This is a smart thing if we are going to emotionally and physically survive growing up.

Protecting ourselves from pain is part of our built-in limbic/cellular survival response. We implement a way of protecting ourselves against an experience when we feel something is dangerous to our ongoing existence. Growing up is hard to do. As I said early on, we are all simply doing the best we can with what life brings us.

A (w)hole Play Opportunity for You

Take a moment, if you wish, and on your same original (w)hole play paper write three to five feeling words that usually apply when you fall into one of your dark places or (w)holes. You might start by asking, "What do my dark 'pits' feel like?" or "How does this icky moment feel?" or "How do I feel in the pits?" You might ask yourself, "When I fall into a black pit, what do I usually feel?" For example, when I fall into one of my (w)holes, I might feel angry, frustrated, and lonely. Take a few moments to write your feelings in the spiral area on your paper. You may want to lightly draw the spiral onto your paper so you can begin to use the Wisdom WAY map. You will notice in the diagram there is a Spiral below the heart. It is here, in the spiral, where you will list your feelings. (If you wish you may use the feeling word list in the Appendix.)

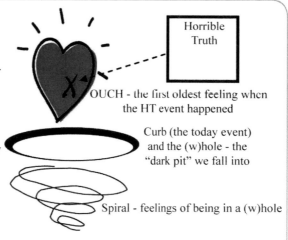

You already have your HT list in the upper right corner of your paper. Now draw a square box around your HT, if you haven't done so already. You are closing the lid on the past.

OUCH - the first oldest feeling when the HT event happened

Curb (the today event) and the (w)hole - the "dark pit" we fall into

Spiral - feelings of being in a (w)hole

Notice: Our Curbs feel the same to us as that first OUCH of our Horrible Truths. Curb moments are great gifts – they show us a (w)hole is present.

In order to be systematic in sorting, we use a pattern for making notes or doing a (w)hole study. Feelings are listed in the spiral or center of the page. This is because the spiral is where we have dumped our feelings in an effort to get rid of them. Our (w)holes are like trash bins filled with old feelings. In all (w)hole studies we write our feelings in the spiral area.

Remember, there is no way to fail. These are your feelings, and no one can say they are wrong. List your feelings on your paper, then set it aside. There is more to learn about the Wisdom of your hidden (W)holeness, which may already be revealing itself to you.

Our Response to the OUCH

The next step is to sort through what we did to get away from the OUCH and the other feelings. What did we do to not ever feel the HT experience again? At this point we are moving into the power of self-revelation. When we dare to sort, we move ourselves gradually into a direct encounter with our earlier decisions. These decisions were hidden from us and by us at an early age; however, they continue to run on automatic pilot, controlling our lives. Revealing them requires courageous sorting, something you are already doing!

Chapter 6: Waking Up to Our Strategic Responses to Life Happening

Let's go back to where it all started. The truth of the Horrible Truth is that we were little, and there were big people in charge of our lives. As children, we have no control over the big people in our lives. This is part of the Horrible Truth. Let's face it, when we are little, they had the power in our world. When we are very little, they are the "gods" of our world. They, the ones with power, are the ones who are not stopping the horrible thing from occurring or, even worse, being the horrible thing, doing the horrible thing, or contributing directly or indirectly to those horrible things. We are little; they are big. They get to say what goes!

Remember "horrible" refers to anything **you** define as horrible. It can be as small as spilling your orange juice or as large as being physically abused. The OUCH isn't in the actual event. The OUCH is how we feel in response to *their* response to us or to *that* event! Only we know how we feel. The point is that the Horrible Truth is yours to name. Now, let us look at what happens in those moments in slow motion. There is a great treasure buried here.

First, in these moments, we **feel powerless** as the horrible feeling experiences move through us. The truth is we *are* powerless! Yes, we are essentially powerless as children to do much to change the events around us. We simply experience them. The adults have more power than we do to impact the events, the structure of our lives, and the process of how things unfold. Instinctively, we do the only thing we can do - **we turn to our own selves**. We are the only person that we have power over. Consequently, we turn our desperate eyes on ourselves and begin to **look for the "cause" of the HT**.

We have one motivation and that is to **not** experience that sensation and emotion again! Without any conscious awareness we are saying, "If I just can find the cause inside of me, I'll have a chance to prevent that experience from happening again! It just has to be me; if it is my fault, then I have hope of changing, controlling, or adjusting things." We don't stop and consider if this is accurate or appropriate or actually useful because we have only one mission: to prevent the HT from occurring again and to do "whatever it takes" to accomplish this mission.

The entire focus becomes "how" to avoid, manage, prevent, or tolerate that horrible experience. And then, each one of us does something quite amazing. We access our ability to alter reality as we know it! We tap into our power to create and recreate. We become creators and re-creators of ourselves. We begin to adjust ourselves so as to please or appease the "gods" in our lives. These "gods" are the big people in our lives. We do this to feel "better," to **not** feel or experience **that** Horrible Truth again! We do this by censoring ourselves. We censor whatever part of ourselves we imagine will prevent further occurrences of the HT OUCH. We make a plan or strategy that we imagine will have a particular effect upon our life experiences and on the big people.

We take steps to "fix" or adjust ourselves so that they won't do _____ again or say _____ or so that _____ won't happen again (whatever the HT is). We create a structure or strategy of hope which we deeply believe will contain the situation and prevent another surprising HT experience. Having realized at a deep level that we are powerless over them, we turn to our inherent power that is "born inside of" each of us! This is the creation-power to adjust ourselves. It is to this inner force that we turn in our horrible moments. Even **if** – and this is a big if – we recognize that what they are doing or saying is wrong, simultaneously we know they have the clout at that moment. They are bigger than us, and we know it. Our power to alter reality as we are experiencing it is inherent in each one of us! Our (w)holes are proof of the potency of our power.

Turning inward towards our power to create, is both great genius and great desperation. This awesome and inherent power to adjust who we are to save ourselves is the pivotal element in the creation of a (w)hole. It is by our own actions upon our own behalf that (w)holes are formed. It is often a limbic experience/decision to recreate ourselves in a manner we imagine will save us. We are not "bad" or "wrong" for doing this. We all have done this over and over again. We are simply doing the best we can to hurt less and save ourselves from more hurt so we can be at ease in life. At this point it is necessary to return to the Universal Story to unfold for you the next segment of the Wisdom WAY map of (W)holeness and empowerment.

As you remember in the beginning, we were born (W)hole and unconscious. Then stuff happened to us (the HT). When that stuff hurt too much (the OUCH), we figure out in our feeling-self or heart a strategy. A large majority of the time, this plan or "strategy of hope" is non-verbal. It is so deeply within our hearts and so instantaneous that we remain unaware of it entirely. We do this using our power to recreate ourselves by our own inner authority. And we do this without consciously knowing it or noticing it. Already, we are beginning to have secrets from ourselves. Already we are moving into the dark. Already we are creating our hidey (w)holes in which we can imagine we are "safe" from life.

Essentially our interior process, if it were put into words, might sound like this: "If I just get rid of that bad part of me that I think is causing them to act like this or be like this towards me, then the pain (HT OUCH) won't happen again." Doesn't this make sense? After all, we just want to stop hurting, so we do the only thing we have the power to do – we make it about us, not them. This shift in focus occurs at a deep felt level inside of us.

Once this shift has occurred, all sorts of options open up to us. What geniuses we are! We find possibilities in the face of our most horrifying moments. The internal creative genius and brilliance of each one of us is astonishing. There is not one student, not one client, not one apprentice, and not one of us that isn't a creative genius. Each of us has designed multiple strategies of hope to ward off the HT experiences. We turned to ourselves since we couldn't control them.

With this shift in place, we now feel the wish for power to do something to prevent a reoccurrence of what hurt. It is no longer about feeling it. We have now shifted from feeling it to thinking about how to prevent it! Now there is hope to manage it, avoid it, change it – anything but experiencing those feelings in that moment. What a relief! We can actually take some action. This isn't a conscious or thought-out decision; rather it is a built-in instinctive response to act on our own behalf to survive. We **all** do this. It is part of being human. It's self-preservation. By turning to our inner power to recreate ourselves, we establish a way to have hope. We create hope for ourselves that we will never, ever feel that again by shifting from *feeling* life to *managing* reality by our own authority. We all need hope!

Good for us for giving ourselves hope.

Consider any of the stories one hears on the news about children and adolescents who have survived war, gang wars, and abandonment by parents. Although horrible, they also attest to the power inherent in us all – the will to do whatever it takes to survive – even to recreate ourselves into the forms we believe will save us. These acts are always from a place of "whatever it takes!" It is the shift from powerless to powerful. It is a shift from feeling life to thinking our way through life.

We shift our attention to where we have the power to act – ourselves. We access the power internally to recreate ourselves in a new image. This is a capacity we are all born with, and it is sometimes called "**learning the right way to be**." Take a moment to think about this. This is brilliant!

We turn to the power we are born with, the **power to grant significance or meaning to an event**. This is a thinking process. We access our power to adjust ourselves based upon the meaning an event, an action, or an experience has in our inner world. The meaning is something **we** attribute to the event. The occurrences by themselves are without a value. Each of us assigns significance to the experiences that come our way. We attribute the cause of the HT to ourselves to create a belief that we have the power to stop the pain. This is how the power to recreate ourselves actually works, even when we are totally unaware that we are doing it.

Simply put, we **presume** that we are the "causal agent," and by this interior perspective shift, we confer upon ourselves the power to alter the situation or behavior around us. Often in the HT, the important people even reinforce this by telling us we are the cause, while in fact, it is the big people who are the primary actors, not us. However, as you may now realize, this is insignificant at this point. It is no longer about what they do, or say, or don't do, or don't say, although this is not insignificant. Rather we shift our internal emphasis to seek out a way to prevent further pain.

Our primary focus **and** conviction shifts to one question: "How can I change, adjust, or alter myself (be less than my (W)hole self) to prevent the HT from occurring again?" Do you notice the hidden assumption, the secret erasure? The other person (the instigator) is now entirely eliminated or erased as a variable in our survival mission, and it now rests solely on our shoulders. They are no longer the primary element in the center of our attention. What we are going to do now with all of our being is "fix" our "broken" (W)holeness. Why? So we won't hurt like that ever again! Each of us, secretly, has come to the conviction that there is an essential "badness" in us. The name we apply to that "bad essence" is particular to each of us. Then with great courage and focus we create our way of eliminating or containing or blaming this "bad essence" for the occurrence of the HT. We do this to insure we do **not** ever feel that HT again!

How we use our re-creative power is exclusive and unique to each of us. That we all access our power to recreate ourselves and correct the imagined flaws in our (W)holeness is a (W)hole Truth – we *all* do this! How we use this creative force, where we apply it, and which HT's become our prime focus is all ours to choose individually. We choose based on what hurts the most. These choices are most commonly unconscious, secret even from ourselves.

Each one of us calls upon our creative powers in the face of our Horrible Truth moments to simply stop the pain, hurt, shame, anger, and especially the profound powerlessness. The surprising thing is that we do this without conscious awareness. We begin to implement a survival strategy of hope that is kept secret even from ourselves, most commonly because it was developed at a non-verbal level. Sometimes it happens in a nanosecond; sometimes it happens over time. In either case it is happening beneath our conscious awareness. Gradually, we become more and more of a mystery to ourselves; we become lost in the dark. We get rid of the bits of ourselves that we have named "bad essences." No wonder we become confusing to ourselves – we are in bits and pieces and parts. This process does not just happen once; it happens over and over again!

I can't count the number of times I have heard clients say, "I just don't know why I am doing this. I know it isn't good for me." Here is the mysterious self, right before our eyes. It isn't that anyone is purposely stupid about themselves; it is simply because we created a strategic methodology we felt would save our lives. It was shaped in our interior selves, usually without any awareness, and then we put it into an "automatic run" mode. Once these recreations or adjustments to our (W)holeness are designed, they continue to operate beneath our awareness on automatic pilot. We censored ourselves in the manner we believed would reduce the danger we felt from those horrible moments. These strategies are plans of hope – hope that the HT experience will be warded off or, at the very least, minimized.

By looking more deeply at what is occurring, as if in slow motion, we can learn a great deal about ourselves which will move us closer to an empowered (W)hole life and our authentic (W)holeness.

In Summary:

We decide to believe that we are the problem because it is too much for us to keep living with the unpredictable vulnerability of the pain of the Horrible Truth. We simply want it to stop. "Anything but that!" is the cry from deep within our hearts. So, our only goal is to make the pain stop. Here is where we begin to exercise this inborn power to recreate ourselves by the action of assigning significance and meaning to the event to save ourselves from further pain. We shift from feeling the Horrible Truth and how vulnerable we are to figuring out and thinking out how to fix the pain by changing or adjusting ourselves. We shift from their impact upon us to our power to recreate ourselves to please or appease them. In the simplest terms, we shift from feeling to fixing.

The Power Point Location Shift

In order to shift from feeling the moment to fixing ourselves, we must create a step of logic that allows us to erase the participation of the other in what is actually happening. This logic step sounds like this: "If I am the problem, then I can fix things so the pain will stop! I'll do whatever it takes so I don't have to feel so powerless. I can keep it from happening again!" I call this logical thought step the **Power Point Location shift**.

The capacity to shift the point-of-power from them to me through an internal choice is a very potent capacity in all of us. This often-little-noticed skill allows us to offer ourselves hope in the face of our personal life-terrors and hurts. How magnificent – we are able to give ourselves hope in situations which often feel hopeless! You will see, as we reveal our inner Wisdom WAY to ourselves, how totally precious our inner brilliance really is – we are all about **saving our lives with hope**. How we create or find hope is one of the secrets we have hidden from ourselves in our (w)holes! I call the entire process of creating strategies of hope our "meaning making in action" or our **Meaning Maker (MM)**. When we create a (w)hole or a space between most of me and that "bad" part, we are not learning consciously; we are surviving automatically. The events themselves are just neutral facts or actions until *we* decide they are horrible and apply the meaning they have for us.

"My mother yelled at me when I was five...all I did was I hit my brother...he was picking on me. I acted how I felt in the moment." Mom said, "You are such a bad little girl. Good girls are nice!" and then she slapped me. She never did this before! I want to be a good girl. I want her to like me again. I don't want her to ever hit me again!"

The Horrible Truth is that Mom yelled and hit. Mom said "You are a bad girl." The OUCH might be a feeling of shame and rejection ("because I was a bad girl"), and maybe even shock at being hit. At this point we decide that we certainly don't want to feel all this again, so we activate our Power Point Location shift and redirect our focus from mom to me. This allows for "hope" of avoiding a repeat of that experience to be established.

In slow motion what is occurring inside of us is this: we say to ourselves, "If I can figure out how to change me, then I can make her change so that she'll never do that horrible thing again and so I don't ever feel so powerless, mad, alone, shocked, confused, and hurt again." So, at this moment we turn to our head (thoughts/beliefs) to manage an HT feeling moment. Our inner process rationalizes, "I just want to figure out how to stop the pain and establish hope so that I can avoid a repeat of the HT moment. The only way I can see how to do this is by fixing what is wrong with me. I want to survive whatever the cost."

The shift we are making is an internal one in which we choose to redirect our attention in such a way as to take on the responsibility and the power to control the other person. Children "know" Santa is real and in the same way, children "know" that they can make it "all better" by changing themselves. From an adult viewpoint, we know that truly we have no power to *make* another person do something, yet for a child this is not clear. For example, even if someone has a gun to your head, you still, in fact, retain your choice to acquiesce or not. Even if someone yells at you, you still have a choice to react or not. Many stories of heroic action are based on the choices made even in the face of a great threat.

My point is this – as children we are heroic another way. Each of us as children take on the entire job. What heroes we all are! We shift the power to our own shoulders – even though this is neither realistic nor possible – and begin to live from this very creative and brave position, all for the purpose of **saving our lives with hope.** This is the "hope" of a child, the "hope" of the innocent.

As children we believe that by changing ourselves, they will change. Doesn't this seem like it makes sense? When we are "good," they are "happy," or at least that is what we are told. This confusion between them and us is a normal developmental stage and is encouraged by how much of parenting occurs. How often have we heard our parents or other big people say things like, "They are making me nuts!" or "If the kids would just quiet down…" Notice they assign a power to the little people for the big people's feelings. Yes, even the big people are confused here, and yes, they, too, have (w)holes. Again, we see the need for sorting!

So, if we look back at our example of a Horrible Truth, we now know that at a visceral level, a gut level, a level without words, we created a plan then acted upon it. Here is one way our strategy might sound if words were applied to it: "Expressing my anger is wrong, so I won't ever do that again! I'll just smile instead. Then mom will like me. I'll be a nice girl, and the HT won't happen again." Most of the child's original (W)holeness is still allowed **except** for the anger/passion expression. Do you notice how the original entirety of the child is now a bit less than (W)hole? This strategy of hope is called our **Meaning Making** (MM) or **Meaning Maker** at work.

In addition, going back to our example, the same situation could occur to another child, and her strategic response (Meaning Making) could be entirely different. Her strategy might be, "When I grow up, I will never let anyone get away with anything like my brother did. For now I will bide my time and fake it, but later I'll show them." You can just imagine what that might look like twenty-five years later in the boardroom. Sometimes this Meaning Making strategy addresses both a current plan and a future plan, as in this example. Most typically, the Meaning Making plan is primarily directed towards "solving" the current Horrible Truth threat, without paying much attention to what will occur later in life.

When this approach of restricting or excluding parts of ourselves feels successful, it then becomes a life strategy. We will automatically apply it whenever any angry feelings start to arise. We could imagine that it operates just the way a smoke detector does. The room fills with enough smoke, and the alarm is triggered. If our anger reaches a certain level, we automatically put on a happy face. We may be completely unaware of this response while others around us may be aware of the incongruity.

Often I will hear an adult partner say of the other, "His words say one thing, but his face/actions say another." Remember, once we make these creative strategies, they run on automatic pilot. There is no expiration time. The Meaning Making systems keep running beneath our awareness until we allow ourselves to move into greater consciousness. Until we sort ourselves out, we stay caught in the dark and lost in automatic! The Wisdom WAY skeleton empowers us to reveal greater and greater bits of our hidden strategies to ourselves and thus, empowers our recognition. Revealing to an ever greater extent the mysteries of ourselves to ourselves is an essential element of empowerment. As we gradually make sense to ourselves, we liberate our empowerment and come awake again as our (W)hole Selves.

Now, the tricky part about all this is we don't know we are creating strategies that require us to reject aspects or expressions of ourselves. Again, this contributes to the mystery of ourselves. We just block off access to the parts of ourselves we have determined are the cause of the pain. We are usually not aware of this maneuver. It is like the automatic transmission in a car – we don't have to pay attention to the gears; the shifting happens automatically. How brilliant we all are! Inside each of us, unbeknownst to us, we have this power to create strategies that help us feel safe or not in danger of more pain and powerful enough to stop the Horrible Truth from ever happening again. Keep in mind that the essential element of the Horrible Truth is the naked raw powerless vulnerability we experience in those moments.

This built-in power to create survival plans by recreating ourselves (moving from (W)holeness to fixed/adjusted (W)holeness) is all we have to respond with when faced with our raw vulnerability. We are all born with this power, regardless of circumstance, race, country, or culture. It is the power to grant significance, or assign meaning, to events in whatever way serves our perceived advantage. We are simply teaching ourselves how to be alive "safely" in this world of surprises, some of which are painful. It is worth noting that this same capacity underlies our ability to learn. For example, if we touch a hot stove and it hurts, we don't touch it again. If we reach out to Grammy and she hugs us back and laughs with us, we do it again. We move towards what feels good, and we move away from what hurts – we shift so that we can fix the problem, which we have determined is us.

In the case of creating a (w)hole or a space between all of me and that "bad" part, we are not learning consciously; we are surviving automatically. The events themselves are just neutral facts or actions until *we* decide they are horrible and apply the meaning they have for us.

Let us now turn to the implementation of whatever strategy we might have constructed at the time. How do we ensure that the strategy is enacted? What do we do with the bad part of ourselves that apparently caused this horrible thing to happen? This is where we begin to look at the core anatomy of a (w)hole .

The moment the strategy is created and implemented, a (w)hole is formed. Remember, a (w)hole is a space between parts of ourselves. A (w)hole is a void or an empty place or a pit.

A (w)hole Is a Space Between

A (w)hole is a space between "most of us" and the "blamed part/expression" of us.

Something felt horrible; we wanted to avoid that experience again. We shifted the power from them to us and assigned blame to that part of us we believed was at fault. Through these steps we have determined that we will not allow ourselves to feel that way (i.e., mad) or

act that way (i.e., hit) ever again. We can be and express anything else, but we definitely cannot be or express *that*. Having figured this out and identified the cause of the problem based on that simple step of logic, all that is left to do is push away, reject, or disallow that expression of ourselves. In effect, we make a space between what we allow ourselves to be or express and what is absolutely not allowed in our repertoire. The effect is that we feel a sense of relief, a sense of power, a sense of safety, and we are able to move on, none the wiser for our newly created strategic plan for pain management. Essentially, we have recreated ourselves by disallowing an expression of our original (W)holeness and creating a (w)hole.

Of course, we have no need to do this IF the "big people" in our lives stop and teach us different ways to express ourselves. My sister, Dorie Cameron and her friend Karen Kuhl, developed an approach called "**Conscious Intentional Parenting,**" with the express purpose of helping children grow up without having to "get rid of" parts of themselves. This approach is an exploration of parenting intentionally on behalf of the child and with awareness of the parent's own values and (w)holes. Sadly, most of us don't grow up within a conscious intentional parental family.

Let us look at what we do again. What we have done is identified and rejected a part of ourselves which we have determined (for very good reason) is a problem. Our universal AND particular solution sequence goes like this:

- We are born (W)hole, and then we encounter our HT experience.

- We feel powerless, vulnerable, and unsafe – in danger.

- We make the Power Point Location shift from "them" to ourselves to establish "hope" and to save ourselves from a repeat of the HT.

- At this point we create our Meaning Making solution by identifying the bad part of ourselves which we think or believe is the problem.

- Next, we implement our solution by rejecting, judging, and pushing away that "bad" expression of ourselves.

- The result: We feel relief and now have hope of being able to avoid the Horrible Truth again.

- We set this reconstruction of ourselves to run on automatic pilot.

- We then move into the next moment with a sense of security.

Because we can feel such relief by exercising our recreation powers, we now have hope. We feel and believe our solution is successful, and because it **seems** to really work, we simply repeat the same process over again. So, whenever "horrible" stuff happens, we'll just make another space between what is still "OK" and what is more of the "bad stuff" of us. This process is called *"making a (w)hole."*

Makes sense, doesn't it? If something seems to work, why would we stop doing it? And so it is that we arrive in our adulthood with many parts of us disallowed while imagining that we are in full command of our (W)hole faculties. **The (W)hole Truth is that we are living from a fraction of who we really are**, and we are in the dark about much of our own magnificence.

"Collapsing (w)holes" is how to reverse this process. First we created (w)holes to have hope in the face of a Horrible Truth; now it is time to bring hope back into our lives by collapsing these same (w)holes. Both of these are Acts of Hope. Our (w)hole creations are the desperate Acts of Hope of a child. Our (w)hole collapsing is the conscious Act of Hope of the adult. Both are possible because of our inherent power to create. We all have this power. We each apply it differently.

Because (w)hole creations are particular and unique to each of us, the process of "(w)hole collapsing" must also be particular to each (w)hole creator. It is for this reason that anyone else's answers don't completely work for us. The Wisdom WAY provides a road-map, so to speak, for **your** answers on the way to unveiling *your* (W)holeness.

There is also another place we see Meaning Making occur in our lives. This Meaning Making creation response process happens repeatedly inside of each of us as we are growing up. This is the part of MM called "socialization." Obviously, we can see that it is important not to move into judgment of how we make meaning for ourselves but rather to move into awareness of all the places MM may be "driving our lives" without our awareness. Making Meaning is a large portion of what shapes how we express ourselves because Curbs and Horrible Truths keep occurring in our young lives. We simply don't want to feel so powerless and vulnerable. It's too scary, so we adjust and alter and limit ourselves in "hopes" of minimizing painful experiences.

So, now you know how this process works. In essence it is a logic shift. Some call this "magical thinking" while others refer to it as "lack of differentiation between subject and object." We magically shift where the power really is (with "them") to acting as if the power is ours. We internally shift the power location from them to us, and then we move into action on behalf of our own survival. Remember, this is an internal shift, not an actual change in the external situation.

The power was theirs (HT), and we didn't like what happened and what they did, said, didn't do, or didn't say, so we created a belief system or a Meaning Making strategy that gave us our power back. This is the essential element needed to transition from the experience of raw, vulnerable powerlessness to an imagined place of power (survival). This shift gives us hope that the HT will not have to be endured again or as often or as traumatically. It is important to understand that our feeling of powerlessness is the central trigger for our inherent survival mechanisms.

Once the logic shift has occurred, we decide that now it is up to us to change in order to ensure the HT will not be repeated. The responsibility of the other is dropped from the picture. The responsibility for HT prevention and fixing the cause is now squarely on our shoulders. The power is now in our hands. The next step is to determine what part or parts in us caused the Horrible Truth to occur. We must become clear as to what the offensive element is within us; otherwise, our strategy will not work.

What Part of Me Will I Blame?

Here is the next big question in our Meaning Making Process: How do we choose what part of us to assign blame to? The system used to figure out what part of us is the bad part is what I am referring to as the **Meaning Making** system (or simply MM). No matter what the Horrible Truth is, what actually creates an effect and alters who we allow ourselves to be is our power to make meaning or grant significance to self and other. This is the process by which we make, select, or clarify which part of us is the "bad guy." Of course, by now you can see, the meaning we make is always about us and against some part of our being – how we "ought to be" or "shouldn't be." Either way it is about us because then we have the power to affect some control.

This system of Making Meaning is **unique in its content**. It's particular content is different for each of us. Looking more closely at this survival system or Meaning Making system, we see it is an inner thought process that allows us to make sense of our world moment by moment as we encounter it. Of course, this Meaning Making system isn't a separate organ or actual personality; however, I have found it is easier, more fun, and quite practical to imagine that the Meaning Maker is the part of us that makes sense of things for the sole purpose of establishing and maintaining safety from direct experience.

Personally, I like to imagine it as a friendly, helpful gnome-like creature living inside of us. It is not something acting from meanness; it is simply trying to help us. I encourage you to create your own personalized image of your Meaning Maker. Regardless of how silly this may sound, it is a very powerful step in empowering our (W)holeness. Our inner selves heal through story and images far more quickly than through words. Gift yourself a moment and create an image of your own Maker of Meaning.

What is a **Meaning Maker**? Essentially, the Meaning Maker is a strategic planner acting on our behalf. The central element of any plan developed by the MM will be to get rid of the part or feeling or expression of us which we have determined to be the cause of the HT. The prime motivation of the MM is to preserve the "hope" that the HT experience will not be repeated. The core implementation for any MM strategy is to create a (w)hole or space between what is allowed and what has been determined as the "problematic element" within us.

The Strategic Formula of All Meaning Making Plans

Let us move into a closer look at our Meaning Making strategy. There is a basic formula or framework hidden inside all the survival plans designed by our Meaning Maker. It is our "if-then" bargaining effort to establish our safety from the HT. The particular MM deals we make are always unique to each of us, even if our HT facts sound the same. The wisdom of this approach is that it both recognizes our total uniqueness while also allowing for revealing our sameness or "oneness." What meaning we make of our HT and how we recreated ourselves is where all the answers to our (W)holeness lies. We all make meaning; we are all creators! In fact, we have been creating our reality for as long as we have been alive. We are all unique in the "colors" we use to paint our own unique image of ourselves as we respond to the HT. We allow the orange and blue of us, while pushing away the red and green, if we were to use a "color" analogy. We get to be orange and blue, and across a space or (w)hole we push the reds and greens. Do you feel, see, and understand that we then would be less than our glorious (w)hole rainbow self?

The (W)hole Point of the Wisdom WAY is to be all your colors! Frankly, we all like this idea until we begin to look directly at the "pushed away" colors. Here is where our courage of heart is required. If you want empowered aliveness, then it is all about looking at the parts of yourself you have pushed away.

By now you know that all life (w)holes you have fallen into are created by your Meaning Maker. It did this by judging and assigning blame to aspects of the self that were determined to be the cause of the HT's occurrence. This formula pivots upon the Power Point Location shift from them to me. The core premise of the Meaning Making is that the only power to prevent Horrible Truth experiences from reoccurring rests solely on the shoulders of the one suffering from the horror, that is to say, you.

The central belief buried in **all** Meaning Making strategies is the conviction that changing yourself can actually cause a change in "them." Another way to say this is, "If I change, then they will be different from how they are right now." Be careful here. It is true that how we choose to act has an effect on another person's choices; however, it is not the direct cause. The other person retains full free will to respond as they choose. So read the central belief of the MM again. "If I change, then they will **have to be** different than how they are choosing to be."

Do you notice the magic-like power that the child takes on once the Power Point Location has shifted? In (w)hole creation we absolutely believe we can change them by exercising our power to change or censor ourselves. As we move deeper into the Wisdom WAY map, the significance of sorting becomes increasingly apparent. Sorting out our authentic power from our magical idea of power, sorting out "us" from "them," sorting out yesterday from today is the courageous action of revealing ourselves to ourselves.

Now, let's examine the **confusion of power** which is hidden in all Meaning Making strategic plans. Authentic Power is the power we each have to censor parts of ourselves. This is the power to recreate ourselves anytime we wish. We can choose how we will be, what we will do, and what we won't allow ourselves to express. The magical, false power is based on the belief that a change in us will guarantee a change in the other person. Do you see and feel the confusion?

What a creative and imaginative approach to warding off powerlessness and vulnerability! We have successfully moved ourselves emotionally from the small, vulnerable, powerless position to the one who can change everyone. It is the innocence and naïveté of a child. It is the desire of a child to live. It is the power of belief put into action on behalf of survival.

Our Meaning Maker applies the shift in Power Point Location with great creativity and finesse. Because of the simplicity of the formula's pattern, it is usable in any and all Horrible Truth situations. How incredible! How many systems of application are you aware of that can be applied in all conditions? Repetitive use of this methodology for resolving powerlessness over the course of our lifetime reinforces its usefulness. At least it seems to work until, as an adult, we keep falling into the (w)holes we made so long ago. At least it seems to work until, as an adult, we experience ourselves as lacking vitality, creativity, boldness, and true (W)holeness. At least it seems to work until we stop and look at our lives, only to realize how we have limited ourselves.

The MM formula is an "if – then" type of statement in which we fill in the blanks as they apply to our particular situation. So, let's look closely at the Meaning Maker's strategic template. There are four steps within this heart logic:

1. If I _____(censor myself, change myself, limit myself this way – i.e., only do this or only be that)

2. Then they will _____(Change, be other than who they are being, respond differently to us – i.e., be happy, be proud, etc.)

3. And they will get _____(something we think or imagine that they want, i.e., a kid that they are proud of, the freedom they want, etc.)

4. And I will get _____ (what I am longing to have – to be loved, to be safe, relief, attention, etc.)

In shorthand I might write it like this:

If **I censor**/limit myself this way (get rid of the "bad" parts and keep the "good" parts),
Then **they** will **change** from who they are to who **I want** them to be, and
They get what I think they want,
And **I will get** what I want from them.

If I make it even shorter, I would write:

If I fix me this way,
> Then they will change.
> They get what they want,
And I get what I want.

The Meaning Maker has two bargaining points:

1. If I change, then you'll change.
2. If you get what you want (what I imagine you want), then you'll give me what I want.

Sometimes all "they" want is for us to "do it" their way, and sometimes they just want us to get out of the way. But either way, it's for us to be less than all of who we are.

Because the particular content of every (w)hole and every Meaning Making is unique, what follows is a discussion intended to flesh out the core elements of the MM strategic pattern. You alone can fill in your particular MM content. Again, we return to sorting as a primary activity which requires us to move ever more deeply into curiosity without judgment.

Initially every (w)hole has its own MM; however, over time, you will discover that there are core MM's in which most of your (w)holes reside. In the beginning, it is most helpful to iden- tify each MM for every (w)hole. First read through this section, then begin to apply your new understanding when you get to the next (w)hole play opportunity, just ahead.

A key point of identifying your Meaning Maker strategies is to **always state them in the positive**. The unconscious mind does not hear negatives. By "negatives" I mean the words "never," "not," "don't," "won't," etc. to describe how you will be censoring yourself. For example, consider the statement: "If I don't talk..." Do you see the "don't?" It is more useful for us to say "If I stay quiet..." or "If I am always quiet..."

Express your Meaning Making strategy in terms of things you will do, or say, or be, and not as things you won't do, say, or be. This will keep your strategy more clear for you and will make the (w)hole more quickly evident. At one point, a teacher I had suggested the "Dead Man" test. If a dead person can do what you wrote, it isn't alive enough (i.e., the dead can "not talk," while a dead person can't "talk.") Our Meaning Making strategies must be alive, otherwise why would we still be implementing them?

We design our Meaning Maker strategies to be **win-win situations** for them and for us. This is because, as a child, we need those big people to survive and to be happy. Our lives depended upon it, right? We want the big people to be happy so that they are not hurtful and, better yet, are loving to us. Our MM strategy of hope is a negotiation we make "secretly" inside of ourselves to insure we are "safe" from the horrifying OUCH experience. As a creative negotiator, the child in us knows that both parties must have a "win." Even though all this occurs internally, as kids we are still proactively generous. We want the negotiations to be successful!

As kids, we imagine what will make the adults in our world happy, and then we adjust ourselves to satisfy the "Big People" in our lives. As kids, we've taken on a large responsibility to "fix" this HT mess. We do it all by ourselves. We don't ask for anyone's input, ideas, or suggestions. We don't hold a meeting to discuss it. We don't hire a consultant. We simply figure it all out by ourselves! So we must keep in mind that the little person is often in grave error or great confusion about the adult's needs or situation because who really knows what another person needs or wants unless he/she says so? However, that doesn't change the power of this automatic operative strategy designed to alter the other through the power of self-censorship.

The MM plan must allow for both:

The (w)hole creator's (that's you) relief from the powerlessness of the HT experiences (this relief is hope) *and*

The perceived, continued and happy existence of those upon whom we are dependent.

Ideally, we get some version of love; however, that version of love can look different from how we normally think of it. For example, it could mean we'll be safe from being hit (safe from danger), or it could mean we'll get to stay (they won't get rid of us). The key is that the plan seems to improve our situation.

Within the parameters of the MM plan, the **censoring of parts of our self** that makes us less than we are but safer from the HT is designed to create a direct change in the other – their behavior and their responses around us. This change in the other is the (W)hole point of the MM strategy. After all, the (w)hole creator (you) is acting to make life's contextual experience less confusing, less scary, less painful, or less lonely. For example, I will create imaginary friends so I won't feel the pain of loneliness ("get rid of real relating"). Or, I will create a mental escape route out of my bedroom so I don't feel the pain of the craziness going on downstairs in my family ("get rid of being present"). I am censoring a part of me so that I am removed from the pain of the HT.

In essence, we need things to be equitable so we'll get what we want. We want to be powerful instead of vulnerable. We want them to be different than how they are, and we want something we feel we are not getting, be it love, safety, or even a mom who plays with us rather than one who yells or ignores us. So why not sweeten the deal and make an effort to build in a payoff for the other person? What a great idea! Yes, the system presumes and intends a win-win or, we could say, a payoff so we can make sure we get what we want and prevent further occurrences of the pain of the HT by "stopping" the HT events themselves. Imagine a "big person" embarrassed you for laughing too loud. This hurts. Wouldn't it make complete sense to decide to only laugh quietly from then on? Then THEY get a quiet laugher, and YOU get to be "safe" from the humiliation of embarrassment.

However, if it becomes apparent that the MM system is less than successful and they are not getting all we imagine they want, (i.e., no matter what we do, they are still angry with us), we will do all we can to adjust who we are (continually reducing ourselves to almost nothing) to be safe from the risk of a repeat of the HT. The essential motivation in all MM is the survival of the (w)hole creator. You and I are the creators of our (w)holes, not them.

The creator of all Meaning Making plans is you. Every (w)hole has a MM strategy. To fully understand the potency of the Meaning Maker, it is important to feel it, not just cognitively access it. Sometimes stories can help us feel the truth of a learning so that it moves from a thought to a feeling. This can allow us to move into a deeper understanding of a process because we can listen in while not being active participants.

A Story About Meaning Making

Here is a story to invoke your felt understanding of the Meaning Maker. It is one of my most favorite MM examples. (*A true story with all identifying information removed.*) Once there was a boy, about six or so years old. He was standing by his window at night before getting into bed, and there was a very big thunderstorm raging outside. Suddenly, out of the sky there came a huge bolt of lightning, which hit the top of the telephone pole across the street from him. Flash! At the very same time, he sneezed really hard. The telephone pole was ablaze, and sparks were flying everywhere! The lights went out. He gasped. It was really scary. He was shocked and terrified. What had happened? He was alone in the dark, and the dark scared him. Then there was an explosion; he could still see the flames of the telephone pole. He couldn't move, but he desperately wanted to run. This was dreadful and horrible!

And in this moment, he knew he never, ever wanted to have that horrible thing happen again. "Someone could get killed!" "I could die." "My family could die, and I'd be all alone!" You can only imagine all the thoughts that went flying through his mind. These thoughts and feelings moved through him so fast that only in retrospect would they even have words. So, without knowing it he (his internal Meaning Maker) instinctively assessed the situation, assigned "blame," and decided that his sneezing was what had caused the lightning. It would have been intolerable in that moment to believe, to feel, and to know that lightning can strike at any time without warning. This would be the ultimate height of powerlessness and vulnerability. He *had to* be the one with the power, for only then could any preventative action be taken.

So, the Power Point Location was shifted from lightning and nature in action (unpredictable, sudden, and dangerous) to his sneezing. By making this shift, the little boy had re-established his power to act on his own behalf to survive. Now, something could actually be done about the HT. He knew what part of him he would have to disallow so that he would not be in danger of lightning striking without warning.

Now, this next sequence is very important as an example of what every single one of us has done over and over and over again. Until he shifted into believing he had caused the danger, there was inside of him a dreadful feeling of vulnerability and the idea that lightning could happen at any time. That would mean that he would have no power to stop it or even know when it was coming and prepare for it, and there was no way to keep safe. With the Power Point Location shifted, then his MM could sort through things to arrive at a strategy of hope to prevent such a disaster in the future. If the MM had words, it might have sounded like this, "Hmmm, if my sneezing caused the dangerous lightning, then I must never, ever sneeze again!"

We can see now what his Meaning Maker strategy was. "If I make sure that I stay healthy (never sneeze, prevent all sneezing), then lighting won't strike out of the blue, maybe even killing me or them. They'll get to be safe from the lightning (which I am "sure" they want), and I'll be safe from that scary lightning (which could cause their deaths or mine). I get to keep my world safe (the big people I need and love) **and** I get to be safe from the scary, unpredictable lightning. Notice the "stay healthy" also has a definition of non-sneezing, which ignores the fact that sneezing is a healthy body response.

Do you see and feel his care and big-hearted logic? He wanted to live, no matter what part of him he had to push away. Whatever it took! He also wanted them to live because he loved them and needed them. Also he wanted no more scary lightning. We might write it more simply:

If I keep myself healthy so that sneezing will never happen (censor sneezing),
Lightning will not happen (change of the other, in this case it's nature).
They get to live safely (by being protected from a lightning strike),
And I will get to live, be safe from lightning, and keep my family.

Do you feel how simple, how obvious this sequence is?

If we were to draw it on out on the Wisdom WAY map, it would look like this:

Internally, the relief kicked in; the MM had resolved the potentiality of a repeat HT "lightning strike," and the pain of being vulnerable and powerless was removed. Sneezing became the rejected or disallowed part of himself. The MM system went on auto-pilot by keeping a space or a (w)hole between all he could be, do, and feel, and sneezing. Now, he could avoid the risk of lightning.

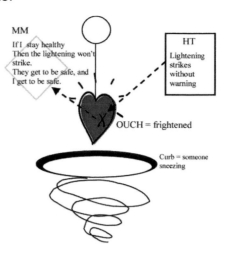

None of this was placed into words or even came close to his conscious awareness, but that does not mean it didn't radically affect his way of being in the world. Now he had to make sure to implement the strategy designed by his MM. He began to avoid people with colds. He always had to have tissues with him. As he got older, he began stealing cold medication. His family couldn't figure him out. "What is wrong with him?" they would ask themselves. They laughed at him when he would cry or get anxious if they sneezed. They got mad at him when he would beg them not to sneeze. He didn't understand it either. He just *knew* somewhere inside of himself that sneezing must be avoided at all cost.

His hidden motivation was actually quite a loving act. He was simply trying to keep everyone he loved alive and safe, including and especially himself. This is the kind of "heart-courage" in which we all engage. While the particulars for each of us are different, the essential actions, conclusions, Power Point shifts, and MM strategy formulation are the same. He didn't want anyone he loved to be struck by lightning, and if he was the cause of such occurrences, then he could make sure to never sneeze again. He wanted his dear family to live no matter what he had to do to insure this was so. What love! What creativity! He also didn't want to get hit by lightning himself; he also wanted to live. That is the life force in action.

Fast forward twenty years. The boy grew up, and although much of his life was fine, he was never free from having to make sure he didn't sneeze. He was subtly bound by this mysterious conviction. Despite its obvious lack of adult logic, he was unable to talk himself out of this fear. He was unable to calm himself when someone sneezed, and he had tried it all. The adult that he had become had no idea what made him so anxious about sneezing. He just knew he always did all he could to avoid it at every turn. He was a mystery to himself. Sometimes he even wondered if he was crazy.

Some folks called it anxiety; others said it was panic attacks, and still others told him it was a conversion disorder, maybe. But this didn't help at all. His life was affected by this, and no amount of studying, workshops, or therapies were changing this for him. He had been given the choice of medication to manage the anxiety, the choice of meditation to relax, the option of surgery to widen and alter his nasal passages to minimize the possibility of sneezing, and the choice of emersion therapy in which they would induce sneezing until he got over it.

None of these treatments helped. Unbeknownst to him, his MM strategy, his own creation from the long ago past, had been established as a "given" about how to survive life. This is a great example of how our MM strategies are primary "givens" or premises so buried as to leave us blind to their existence. No wonder we are confusing to ourselves! Despite all the various processes he engaged in to help him with his problem, he would inevitably find himself back once again doing "sneeze monitoring and prevention behaviors" (a phrase he had developed to summarize his problem). And if he did happen to sneeze because there were a few times when he just couldn't stop the sneezing, he would fall into a big black funk! He would feel terrible, anxious, fearful, and guilty for no reason he could understand. He made no sense to himself or to anyone else. But that didn't matter. What mattered was not sneezing. It was all quite exhausting and frustrating and frankly a bit embarrassing. He had no idea he was attempting to control lightning. So, for quite a long time he simply continued on managing, going around and around the same old stuff.

Yes, this example may seem a little silly and unusual; however, each of us in our own way has come to decisions that being or doing or expressing or feeling certain things are simply not acceptable. These mysterious decisions rule our lives until we sort through what happened. Sorting without judgment is a primary tool to (w)hole healing and (w)hole collapse. We sort without judgment through being curious.

When the mystery of ourselves is revealed to us and we can feel and see how much sense we make, there is an awakening to ourselves that occurs without effort. Yes, we make sense! The mysteries we have been to ourselves are revealed. We are empowered to show ourselves to ourselves a bit at a time until we are revealed as (W)hole, and then we remember our (W)hole selves. When we make sense to ourselves and we are able to soften and receive ourselves – (w)holes and all – then we step into a place of empowered choice.

As folks begin to feel the potency of the Wisdom WAY, they sometimes want to rush forward. If we move too fast, there isn't time for deep digesting and authentic interior felt changes. We ripen into (W)holeness until we just know ourselves as (W)hole, (w)holes, and all. I encourage you to let yourself ripen as you continue to read.

You are already familiar with "**Memory Lane**," the similarity of feelings between when we trip on a Curb of today and the feelings we had when the HT was first occurring. There is a feeling cord between today and yesterday, which I have called "Memory Lane." There is also what I like to call a felt pathway or "a WAY our heart logic flows" between the HT, the OUCH, and the MM. This is the felt-pathway from your big sensitive open heart and its initial felt response to the HT moment (OUCH) to your MM plan. It is a cellular, emotional, and cognitive memory, and it is an emotional and logic pathway. Each of us repeatedly walks down this heart-logic each time we trip on a Curb (in today) which feels similar in nature to the HT events. If you let yourself trace this route and feel each step of the way, you are truly accessing the original re-creation wisdom and motivation which resulted in your creating a (w)hole. This pathway, in short, runs from the HT to the OUCH to the MM. It is established based on a "logic of the heart" and the "logic" of a child's mind.

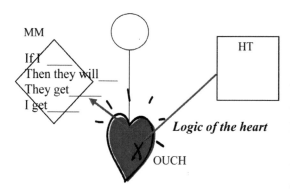

MM

If I ____
Then they will____
They get____
I get____

HT

Logic of the heart

OUCH

Being able to feel this heart logic is a great litmus test for your (w)hole study. Can you feel how brilliant the inner felt logic was from a child's viewpoint? Can you feel the hope, the yearning, the "whatever it takes" motivation? Can you feel and follow the logic underneath the negotiation of the Meaning Maker? These are the questions to ask yourself as you reveal your own MM and your own "WAY of heart logic."

The key to revealing the mysteries of ourselves is to begin where we all are – in our (w)holes. Just pick one, and begin to sort. The rest begins to fall into place.

A (w)hole Play Opportunity for You

Take a moment and review each of the sheets you have written on. Look at your list of Horrible Truths and Curbs, look at your page with all your concerns and issues. Select one of the HT's you have listed which particularly strikes you, or perhaps there is a new one that has come to mind as you have been reading. Or you may select a current Curb that is "touchy" or challenging you right now. Then look at your HT list and ask yourself, "What is it about this Curb that is familiar?" Either way, you are aiming to identify an HT, a Curb that feels similar, and the OUCH feeling.

It is helpful to begin with an HT that occurred when you were younger. Perhaps you might want to circle it or highlight it so you will know which one you are choosing to focus on in this moment.

On the next page is a basic diagram of the Wisdom WAY map of a (w)hole with all the parts you have come to know labeled. Just copy it over onto a blank sheet of paper in the same manner it is written. Use up the whole piece of paper so there is room for you to write. Please be careful to be particular as you fill in your unique answers – the details matter.

In the box called the Horrible Truth (HT), write the one HT you are focusing on. Keep it simple, like a news bulletin. For example, I might write "Father killed himself." It would not serve me to write the entire story of how and why he chose suicide. Remember, the HT is only about the other people, not you or me, so I wouldn't write something like

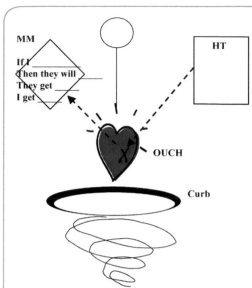

"Father died by suicide." Keep your HT short, simple, and essential. You don't need to write it all down – you have already lived it. The entire story of the events leading up to the core HT are also mostly irrelevant since we can't change the past. What is important is to start someplace. The HT is an easy place to start. The Curb is simply a today version of your HT. So, begin the way that makes the most sense to you. The HT isn't the point; the Curb isn't the point; it is the beginning.

Now, on the heart with the big "X," write what it felt like back when you were a kid when this particular HT happened. This is the OUCH. Feel the OUCH. Perhaps you felt afraid or ashamed or scared or hurt or embarrassed. Be sure it is a tender place in your heart. For example, I might write "scared or lonely or left behind."

If you wish, you may make a note of the most recent time you felt similar feelings. This is the "Curb." You may write that at the edge of the (w)hole. Sometimes identifying the Curb helps us give a name to the OUCH since today's feelings may, at first, be easier than recalling yesterday's feelings.

Then draw a diamond shape in the upper left corner. This is the symbol I use for the MM. Our Meaning Maker strategy is about bargaining - it is an exchange: "IF I do/say/ be only…, THEN they will change this way (the way I want them to be). They get something I think they want, and I will get what I want." The MM operates from "if-then" thinking. This shape is the shape for the "if-then" box in schematics. For consistency and to allow for the depth of this frame to reveal itself, draw this always in the upper left corner of your paper.

Now, using the Meaning Making strategic formula (MM), jot down what you imagine your particular strategy might have been for preventing a recurrence of this particular HT. If you are unsure, just take a good guess. There is no way to fail, only to gain more clarity as you sort things out. Remember, it is easier to figure out your MM when your HT is a short simple sentence. For example, for my MM I might write:

> If I am very nice and do everything perfectly,
> Then he'll come back from the dead (*he'll* change)
> He will get to be alive again (just as I imagine he would want)

And I'll get my dad back.

Write your final answer in the upper left-hand corner of your paper, in the diamond shape. (I recommend using some scrap paper to just jot down all the thoughts that come to you. When you are satisfied, put your "final for the moment" answer on your paper in the top left corner.):

1. If I am only this_____ (or if I only do_____).
2. Then they will _____ (be this way).
3. They get _____(what I imagine they want),
4. And I will get _____ (what I want from them).

This can be a bit of a challenge to figure out at first, so don't worry if you cannot figure it out exactly. Just stay curious, drop all judgments, and enter into a playful mindset. "I wonder what my personal MM strategy could have been?" "If I let myself see this creation of mine, what might I see?" Be even a bit silly about it so that you open up to the mystery of you, waiting to show its face. Just give it your best shot, knowing that you can change it at any time. Remember, there's no way to fail!

I have numbered them so you remember that points two and three are about the other people, while points one and four are about you. Remember it is from a child's viewpoint, and it is about what the child imagines the other person would want. Do not judge the child or the strategy as an adult would. This serves no purpose because it was the child of us that created these brilliant strategies to save our lives.

Showing ourselves to ourselves, letting our mysteries reveal themselves, isn't always comfortable. Sometimes it can be a bit surprising or even shocking! Breathe deeply and get a bit silly about it all. After all, any (w)hole you have fallen into is one you created years ago. Frankly, it's old news. What is new is letting yourself see yourself. What is new is seeing how much sense you really do make!

In order to unveil your particular "space between" or (w)hole, we must return to the Universal Story for just a moment.

Chapter 7: Waking Up to How We Broke Ourselves Into Bits and Pieces

There Are Two Sides to Every (w)hole.

Now, let us look again at the (W)hole Universal Story. This is what we know so far:

We are born (W)hole and unconscious.

Life happens. Things happen. Other people do and say things.

Some of these things feel horrible for us (HT).

We hurt; we get scared. We have painful feelings about the stuff that happens (OUCH).

We don't want to have these painful feelings.

We want to stop the pain, fear, shame, terror, and especially the awful feelings of being powerless and vulnerable.

But, we have no power over the other people and what they do or say (they have free will) and as a kid they are bigger than we are.

We only have power over ourselves.

We have the power to recreate ourselves from the inside out.

So we use it. How smart we are!

We shift the focus from them to us. It is instinctive in all of us.

We save ourselves with "hope."

We engage the Power Point Location shift mechanism we all have.

We engage our Meaning Maker and create a strategy to dodge, avoid, or prevent that which hurts us, frightens us, or scares us. (MM)

Now we have power to do something about the Horrible Truth! We do this secretly and internally, often without any awareness.

We simply get rid of the identified "bad part" of me. This is the part we have secretly assessed and decided is the cause of the HT. This can also be something we are told we "ought to be but aren't." (A failure on our part according to them.) However, the "blame" is established, and this "bad" part of us is disallowed or pushed away (the Not Allowed to be Me part).

We begin to live as if we don't have that part (the only part of Me I can be).

We create a (w)hole, a space between parts of our original (W)hole self we accept as allowable to express and the parts we push away as disallowed.

This is what we have explored so far; however, the Universal Story continues.

The Universal Story Continues

Remember our earlier definition of a (w)hole as a space between parts of ourselves? You may have noticed that in our Meaning Making plan, there is a part or an expression of us that we push away because it is the part that we believe caused the HT to happen. We push this part to the far side of the (w)hole or space. We push it as far away from us as possible. The parts we push away are called the "Not Allowed to be expressed parts of Me," or the "Not Me" for short. These are listed down the right side of the (w)hole study. These are the parts of us that will interfere with our MM strategy, our plan of hope. We believe that we cannot be or feel or express these parts because doing so could make the HT happen all over again, and that is something we desperately want to avoid. We label these parts the **"Not Me."**

You may have also noticed that the Meaning Making strategy tells us what parts of us we can keep. The parts we "get to keep" are the parts we can continue to allow ourselves to express. These are the parts that seemingly do not elicit Horrible Truth experiences. These are also the "safe" parts of us that will not interfere with our MM strategy. These are the parts of us we believe did not cause the HT to happen. These allowed parts are listed on the left side of your (w)hole and are called the "Allowed to be expressed parts of Me" parts or "Me," for short. These are the parts we present to the world and to ourselves as acceptable. We label these parts **"Me."**

Each time our Meaning Maker assesses a Horrible Truth situation and determines the offending part, it places it on the "Not Me" side of a space. By doing this we have created a (w)hole. A (w)hole is a felt space in our hearts. The feeling of falling into a (w)hole occurs each time we are faced with a situation that invites us or challenges us to access the "Not Me" parts of ourselves. We feel discomfort when we are pushed to express a part of ourselves that we have previously named as "Not Allowed to be expressed, felt, or acted upon." In essence, each time we feel ourselves fall into a (w)hole, we are risking the possibility of breaking the internal rules of safety and survival we have previously established. It is feels like we have accidentally taken the plane off auto-pilot and find ourselves in the pilot seat, but we don't know how to fly! This is one way to describe the feeling of falling into a Life (w)hole.

Now, consider for just a moment the Meaning Making strategy that the young boy created in response to the lightning without knowing it. There were all of the healthy parts of him on one side, and sneezing was pushed over onto the other side. Let us say, for example, that this young boy grew up to be a chef (I am making this part up), and whenever he had to sniff a dish he had made, essentially risking sniffing pepper, he would fall into a (w)hole. How would he know he fell into a (w)hole? He might have feelings of tension, anxiety, and possibly even anger which surface for no apparent logical reason. Or, instead of becoming a chef, he might have chosen a career based on his avoidance of that feeling of anxiousness. He might have become an accountant who worked at home in a sterile environment of his own creation to reduce the risk of sneezing. Remember, the reasons for many of our life decisions are not fully conscious – the reasons are buried in our (w)holes. No wonder we haven't felt free and fully empowered – we haven't been! Our (w)holes and our Meaning Maker have been in charge of us!

So now, if we look closely at the anatomy of a (w)hole, we see there is one side, a space, and then the other side. We can imagine this space as a pothole, which we can fall into. In the form of a simple diagram, the anatomy of a life (w)hole is:

Remember, "Allowed to be expressed parts of Me" is on one side of the space and "Not Allowed to be expressed parts of Me" is on the other side of the space. For short hand we say the "Me" and the "Not Me." Actually, they are all parts of you; however, one expression is allowed and the other is not.

We use vital life force to keep the space intact so that we are only being the "Me" parts and studiously avoiding the "Not Me" parts." This, in essence, is what creates the "issues" we have all so urgently sought to heal or resolve. They are (w)holes in the fabric of our expressions of our selves. They are the spaces we keep in place and are why we feel broken rather than (W)hole. When there are elements of who we are that are disallowed, by definition we are *less than* who we are. We are not (W)hole! Conversely as we allow or welcome home these dis-owned parts of ourselves, we are more of who we are – (W)hole.

For example, sometimes we push away or identify a skill or talent as "bad" or disal-lowed. An individual came to me a few years back who loved to sing and was very talented. However, she struggled greatly. She was not confident with her obvious talent and suppressed it (*again a true story with identifying elements removed*). In her (w)hole work we discovered that there was a music teacher who this (then) little girl adored. The teacher mentored this little girl for several years. They were years filled with joy-filled singing. This teacher then suddenly and abruptly cut the girl out of the lead role of the school musical after first giving it to her. This occurred without explanation. This was confusing. She loved to sing, and her teacher had been like a second mom.

What had made this horrible thing happen (the HT)? It's mysterious, and there didn't seem to be any clear reason. To make matters worse, the teacher would not even discuss it. Now, it really did feel crazy to the little girl, and it was also very painful. Her interior Meaning Maker rose up on her behalf, and its process sounded something like this: "It must have been something I did." "What was it?" "What could it have been?" The little girl's MM – after great inner turmoil – comes to the conclusion that her BIG joy of singing was somehow at fault.

The little girl's Meaning Maker concluded that it isn't okay to do what you love to do because it mysteriously causes people to reject you. Although she still didn't have a sense of why, it no longer mattered. Having a solution, a resolution, an explanation, and a plan of action is all that matters in this big OUCH moment, when Horrible Truth events occur.

If I said this more simply, it would sound like this: "Make sense of this no matter what!" This is the mission of our interior Meaning Maker! It really doesn't matter at that moment if the conclusion makes adult sense – only that there is an explanation of some sorts!

The blame or cause has been assigned. An explanation has been arrived at, and this allows for a strategy of hope to form. In this example, the clear MM strategy was to "not sing alone – sing only in a group." After all, she didn't want to be rejected, and she wanted her teacher to like her again. So, she stopped singing except for background harmony. It was safe to sing as long as she could hide in a group, and it was "obviously" not safe to be standing up alone in a bold full-voice manner. She made a (w)hole. She could do or be anything else, but she could not sing big by herself.

Pause a moment, and notice the word "**Obviously.**" Whenever any one of us encounters a thought or a belief or a sentence in which we say something like, "Obviously, I could not do, not be, not say….," there is a (w)hole here!

Let the word "Obviously" be a gift to yourself. Let it be an invitation to get curious without judgment and look at the self-expression you so "obviously" can't be! This is a "Not Me!" Surprise! You have found a (w)hole!

It was sixteen years later that this woman with this "*only sing in a group*" (w)hole came to a two-day intensive (W)hole Shop. She wrestled with the Horrible Truth and the Meaning Making system she had devised. On the second day of the program, she stood up and sang her own song, one that she had written the night before! **When we make sense to ourselves, we can choose again**. So she did. She went on to write and sing several more songs, and shortly thereafter, she recorded her first CD. (If you wish to hear her amazing, healing voice, contact me at The (W)hole Point Institute, and I will direct you to her CD's – with her permission.)

Read this sentence again: When we make sense to ourselves, we can choose again! One of the gifts of the Wisdom WAY map is how quickly we make sense of our own life decisions. If we are judging ourselves for this choice or that behavior, there is no room, no space for new decisions! Consequently, as your own Meaning Making strategies become clear, without any effort on your part, new possibilities arise! This means that more life force can flow through you, and your aliveness expands. Now is the time to wake up and step into your (W)hole Life – at first we do this one (w)hole at a time.

Now that we have unveiled more of how we create our (w)holes and more elements of the Wisdom WAY map, it is time for you to begin to reveal yourself to yourself.

Notice the image. It is the map of (w)holes as you know it so far. This Wisdom WAY map, which is a Universal map or "story," comes alive as you input YOUR particular experiences.

Take a moment, and look at the image. You will see your original (W)holeness at the very top in the symbol of a circle. We were born (W)hole and unconscious – as if we were born with a lollipop in our hands that said, "Here I am! Aren't I great?" You will see the Horrible Truth (HT) box up in the upper right hand corner. You know all about your yesterday (the HT), so nothing more needs to be said. Whatever is written in this box is all about *them* and not about you.

You will see a big, sensitive, alive heart right below it. Imagine a new born baby – this big heart in the middle of the diagram is the complete open-hearted

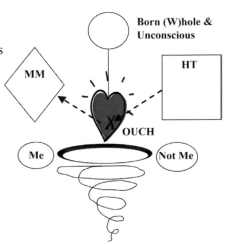

nakedness of us as infants. You will see an "X" on the heart signifying the OUCH of the Horrible Truth moment. Notice the dotted line that goes from the HT box to the heart. This is to represent that the HT events touched our hearts and had an impact called the OUCH (X). You will then see that a dotted line goes from the "X" to the Meaning Making diamond in the left hand corner. This dotted line represents our naked raw feelings of vulnerability and powerlessness and our urgent need to make sense of what has happened and then find a way to prevent a reoccurrence of that Horrible Truth event. This line also indicates the Power Point Location shift from "them" to "us." This "desperate-to-save-ourselves-from-the-HT" feeling activates the Meaning Making program. Remember, the diamond shape is an "If-then" negotiation shape. The diamond shape represents our MM solution or strategy for making sure that *that* horrible thing never happens again.

Then you will notice there is an oval or (w)hole, and on either side are two smaller circles. These represent the "Me" part on the left side and the "Not Me" part on the right side of the oval. The space between these two parts of your (W)holeness is the (w)hole itself. You will also notice the Curb or line around the edge of the (w)hole. This is a way to represent the events in today which operate as Curbs, tripping you into an awareness of a (w)hole you created ever so long ago.

A (w)hole Play Opportunity for You

Make a rough sketch of this more comprehensive skeleton on a new piece of paper. It is not yet the complete Wisdom WAY map; however, you now have enough of the map to begin to show yourself a (w)hole.

Now, using all your notes from your earlier pieces of paper – the one where you listed your concerns, the one where you listed some Horrible Truths and Curbs, and the one you guessed at some of your MM strategies – pick one Curb or one Horrible Truth, and write it at the proper location on the Wisdom WAY map. Take a guess as to the OUCH – that deepest of all feelings or the feeling that just "sticks inside of you." Write it on the "X" of the OUCH.

Now … pause … feel "Memory Lane," the felt path from the Curb to the Horrible Truth. Can you feel the similarities? Can you feel how it seems the same in a way? If so, proceed. If not go back and mull a bit more until you can feel the similarity between the Curb you picked and the Horrible Truth you picked.

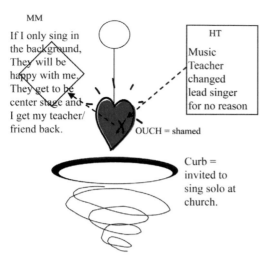

MM

If I only sing in the background, They will be happy with me, They get to be center stage and I get my teacher/friend back.

HT

Music Teacher changed lead singer for no reason

OUCH = shamed

Curb = invited to sing solo at church.

Let's look at an example so you can see what you will be doing next with your precious (w)hole. Let's go back to the woman who didn't dare sing BIG. She might write in the HT box – "Music Teacher wouldn't talk for no reason" or "Music Teacher changed lead singer for no reason" or "Music Teacher excluded me" or whatever *she* felt was the heart of the Horrible Truth for her. Remember, YOU are the expert of you!

Here is one way "the woman who didn't dare sing" *might* begin to "Spiral" or move through her (w)hole. Perhaps she would write on the Curb "Invited to sing a solo at the church musical." Perhaps she would write on the OUCH "Shamed." Perhaps she would write in the MM diamond, "If I only sing harmony in the background, then they will be happy with me. They get to be center stage (what I imagine the Music Teacher wanted), and I'll get my teacher to be my friend again. In this example, in order to implement the MM strategy – she would push away the option of "Singing solos" and "Loving to be musically BIG" to the far side of the (w)hole. This would be her "Not Me." On the "Me" side of her (w)hole she might write, "Singing harmony" and "Staying in the background."

Continuing Your (w)hole Play Opportunity

Look at your paper where you began your first (w)hole study by filling in your Curb, HT, and OUCH. Now, take a guess at your Meaning Making strategy. Write it in the diamond shape. Don't worry about doing it perfectly.

As you look at your MM strategy, notice that the first line tells you what you can *only* do, while implied is what you *cannot* allow yourself to do. This tells you what your "Me" is and what your "Not Me" is.

Now, it really pays to be particular here. What parts of you do you think you had to push away in order to implement this strategy? Another way to do this is to begin by writing a list of all the things you long to be or hate to be on the right side of the (w)hole labeled "Not Me." These are all the parts that you have not allowed yourself to be or to express as you because they would interfere with the MM strategy. From the example of the woman who didn't dare to sing BIG, she may have listed on her "Not Me" side parts such as "Big voice," "Being center stage," and "Singing my way."

> Once you have listed a few "Not Me" parts, then move to the left side of the (w)hole, the side labeled "Me." Write all the parts you do let yourself be, express, and feel. These are the parts of you that will not interfere with your strategy. Often these two sides of the (w)hole are opposites, and this can be a helpful way to begin to create the motion between the two sides of the (w)hole as well as a way to get a rich list for each side. Look for opposites. From our example, the girl who wouldn't dare to sing BIG may have listed on her "Me" side parts such as "Small voice," "Blend in with the others," "Singing the way they tell me to." If you want to get even more particular, circle the elements on the "Me" side and the "Not Me" side that feel directly linked to the Curb and the HT.

Take some time now and begin to sketch out your first (w)hole study. Remember, there is no way to fail. Let yourself begin to feel the (W)hole Truth that there are spaces between parts of you and that perhaps, just perhaps, you aren't so mysterious after all.

At first it takes time to establish the sorting process. Sorting slowly at first, we teach ourselves how to recognize the difference between a Horrible Truth and a Meaning Maker, the difference between a "Me" part and a "Not Me" part, the difference between a Curb and a Horrible Truth. Sometimes, because we are little and desperate when we are creating our (w)hole solutions, the event itself becomes merged with the Meaning we are making of the event, until they are actually experienced as one element. Since there are actually two elements (HT & MM), no matter how much we investigate our issues, if the foundational premise is faulty, we'll get stuck. The event (IIT) is not the same thing as the significance or MM one has assigned to the occurrence.

You will begin to recognize the wisdom and wonderful creativity you applied to create the space between this part and that part of you. Every (w)hole is your own brilliant creative powers in action. Remember, YOU created each of these strategies of hope and thus, each of your (w)holes, which are just the implementation of your Meaning Maker. YOU are the creator. You had no help! You did it all alone! You did this when you were LITTLE! Appreciate yourself with every (w)hole you begin to recognize. Each one is evidence of both your creative genius and your tender heart's precious choice for hope.

What do you feel as you look at all your parts on both sides of this (w)hole? This is a key point to notice. Give yourself some credit. It takes guts to look directly at the secrets we have kept from ourselves. One never knows what will be revealed. Allowing yourself to be surprised as well as impressed with yourself is part of (w)hole play and (w)hole collapsing.

Take a moment to breathe in the wonder of you revealing yourself to yourself.

Chapter 8: Waking Up to the Mysteries of the Spiral Pathway

There is a secret about (w)holes which is now no longer a secret because I've already spilled the beans. You have seen it drawn on the diagrams earlier. Earlier still, you also may have noticed I had you write your feelings down the center of the page. All of us have felt the space between the two sides of the (w)hole each time we "fell into the pits." We felt "awful," "sad," "hurt," "angry," and a (W)hole bunch of other feelings. In fact, when we fall into the dark (w)holes, we feel all sorts of feelings because when we created the (w)hole, we dumped all of the feelings we didn't want to feel down into the (w)hole. Falling into a (w)hole is sometimes likened to falling into a big vat of feelings. At this point you know the secret. It may feel like a vat of feelings, but when we know how to turn on the light, a spiral path is revealed. The secret is all (w)holes are collapsed spirals; the only thing missing is the light.

As I mentioned earlier, (w)holes may be likened to the old Slinky™ toy. The spiral wiring is not obvious when it is sitting on a table. What is obvious is that it is "closed up," and there is a space in the middle of it. I call this space a (w)hole. Oftentimes we imagine (w)holes to be deep, dark places.

What makes (w)holes feel "dark?" They feel dark because the path of light has collapsed upon itself and thus, is hidden. For light to penetrate a (w)hole, we need to open up the spiral. The tool we use to do this is "curiosity without judgment." When we apply the art of "curiosity without judgment" to the Wisdom WAY map by simply filling in our particulars, the collapsed spiral opens up! It's that simple. It is at this moment that our personal "wisdom path" is revealed to us. Sometimes this can be really scary. Sometimes we just simply do not want to look. And sometimes, we're really anxious about what we might find.

Each (w)hole we stumble upon is an invitation to open your spiral-being to the light of your own wisdom! Drawing the Wisdom WAY map, picking a Curb or a Horrible Truth, and beginning to fill in **your** wisdom elements using curiosity without judgment opens the spiral and allows in the light. In this way **you** are bringing your light into your own dark places! In this way you are empowering yourself to step into your (W)hole life!

Now you know the mystery of ourselves. (W)holes are actually compressed spirals, and when we extend the spiral and open ourselves up through curiosity without judgment, the spiral pathway of our own (W)holeness is revealed. This spiral path is another element of a (w)hole. When we are mapping out a (w)hole, we write our feelings on the spiral of the map. We do this because when we create a (w)hole, we are working hard to "get away from" how we feel. The solution? Dump the feelings into the (w)hole, much as we dump garbage into the trash can.

Since then, what we have typically done is go around and around the edge of our (w)holes, trying desperately to not fall in or getting out as fast as possible if we do! Essentially, we are going from one side of the (w)hole to the other. I call this **oscillating** – moving back and forth without direction. Remember, when we find ourselves in a (w)hole, we've just been invited to be one of those parts we decided we absolutely cannot be. We're suddenly on the "Not Me" side of the (w)hole, and it feels awful because now our strategy is in danger. We find ourselves scrambling back to the "Me" side, which will essentially move us outside of the (w)hole. All of us will and have oscillated in our (w)holes. In a state of oscillation we have felt "stuck in the pits," "no way out of this issue," "hopeless," "frustrated," and "confused."

However, now that we know that the Spiral of our heart can open up and reveal a path, we no longer need to be paralyzed in oscillation. What great news. Knowing this secret, we can open up the spiral, follow our wisdom pathway home, and reveal our (W)hole selves to ourselves. If we don't know this secret, we will spend our lifetime falling in and climbing out of (w)holes, telling ourselves all sorts of stories about how we are in the same mess again. Oscillating means you will miss out on your precious (W)hole Life!

Yes, hidden in every (w)hole you fall into is your spiral path or your WAY of Wisdom laid out for you at the time the (w)hole was created. The path was created by the Meaning Making process you, yourself, created to prevent or at least manage the Horrible Truth that happened. This pathway is the way back to (W)holeness, which is our natural state. Each and every (w)hole we create has this spiral pathway. It is automatically invoked into being whenever we create a Meaning Making strategy of hope. Each time we "push away" or "disallow" a part of ourselves, our inner wisdom insures that whenever we choose, that orphaned part of us can come home. All our disowned parts are just waiting for our welcome home. It is as if each part you have pushed away is a breadcrumb you can follow to wake up your own (W)holeness. This path of wisdom isn't about my wisdom; it is your wisdom and your brilliant creations. This path cannot be traveled by merely thinking about it or through just a cognitive understanding of it because this alone will change nothing. Your (w)holes were created by you in response to what you were feeling; therefore, your feelings must also be a part of your (w)hole awakening. To walk the wisdom of your own WAY requires your felt participation. This unmasking of the hidden spirals of your life offers you a key to your own (W)holeness.

For your spiral paths to be fully revealed, it simply requires a full familiarity with the framework. We are building a solid foundational understanding of why we created (w)holes, how we created them, and what all the wisdom elements or parts are of any (w)hole. The effect is to empower us to sort out all the stuff of our lives.

This has nothing to do with "fixing" anything about us. (W)holeness is all about being all of who we are. The difficulty has been that we weren't aware of what we had done with all our parts. Some of our parts, feelings, and behaviors we have kept. Some of our parts we have pushed away. We have created strategies to try and prevent HT reoccurrences. Some of us have been hiding in the dark (w)hole, hoping to be found and yet, terrified of being found. Our (W)holeness, the (W)HOLE of US, is found in each (w)hole we fall into.

Now, we know we created these spaces to save our lives. The good news is that our disowned orphaned parts are just waiting for us to open our hearts and welcome them home. We are not broken! The difficulties are due to the gaps in our consciousness. The difficulties are due to our initial Acts of Hope, designed to save our lives from our Horrible Truths. Now is the time for the Act of Hope of Waking up to our (W)hole Lives! (W)holeness isn't about "fixing," or "correcting" because we are not broken, and there's nothing "wrong" about us. (W)holeness is all about revealing ourselves to ourselves over and over again, and in doing so, we expand into all we can be without hesitation, without apology, without holding back. (W)holeness and living a (W)hole life is all about embracing who we are! We can do this by Intentionally Spiraling one (w)hole at a time until there is a Cascade of (W)holeness!

So, when in doubt, stay curious. Drop all your judgments about yourself, the (w)hole, the feelings, and everything else. Just let it all be. Nothing is wrong with you. The only thing you need to do is to sort. Begin to reveal the mystery of yourself to yourself. Then begin to sort the HT from the MM and the Curbs, and the "Me's" from the "Not Me's." This sorting process stops us from going around and around. It creates the motion called Intentional Spiraling – intentionally walking along the spiral pathway towards our (W)holeness.

Intentional Spiraling

Intentional Spiraling is the movement of entering into the (w)hole on purpose by being curious without judgment. Entering a (w)hole with a clear direction is the key, for it provides us with a compass. This direction is our revealed (W)holeness – **ours**, not anyone else's. At the bottom of every (w)hole is a bit of conscious (W)holeness, a bit of our aliveness. Intentional Spiraling is going **into** the (w)hole towards the bottom of it through the movement of mapping our personal Wisdom WAY.

As we are building a solid foundation and orientation within the Wisdom WAY map of (W)holeness, one key to spiraling around a (w)hole is to let the little "ah ha" moments pop in and let them go. There is no great effort needed, just gentle, persistent curiosity. Patience helps. These (w)holes were created a long time ago, and you have been living in and around them for a long time.

The (w)holes we have created are gaps in the flow of our being. These gaps or hiccups in the flow of our life force are the result of the dismemberment of our original (W)holeness. These gaps are created each time we assessed a life moment as horrible (HT), shifted the Power Point from them to us, established a particular part for self-blame (MM), and then implemented the judgment by disallowing or pushing away the "Not Allowed to be Me" part of us.

These (w)holes operate like static or blips or blank spaces in the flow of our life force. One analogy I particularly like is the experience of talking to someone who is using a cell phone too far from the nearest cell tower. We can hear bits and pieces of what they are saying but not the whole sentence. This is exactly the same effect (w)holes have in our hearts and in our lives and upon our Life Force itself. We can't hear, act from, or much less be our (W)holeness when all we have access to is bits and pieces of ourselves. (W)holeness requires ALL of US, while our (w)holes keep all the bits and pieces and parts of ourselves separate. It is that basic.

When we feel "in the pits" or in the black (w)hole again, what has occurred is that we have stumbled into a void in our energy field. It is simply a (w)hole in our (W)holeness. What makes falling into these spaces painful is the felt experience that we are being or are being asked to be a part of us that we have disallowed. We are experiencing a demand or push to break the very Meaning Making strategy we designed to save ourselves as children. The dilemma is that the MM is now interfering with our lives as adults. No wonder we all react when we fall in! Each (w)hole is a collision between two time zones – the age we created the (w)hole and the MM plan, and the age we are today! No wonder it feels like we are at risk. In a funny way we are – we are at risk of becoming (W)hole. We are at risk of more of us coming back into our own awareness, today. We are at risk for having to take responsibility for our (W)hole lives: then and now. We are challenging ourselves to recognize our own creations! We are especially at risk for having feelings. The path of (W)holeness is all about feelings.

Becoming (W)hole is about discovering **lost feelings**. It is about revealing how much we judge our own feelings. It is about feeling our feelings – **all** of them. We will inevitably be pushed by life into situations that invite us or coerce us to access the "Not Allowed Me" expressions of ourselves. When this occurs, the feeling is of falling head first into the vat of old, moldy, yet familiar, feelings. These are the feelings we had at the moment of the HT. No wonder our (w)holes hurt! Besides, there is more than one feeling in any one (w)hole!

We actually do not feel just one feeling at a time. It is more like a flow of various shades and hues of colors or feelings all blending together. We might call it a single name, while in truth there are many feeling elements present. These (w)hole feeling constellations are what we didn't want to feel ever again, so the MM quite conveniently dropped them into the space between the two parts of ourselves. Every (w)hole serves as a "holding bin" for feelings which were experienced at the time of the OUCH.

A bit of truth: No part of our original (W)holeness is ever lost. Every element is held in waiting until we choose to embrace it once again. It is important to understand that we can't actually get rid of any part or a feeling, but we can do a very good job of hiding these parts from ourselves in all sorts of places. None of us have to work to be (W)hole. The "work" is to simply open the door and let all our parts integrate. The Wisdom WAY map is the "Hands & Feet" for doing this – one (w)hole at a time – embracing one "Not Allowed Me" part at a time. You are now beginning to see, I hope, that every Wisdom WAY element offers many gifts, which are expressions of you held in waiting for their own unveiling. Sorting is the basic practice which invites (W)holeness to reveal itself. We open the spiral by sorting using the Wisdom WAY map.

As we open the Spiral, we discover the surprise of ourselves. The (w)hole isn't just a space; it is a storage vat. The spiral of the (w)hole operates like a great bin of unfelt, disowned, painful, shameful, judged, abandoned, or rejected feelings. To date we have not wanted to peek inside because we were afraid. Of course, it is scary to go poking around in a dark pit. However, now you are beginning to have an understanding of what (w)holes are all about, and you have a map so that you can find your way around, and you know how to open the spiral to let the light in.

Let us look at an example as a way to review all that you now know about (w)holes and how they are created and how they feel. Let us say that someone has experienced her mother yelling at her for playing "too loudly and enthusiastically" (mom's judgment of her). Her mom said, "Maybe I'll just give you to the neighbors." In an instant the child feels the horror of that possibility. This moment has become a HT.

The child in us doesn't know this was only an expression of mom's frustrations. "Maybe," the child feels and thinks, "she really will give me away. How horrible that would be? I love my mom!" The Meaning Maker jumps in automatically, with no effort required, and pushes to the far side of the (w)hole "loud and enthusiastic expressions" based on the Meaning Making template of survival:

> If I am very quiet and contained,
> Then mom will be happy.
> And Mom will get a kid she wants to keep,
> And I will get to stay. (Mom will keep me)

The MM is a negotiation. The price paid is the price of passionate, loud, enthusiastic expressions so the mom will now be happy. The Product: she will keep Me. Can you feel the pay-off for the (w)hole creator? The child is now relieved of the horrible terrifying feeling that mom might really give her away. What a relief! There is a plan, a response, and a solution all neatly designed by the Meaning Maker. There is no more imminent threat of danger and the (w)hole creator, the child, can relax. It is set up to run on automatic pilot, and so it does. Then what happens?

The feelings of shame, fear, and badness have been dropped into the Spiral space of the (w)hole. This person now grows up and is usually very quiet. In high school, she desperately wants to join the cheerleading squad but just can't seem to. She finds herself thinking, "They are just so loud. I could never do that, but they look like they are having so much fun." The secret she is keeping about herself is that this (w)hole, created so long ago, is still running the show and running her life and limiting her choices. She isn't aware of the connection between then and now. She only feels discomfort – longing and judgments and fears and sadness – so she avoids the very things that might awaken her "Not Allowed to be Me" part

Later on in her life, in her job as a research chemist, she is asked to give talks about her revolutionary discoveries and declines the offers. "I just can't get up there and make a bunch of noise about what I have discovered. If they want to know, they can read my articles. Anyway it just isn't proper for folks to be so noisy about their accomplishments." And so it goes. Many opportunities are missed or avoided all together because the Meaning Maker is still on auto-pilot, and she is unconsciously abiding by the original strategy.

Do you see how her (w)hole is in charge of her life? Our (w)holes prevent or discourage us from making choices that require the (W)hole of us to show up. The sad truth is that our (w)holes narrow our lives until there are very few ways left for us to be. This is the cumulative effect of creating (w)hole after (w)hole after (w)hole. Once we see that it "works" to make the pain stop, we simply repeat the same process.

Intentional Spiraling is, in part, a heart-felt choice to stop going around and around and instead, purposefully go within to sort through the Meaning Making strategies so we can reintroduce ourselves to all of our parts. Intentional Spiraling is all about daring to go into a particular (w)hole intentionally, on purpose. Intentional Spiraling is choosing to reveal ourselves to ourselves. Intentional Spiraling is the decision to be willing to be surprised by and to accept who we discover!

Let's face it, we already know there are parts of us that we've tossed aside. By the word "**intention**" I mean to make a choice or decision on purpose. Intentional Spiraling is to purposefully decide to move within so as to reveal our own (W)holeness to ourselves. (W)holeness is **not** outside of us; it is inside of us. We have to go into that dark, creepy place and take our parts back. This isn't about wishing or hoping or longing for or blaming others or settling. The very first step in Intentional Spiraling is to **choose to look inside** yourself rather than outside of yourself. Spiraling is a pattern of empowering motion inside a (w)hole.

(w)holes Are the Holders of the Secrets

Our (w)holes are where we put all the secrets about ourselves that we wished to keep from ourselves. These secrets are about all of who we are. Your (w)holes are the secrets you have been keeping from yourself for years, maybe even your entire lifetime! Our (w)holes are hidey-holes. They serve to keep us blind to our magnificent (W)holeness. So be prepared. Intentionally Spiraling a (w)hole is all about daring to tell yourself those secrets. There isn't any place to hide when you choose to spiral (w)holes intentionally because everything of the (w)hole is available to be revealed to you. Revealing yourself to yourself is the greatest adventure, the wildest ride, and the most freeing of activities.

Determine to be curious. Be curious without judgment about whatever you see or learn. Judgments are decisions about the acceptability or non-acceptability of expressions of ourselves and others. These evaluations appear as labels of black or white, good or bad, right or wrong, should or shouldn't. Judgments block and distort our vision and only serve to hold us firmly in these (w)holes of our own making. Judgment is what the Meaning Maker uses to separate parts of us by evaluating them as "OK" or "Not OK." Judgment is the tool of the Meaning Maker. Judgment also has the impact of contraction.

Any time you are using judgment against yourself or another, you are already in the clutches of your Meaning Maker, not wanting to look at the painful feelings you have successfully suppressed until now. The effect is to tighten up. This tightening contracts the Spiral, and it once again becomes a black pit with no light. Curiosity without judgment is the practice that allows us to look at our feelings and to move into our (w)holes. A truth of Intentional Spiraling is that it is up to us to chose whether to allow light into the dark places of our heart or not!

You have been developing this skill of Intentional Spiraling (sorting with curiosity while dropping judgment) as you have been learning the Wisdom WAY map. In effect, Intentional Spiraling allows light to be shed on the mysterious ways we have limited our self or hidden from ourselves. With this skill, you open up the compressed spiral of any (w)hole, allowing light to enter the dark mysteries of that pit with which you have become so intimately acquainted. Enlightenment is all about turning on a light in the darkness – not changing who you will reveal!

What Is at the Bottom of Each (w)hole or Spiral?

At the bottom of every spiral in every one of our (w)holes is a bit of your (W)holeness or "Radiance," as I like to call it. **Radiance** is (W)holeness awakened, empowered, revealed, and embodied. Radiance is always unique because we are unique. Radiance is you being all of you. Radiance is all of you alive! Radiance is your (W)hole Life, awake as you. Radiance is your life force flowing.

Infants are bundles of Radiance! Radiance is your life force, your vitality, your aliveness, your (W)holeness awake. When we create a (w)hole, we drop a bit of our life force down into the (w)hole. We create those gaps in the flow of our life force. Instead of being available for us to use, this bit of life force energy is used to keep the space between our parts in place, and it is experienced as a gap in our ease of moving through life. Is it any wonder that we have less and less energy as we get older and become more (w)hole-ridden?

Radiance comes alive and becomes available to us when we begin to say "yes" to those pushed away parts of ourselves. Radiance is the light of our being joyfully alive as who we really are. Radiance is not about efforting; it is about adopting all the "orphans" of our (W)holeness. Radiance isn't "achieved." Radiance is revealed! Radiance isn't about "fixing." Radiance is all about embracing and welcoming. Radiance isn't the spaces between parts or expressions of ourselves. Radiance is conscious (W)holeness – all parts welcomed. Radiance is what you sense from someone who is at ease with who they are and at ease with you being who you are! Radiance is a (W)hole Life come alive!

Movements of a (W)hole Life Waking Up

When we are going around and around in a (w)hole, we are **oscillating.** We all are quite adept at this type of life motion. In fact, it is a "false aliveness," for it takes us nowhere but around and around, back and forth. Oscillation is the motion of back and forth between the two sides of (w)hole without any focus or direction. We are oscillating when we fall in a (w)hole and can't orient ourselves or begin to sort. We are oscillating when we effort and try but don't go anywhere. Often this feels like flailing around, groping in the dark, or frozen in flight-fear. However it feels to you, the key point to recognize is that when you are oscillating, you are going nowhere, as there is no focus, just a huge wad of "icky" familiar feelings. When you are oscillating, you are in a (w)hole!

Pulsating is the motion of going back and forth between the two sides of a (w)hole with the purpose of (w)hole exploration and in the direction of revealed (W)holeness. We have a direction because we have established a purpose (intent, choice) to get to the bottom of our (w)hole where (W)holeness-revealed awaits us, in particular. We move around and actually go somewhere because we know where we are and where we are moving towards.

When we are oscillating, the spiral of our (w)hole remains collapsed. When we begin to pulsate, the spiral path opens up to reveal more of who we are – radiance waiting for permission to come alive as us.

Intentional Spiraling is the choice and activity **of focusing within and moving towards** the points of tension in your (w)hole. The felt effect of this is to open up or stretch out the Spiral of your (w)hole so you can follow this Spiral path to your (W)holeness. Intentional Spiraling is done using the skill of curiosity without judgment.

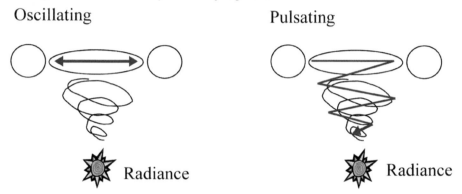

Oscillating   Pulsating

Radiance   Radiance

To summarize: Our focus is to open up the Slinky™ of a compressed space and reveal the (w)hole you have created from your own wisdom. Just choose to go **in**, to go **towards,** and to get **curious**. When we do this, the Spiral naturally, gently, softens and opens itself, revealing the (W)holeness, brilliance, and wisdom of our creations. This doesn't require big pushing and huffing and puffing. It simply invites you into curiosity without judgment.

The Intentional Spiraling Toolbox

Before we go further into the Wisdom WAY map, it is helpful to have a few more practical tools to use as your (w)holes become more noticeable to you. The process of Intentionally Spiraling – going into (w)holes with the clear choice to welcome home the parts we have pushed away – can be sometimes daunting, since we haven't looked into those dark places for a very long time. It helps to lighten up! What do I mean by this? To lighten up is to gently soften with compassion and some humor as you begin to notice all the (w)holes you have created. After all, we are all Holy! This is a given. We don't have to do anything to earn it.

We can lighten up by simply staying curious, dropping judgments, and adding some humor even when a (w)hole is really bothering us. Remember to appreciate yourself for the amazing creator you are and have been over the course of your life. Take a pause and say, "Good for me, I saved my life, and I didn't even know I was doing it!" or "What a surprising way to save my life!" Do this while patting your heart area gently, for your brilliant wiz-kid lives in your heart and has waited a long time to be appreciated for all it has done to save your life.

What makes this appreciation so important? We contract when we get very, very serious. Contraction in our bodies, our psyches, or our hearts makes everything tight and prevents movement. Contracting tightens up the Spiral and prevents the light from permeating the (w)hole. Contracting also freezes things in place. Contracting and freezing in place is what our Meaning Making system is all about. Intentional Spiraling is all about movement. So here are some tools you can use in your Intentional Spiraling process.

Get up and move around. Breathe. Walk. Do something that creates physical movement in every part of you that you can think of. We get stuck in (w)holes. Sometimes we even become filled with tension and immobile; so create motion.

Be curious without judgment. You already know this, but here are some tools to help you be curious. Ask *how, when, where,* and *what* questions such as, "How am I feeling right in this moment?" "When do I remember feeling this way before?" "Where am I? Am I in a (w)hole?" "What (w)hole am I in?" "What just happened to make me feel this way?" There are all sorts of how, when, where, and what questions to ask. The only question you should never ask is "why?" "Why" questions take us straight into our heads. This is not helpful in (w)hole work because (w)holes are not in our heads. They're in our hearts. If we go up into our heads, we're looking for clues to our (w)holes in the wrong place.

Be particular. You know that being particular is important. No one's answers matter but yours. No one's wisdom matters but yours because this is **your** (w)hole and **your** life. Being very particular is part of what empowerment and enlightenment is all about. Here is a simple way to remember *how* to be particular. I call this **The Terms of Endearment**. When you can say "yes" to all five of them, you are on the move in a (w)hole. You can use the fingers on your hand as a reminder. Each finger stands for a particular question and action.

• **Thumb = Be persistent**. "Am I willing to keep spiraling and being curious about this (w)hole even though I am feeling resistant to it?" Thumbs up (yes) or thumbs down (no). If "no," then move to another tool; you are not yet intentional in your choice.

• **Index finger = Be accountable**. "Am I willing to admit this is my (w)hole and my creation? Am I willing to admit I'm responsible and not blame others? Am I willing to be fully accountable for my actions, responses, and impact on others?" Who are you pointing the finger at?

- **Middle finger = Receive**. "Am I willing to ask for help and be open to another's help and suggestions when I'm stuck?" Yes? Or are you really expressing the international sign for "leave me alone," so to speak. This would be a "no."

- **Ring finger = Talk**. "Am I willing to talk about my process and be present with another as I spiral this (w)hole? Am I willing to come out of hiding?" The ring finger connects to your heart and indicates relationship. Are you willing to share your heart logic with another, to relate with another?

- **Small finger = Listen**. "Am I willing to listen to myself or to another?" Sometimes we need to clean out our ears with our pinky finger! "Am I really listening and being open?"

Think in terms of opposites. Have you noticed that the parts of you that you list on the "Me" side of the (w)hole are opposites of the parts that you list on the "Not Me" side? A lot of the time, we know exactly what we are allowed to be. Sometimes it is really unclear what we've not allowed ourselves to be. One thing that can help is to think in terms of opposites.

Laugh about something. Sometimes, we just need to laugh in order to lighten up. Find something that makes you laugh. It can be a picture, something funny you remember from a movie or a television program. It can even be a silly-looking toy. Keep the toy nearby as you do your (w)hole work. When you find yourself stuck and too serious, look at it to make you laugh. If you cannot find anything to use, call someone and ask them to tell you a joke. Laughter creates movement within us and is a fun way to lighten up. We cannot collapse a (w)hole when we are contracted. Lightening up doesn't mean dismissing the importance of something. It just means we have to loosen our grip a bit to let some light in. Lightening up is letting light in.

The Good for Me Mudra. We have bodies, minds, and feelings. When we do something that involves all of these aspects of us at one time, it is quite powerful. We are being (W)hole in that moment. **Mudra** is a term used to describe an activity that incorporates all of yourself in one aligned activity. This is a very easy and simple Mudra to learn. At our two-day intensives, we teach this as a way to support everyone in the Intentional Spiraling process. Put your right hand on your heart (where (w)holes are) and say while gently patting your heart area, "**Good for me, good for me, good for me.**" Be sure to pat your heart three times, and say "Good for me" three times. Our unconscious hears in three's. It may sound silly, but this body-feeling-thought practice, or mudra, has saved lives, so just do it. Even if you don't feel anything, just dare to do it. In time, you will feel your own (W)holeness coming awake inside of you. You might even come to enjoy doing it. (W)holeness awakens in our hearts when we are able to appreciate who we are, right where we are, even when we are smack dab in the middle of a (w)hole.

It reminds our minds, hearts, bodies, and spirits that we are always doing the very best we can with what we know and understand. It is a very powerful way to support yourself. When in doubt, do the Good for Me mudra. It will change your life. By the way, it also has an effect physiologically. You are tapping the thymus which stimulates the immune system and adds to your overall health and vitality.

Good for Me!
Good for Me!
Good for Me!

In addition, if our head is moving in one direction and our heart is moving in another direction, we cannot fully participate in our (w)hole work – there's no connection. When this happens, we cannot move intentionally towards where we are going. When we are mixed up, going in all sorts of directions, we are out-of-alignment with ourselves. This simple and potent Good for Me mudra helps us get into alignment again.

In case you are wondering, in Buddhism and Hinduism "Mudra" is a symbolic series of gestures of the hands and fingers used in ceremonies and dance. For our purpose it represents having your mind, your heart, your body, and your words all matching, going in one direction. It is choice and action and sensation all in the moment you do it. It is a little bit of (W)holeness happening right in a (w)hole. This is very important in (w)hole work. It is helpful to align ourselves intentionally. This mudra does just this. In Intentional Spiraling we choose for our hearts to feel the truth of the (w)hole and for our heads to help us sort through all the stuff we find in our (w)holes. Our heads are not judging or thinking about "our stuff," instead, they are sorting.

Use this tool every chance you get. You will find that giving yourself a "Good for Me" pat can feel as good as someone else giving you a "pat on the back." You will find yourself saying "Good for you" to others. When you can do this in the presence of others, you will know you have "got it." It is the most powerful of all the tools I have told you so far! If you use the "Good for Me" mudra tool daily, your life will change.

Sorting Feeling Elements

Feelings are internal. Actions are choices we make about how to express a feeling. A significant element of (w)hole healing involves access to and clarity about our feelings. There are some distinctions that are helpful to have clearly on the table. *How* we express ourselves is different from the legitimacy of our feelings. Both of these are different from the inherent value of you. Sorting these out from one another will support your process of (w)hole healing.

The truth is that all feelings are facts. What you feel is what you feel. They are your facts about your feelings; I call them your **feeling-facts**. You are the only one who knows how you feel. You are the only one responsible for choosing how you will treat your own feelings. These feelings of ours are facts that are incontrovertible. They are simply how we are truly feeling at a particular time. Feelings or emotions are experiences that arise from inside of you. Only you can be the sole expert of your experience. Feelings are internal to you. You give them meaning. You give them power.

It is *how* we express these feelings that elicits responses from those around us. Let us look at an example. If I am angry and throw something, that does not change the value of who I am and the truth of my anger. Yes, I am feeling angry. The anger is the truth of what I am feeling. Anger would be my feeling fact at that moment. Feeling is an internal activity. An outer activity is *how* we are expressing that internal experience. Throwing something is *how* my feeling is being expressed. These are two different things. There is the feeling fact, and there is the manner in which we choose to express the feeling, if at all. One is an internal experience. The other is an external action. One is a fact of what we are feeling. The other is our choice of how we act upon that feeling. It is helpful to keep these sorted out as we do (w)hole spiraling. Sorting effectively, as I have said, is part of the "skill set" of Intentional Spiraling. Sorting a feeling from an action is part of Intentional Spiraling.

The Horrible Truth is the actions, words, deeds, or lack of them done by the other. The Horrible Truths are *how* those people expressed what they were feeling. The OUCH and the emotions in the Spiral are *what* we are feeling. These are internal to us, often hidden even from ourselves. Our Meaning Makings are thoughts, not feelings, nor are they actions. Our Meaning Makings are a plan of action.

Now that you know feelings and the forms of expression one chooses are two distinct items and how that is related to our (w)holes, let us move more deeply into another element of our (w)hole creations.

Our (w)hole Enforcers

As you now know, the Meaning Maker strategy is the prime directive within any particular (w)hole creation. Its strategic purpose is to dictate to us how we are going to avoid the HT in the future (for all time) and thus, how we are going to live our lives. Look closely at the significance of a strategy that disallows any element of oneself. Any and all opportunities that would require our expressing any of the "Not Allowed to be Me" parts of ourselves must be excluded from our life choices. The Meaning Maker is quite strict about this.

Having decided which parts of ourselves will help us implement the strategy (the parts we should keep) and which parts of ourselves have to be disallowed because they'll interfere with our safety strategy, the Meaning Maker enforces these policies with an iron hand. This will not change unless the entirety of the MM directives, motives, and magical ideas are appreciated and then released.

Here is a Wisdom Truth: Before we can let go of anything we have done to save our lives, we first must appreciate its genius. Whenever there is an approach that has saved our lives, we can assume it is deeply established and fortified so as to withstand any pressures to give way. If we stop and really *feel* and *appreciate* our creation, there is a softening and an opening that allows for a change. This is just another reason why judgments against ourselves are so toxic: they reinforce the very elements we would change.

So, let's look even deeper at how the Meaning Maker ensures its plan will be maintained. After all, this is that part of you that has moved in to save your life.

Once the Meaning Maker has established a safety strategy and sorted our parts into "Allowed" and "Disallowed" containers, the Meaning Maker goes one more step towards protecting us. It creates an enforcer to make sure the (w)hole stays in place and that the "Not Allowed" parts stay on the far side of the (w)hole. I call this enforcer a "**Yuckie**." In more traditional language we might call this the "**negative animus**," the "**super ego**," the "**inner critic**", etc. I have chosen to use the name "Yuckie" because this is exactly what it says! Yuckies say " *Yuck, Ewww, Yuck stay away"* to the "Not Allowed to be expressed parts of Me." The Yuckie uses whatever tools will work from self-abuse to self-judgment to judgment of others to blame to shame to fear to whatever it takes to keep you away from those "Not Allowed" parts. Yuckies have one job only – to be sure you feel that those parts over there are "yuckie" and you want nothing to do with them. Remember, the MM and the Yuckies are all parts of you, too, and the Yuckie is there to help enforce your "safety strategy."

Keep those parts back over there!

Ewwww! Those are Yucko parts!!!

Me

Not Me

From the viewpoint of a Horrible Truth experience, the Yuckie's job makes complete and total sense. The "Not Allowed to be Me" parts are the cause of the HT pain. The most brilliant of all solutions is to just stay away from those nasty parts. However, from the viewpoint of an adult who wishes to be fully alive and living from authentic free will (all aspects of the self available), these Meaning Making strategies become grave obstacles. In some self-growth and self-development processes, this has been called "**having issues**." Issues are places where we are in struggle with ourselves. Yes, we all have "issues." What I say is, "Yes, we all have (w)holes." Our "issues" are proof that we can recreate ourselves and implement these creations with absolute effectiveness. If we could re-create ourselves then, we can re-create ourselves now by collapsing these (w)holes and revealing our (W)holeness. We never lose our free will and power of choice. The only question is how we use it. In the beginning we used our power of creation to make as many (w)holes as we determined would serve us. Now we can use our power of creation to collapse our (w)holes and reclaim our (W)holeness.

We don't make just one (w)hole because there isn't just one Horrible Truth that we encounter in our lives. As we were growing up, the Horrible Truths kept on coming, so we kept on making (w)holes following our Meaning Making survival templates. We did this because it seemed to work. The pain stopped, even if it was just for a while. We did this because it gave us hope. As a result, our lives have become narrower and smaller, and the expressions of who we are have become increasingly restricted because of all the (w)holes we've made. By the time we arrive in adulthood, we are, in effect, ruled by our many Meaning Making strategies.

Because most (w)holes are created without any consciousness or verbalization and because (w)holes are created in a split second of time and because most of them are created when we are quite young, the (W)hole Truth is that these mysterious (w)holes are running our lives. At the same time, we are going around and around trying to free ourselves from our mysterious responses and illogical self-limitations or fears or our "issues."

A (w)hole Point: If you are feeling confused and going around and around – pause. Recognize this is a (w)hole. It's just a (w)hole no matter how bad it feels. Just by making this one comment to yourself, you are already in an empowered position. The global mystery has been solved. You know where you are – upside down and head first in a (w)hole. Breathe, and then begin to sort through things. We sort by stepping out of the (w)hole for a moment and looking at it. We cannot sort if we are head first, upside down in the moldy soup of a (w)hole. Sorting requires the small step out of the (w)hole so you can get your orientation back, get your Wisdom map out and your curiosity ready. This sentence, *"It is just a (w)hole"* is a way to remind ourselves that (w)holes may feel icky, but they are not lethal. It is a way to remind ourselves that every (w)hole has a gift of some part of us at the bottom.

So, what makes a (w)hole hurt? When we are in the (w)hole, we are in pain because we were being, doing, or expressing a "Not Allowed Me" part. We were breaking the rules of our Meaning Maker. This creates discomfort. The MM was put in place to reduce the risks of the Horrible Truth, and here we are breaking the rules established by our MM. The felt experience is our being the "bad" part of us. Then our Yuckie jumps in and makes lots of noise to force us to get back in line.

NOW is the time!

A (w)hole Play Opportunity for You

Take a moment and write on your paper right near the Curb, what your Yuckie says to you. You know. It will sound like blame, shame, self-judging attacks, etc. Your Yuckie may say things like "You are bad." "Why did you do that!?" "How could you be so stupid as to…?"

Now, take a moment. Look at your (w)hole study. Can you let yourself feel the discomfort of a "Not Allowed" part? What if you are that!?! What do you feel when you accidentally act out the "Not Me" side of the (w)hole?

Pause. Appreciate what you are looking at and what you are feeling. It is your creation of brilliance and genius! You made it all alone, unwittingly, without help, long ago, and it has been operating ever since. Can you think of one invention you have ever read about that is self-sustaining, automatic, able to adjust itself, and be applied to any relevant situation, staying durable beyond years, and totally self-contained? That is what every (w)hole of yours is, a work of true determination and genius.

Our Language Tells Us When We Are In a (w)hole!

A quick and easy way to notice that we are in a (w)hole is when we hear ourselves saying things like, "Yes, **but**…." or "I can't because …" or "I won't because…" or "I can do this **but** not that." In addition there are certain words that are signals that a (w)hole may be in charge of the moment. The word "but," the word "or," the word "always," and the word "never," when applied to you and your life, indicate a (w)hole at work.

For example, I might say, "I am pretty **but** not very smart." "I want to do that, **but** I am afraid of what people will think about me." "I can either be smart **or** well-liked, **but** I can't be both!" "I am **always** the one left out." "I **never** feel good about myself."

Take a close look. Do you see what each sentence tells you? "Or" and "but" are the words we put in between the "Allowed to be Me" parts and the "Not Allowed to be Me" parts. "Always" and "never" are the favorite words of the Yuckies.

Signals that we might be in a (w)hole are called (w)hole alerts. We all have our very own, unique signals, and sometimes it is helpful to know about other signals. In the appendix we have provided a short list (see the appendix item called (w)hole signals).

A (w)hole Play Opportunity for You

After looking at the list of (w)hole alerts, take a few moments and write down your own unique list of signals that tell you when you are in a (w)hole.

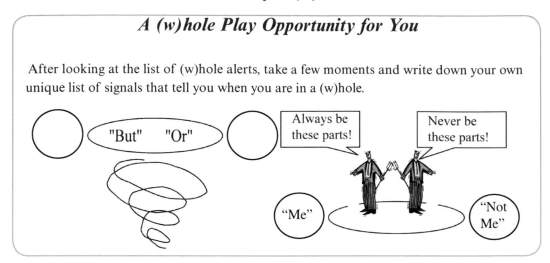

In essence, our lives are in the hands of the Meaning Maker until we reclaim our own authority. Paying attention to our particular (w)hole alert signals is another way to practice curiosity without judgment. Intentional Spiraling is the action of admitting to our own power to create and re-create (w)holes or awaken our (W)holeness. This is only up to us!

Authentic and sustainable authority emanates from our (W)holeness. Self-authority isn't found in the bits and pieces of ourselves that are strewn all over the place. The truth is that significant portions of our life may be under the dictatorship of our Meaning Maker. What a surprise to discover that your life has not been yours but in the hands of your Meaning Maker. You didn't know that, and neither did I. The Wisdom WAY map offers us a way to see the entirety of our lives and the particulars of any one (w)hole. We didn't have a map before. Now we do.

One tendency at this point is to judge our Meaning Maker because we begin to recognize how very profound and pervasive these strategies are in our lives. At times this can be quite shocking for folks, especially those who have believed that they were living by their own dictates. As we begin to recognize our Meaning Makers, it is vitally important to not judge or hate or reject our Meaning Maker. By now you know that this would just create another (w)hole. We create a (w)hole anytime we push away a part, a thought, a feeling, or a realization of our self. Frankly, we all have enough (w)holes, so let's not make more.

This power of ours to create meaning and act upon it has saved our lives emotionally and for many of us, physically. Now is not the time to turn on the very thing that saved us. In fact, now is the time to appreciate all that we have done to save our lives. Our little kid only did the best he/she knew how to do, even though it was all done unconsciously. As you discover and reveal your Meaning Making strategies to yourself, take a moment to appreciate the ingenuity, the courage, and the creativity your Meaning Maker has put forth to save your life. Its intention was never out of malice; it was always done out of great love for you and your life and for survival, itself.

Our Meaning Maker part is a part of us that has loved us beyond anything we might imagine. It has stood on our behalf despite all odds and against all sorts of pressure to give in and give up its strategy. Our Meaning Maker is not a "bad" part of us. It saved us from what felt "horrible." Now, you are ready to see that the Meaning Maker has out-grown its use to us because now it is keeping us from our full (W)holeness. This is the awakened and empowered way to love all of yourself. Additionally, your Meaning Maker is an aspect of yourself which is holding a great many gifts. These gifts are only available to us as we collapse the (w)holes. Hence, there is even more motivation to develop the skill of Intentional Spiraling.

Chapter 9: Waking Up to (w)hole Creation as Free Will in Action

You now know we are the creators of these (w)holes that have saved us and plagued us. This may not be how it feels, for we often feel like the victim of our circumstances and experiences. But the truth, the bald naked truth, is that we created the dark spaces into which we drop. We created the spaces between the "Me" and the "Not Me" parts of ourselves. There is no one to hold responsible but ourselves. There is no one to blame, not even ourselves. Take a big gulp. This can feel tough at first to realize, but I would invite you to appreciate the awesome power it grants you. You are in charge of your (w)holes and your (W)holeness and your (W)hole life.

Yes, others are accountable for their actions. Yes, others are responsible for their choice of behaviors. Yes, it is true that those who acted in ways that felt horrible and horrifying to us are accountable for those actions, for they chose to act in that manner. They have free will. We have free will. Everyone has free will. Using our free will, we created the (w)holes into which we fall.

Remember, the good news is that since we created the (w)holes, we can also collapse them or unmake them, so to speak. To do this we are asked to step into full accountability and recognition that we, ourselves, are the (w)hole creators. There is no room for blame in this process. Blaming ourselves or others is just a sneaky way of not choosing to engage in Intentional Spiraling on behalf of our (W)holeness. As long as we are blaming either ourselves or others, we are not being responsible and we are not in a place of authentic power to do something different. Blaming keeps us in a victim position, a position of powerlessness. Blame is just an excuse to keep going around and around the same old stuff. Blame changes nothing.

Let us look at another example to demonstrate how the Wisdom WAY map is hidden inside a person's story. It actually begins to be fun to listen to yourself or another with an ear for (w)holes. You will find they are simply everywhere. And what makes that so fun? Any (w)hole you can see and sort and Intentionally Spiral is a (w)hole you can collapse. A (w)hole you can collapse becomes a doorway to your Radiance. And let me tell you, Radiance, is great fun and very potent!

This is a (w)hole of a forty-year old man who has found it difficult to be in intimate relationships because, as he said: "I somehow always let them down. I can't keep it all together. I turn out to not be who they think I am."

The event: He was about six years old. His family was a regular kind of family, happy and steady. He was the only child and was very special, or so they all said. He was very happy, and he loved having his parents all to himself. He loved playing and being the kid, being the only kid! One day his mom and dad came home with another kid, a second baby boy. Everyone seemed very happy, and they all told him, "Now you have to be the big brother." His world got turned upside down!

OUCH! Suddenly he was replaced, and he had to be "a big boy!" That hurt a lot! He felt very confused. Wasn't he enough? Weren't they happy with him and how he was? Here was the OUCH moment. He felt really bad, ashamed, and unloved. He was not really sure what he did wrong, but it must have been something. No matter what he tried to do, he still felt little and they wanted a "BIG" boy. Oftentimes, we may not even know any of the names of our feelings. We just know that we feel bad. As adults, we can look back at the Horrible Truth and feel it and then give names to the feelings we had back then. At the time that it happens, the OUCH is just that – "Ouch!"

What is the Horrible Truth? "Baby brother came home," or "Mom and dad had a second kid." What makes this an HT is that it felt horrible to this young boy. In this situation it was totally horrible. He felt his world shatter and his specialness became dependent upon being big. In this case, the child's feelings and thoughts were something like, "I have to be big or else! They will only love me if I am always big." Can you now begin to see the (w)hole forming?

The **Meaning Maker** then moves into high gear by first implementing the Power Point Location shift from them to him. He can now figure out how to change himself so they'll keep loving him and don't replace him or bring more kids home. "I must make them happy! I have to be big." Unconsciously he decided, "It must have been me somehow. I wasn't good enough or the right way for them. They went and got another kid. Now I have to stop being the only kid and start being big." The MM then starts breaking up his (W)holeness into bits and pieces to ensure the danger does not repeat itself.

What does it mean to be big? This boy decided it was *always* being on top of it all, *always* being emotionally steady and strong, *always* having all the answers, *always* being the first one and the best one in everything, *always* confident, *always* certain, *always* independent, *always* focused, *always* being tough, *always* being serious, *always* acting grown-up like an adult, *always* being in charge of it all, *always* figuring it all out himself, and *always* doing it solo. The word "always" helps us to identify what might be on the "Me" side of the (w)hole.

The Meaning Maker system is now going to sort "Big" from everything that is "Not Big." "Not Big" is now what we would call the "Not Me" of this (w)hole. What is "Not Big?" The Meaning Maker decided that "Not Big" was uncertain, emotionally needy, dependent, not knowing the answer, following, relying on anyone, being gentle, being easy-going, being vulnerable and weak, being silly, being tender, being playful, and being a little kid.

We could have written never having needs, never not knowing, never following, never dependent, never soft and vulnerable. You see? The word "never" helps us identify what might be pushed away to the "Not Me" side of the (w)hole. Sometimes it is easier to list the "Not Me's" first, and sometimes it is easier to list the "Me's" first.

The MM strategy is then clarified secretly within the boy:

>If I am always Big (as defined above)

>Then they will not bring home any more kids.

>They get the "Big Brother" kid they want,

>And I will get to still be loved.

…and thus the boy created a (w)hole.

We distance ourselves from the offensive parts of ourselves as determined by the Meaning Maker. The Yuckies are the ones that rise up and shout whenever we start to be one of those "Not Allowed to be Me" parts, and thus, the adult man would become very judgmental of anyone and of himself whenever they were expressing the "Not Allowed to be Me" parts. The rule we unconsciously made is that we *only* get to live on the "Allowed to be Me" side of the (w)hole.

All this was done without his conscious awareness and was then set on auto-pilot. Whenever this man entered into a relationship, he had to be "Big." However, the trouble was that he was human, and no human could ever meet this (the boy's) definition of Big. So, when he would fall into this (w)hole and be the "little kid," the other person would feel tricked. "Who is this? I thought he was a strong, steady, and always ready to do whatever it takes kind of guy?" It was this pattern in relationships (four marriages later) that finally gifted him with the awakening into his true (W)holeness. Now, this man is quite adept at being his (W)hole self for real – both in and out of relationships. Our (w)holes are our greatest gifts, whenever we choose to discover them.

If we drew out the map for this man's (w)hole, it would look like this:

Yes, it is that simple!

We do this over and over again because (w)holes work – for a time anyway. When I say (w)holes work, I mean to say that they *seem* to take away the pain of the experience, they *seem* to offer empowerment, and they *seem* to make sense of the scary surprising Horrible Truth experiences. Yes, (w)hole creating *seems* to work very well until we grow up and find our lives very jumbled, ineffective, and unsatisfying! This is when we discover that (w)holes out-grow their apparent usefulness. It is at this point that we are called to admit and own up to our **authentic potent creative power** in our own lives and to let go of the inherent victimhood of living under the dictatorship of our Meaning Maker.

If I'm always Big, they will not bring any more kids home. They'll get the Big Brother Kid they want and I'll be loved again.

HT: Mom and Dad brought home a baby brother.

OUCH = unloved

On top
Have answers
First/best
Tough
Serious
In charge
My way
Leader

Weak
Emotional
Uncertain
Dependent
Dumb
Follower
Their way
Silly/playful

(W)holes have a very clear purpose. (W)holes are created by us to help us make sense of what just happened (Horrible Truth). They help us feel powerful and not vulnerable and not in jeopardy, and they are designed to never let the hurt happen to us again. The price we pay is we just get rid of the "bad" part of us. What is amazing about each of us is that we create (w)holes without any awareness of the process and without putting conscious words to our thoughts. Then we implement these very potent strategies with a fierce passion, determination, and single-mindedness.

And what is beyond amazing is that each of us has created these powerful strategies without as much as one consultation with another human being. We have implemented them, and then for years, they operate without even one maintenance checkup. All (w)holes run on autopilot even if we keep flying straight into the side of a mountain over and over again, crashing into our lives! It doesn't matter. Once created, (w)holes run without fail and without assistance. Our (w)holes are self-maintaining. This is the reason that we feel often "run around by the nose." Our (w)holes operate independently of what we might consciously choose in any one moment because a (w)hole will always take precedence over a contemporary choice.

Doesn't that make so much sense? (W)holes were originally put in place to save our lives from horrible pain; anything else is secondary. Our (w)holes are our responses to what felt lethal to us.

Can you appreciate the impeccable heart-logic behind (w)hole creation? Can you allow yourself a deep compassion for the kid in yourself who was just trying to manage a hugely complex and confusing world? Can you hold yourself compassionately for all the ways you have created (w)holes to save yourself? Compassion is at the heart of Intentional Spiraling – compassion for ourselves, appreciation for our genius, and acceptance that our urge for life was so huge that we were even willing to cut up our original (W)holeness into bits and pieces to survive.

We create our first hole, and we find that it works. We are relieved of the powerlessness, the vulnerability, and the horror. We're relieved of the pain. We're filled with hope. It's such a success that we do it over and over and over again. We end up being very full of (w)holes – all created to save us from our Horrible Truths. We begin doing it as infants and keep on doing it into adulthood. After all, why change something that seems to be working for us? Being (w)hole creators becomes our chosen method for life management. This process is universal; we all do it.

When we create a (w)hole, as we have over and over, the effect is to blind us to our own (W)holeness, to our own (W)hole Life force.

Chapter 10: Waking Up to the Power of Naming

Naming is a powerful act of creation and re-creation. In almost all of the world's great spiritual wisdom traditions, they point to "God's" naming things as part of how things come into being. Naming is an activity of creating. Naming is also an action of re-creation. Naming is also the Universal Solvent. Thus you may notice, the activities of naming are three fold: Creating, Dissolving & Re-creating. Naming is a choice made from the inner authority of ourselves.

I have personally been named by others as both "Elizabeth" and "Betsy." I have renamed myself as "Althea" and then renamed myself again as "Alaya." (The stories behind this are for another time.) Our names are a summary of who we feel or think ourselves to be. Folks who have known me for a time will say things to me like, "But you don't feel like a Betsy to me" when they have only known me as Alaya. "You are an 'Alaya' to me."

Naming is a potent and sacred act. Naming is the capacity to create our reality, our experiences, and our sense of who we are in any moment. The act of naming something is also embedded in much of our daily life just as our (w)holes are woven throughout the fabric of who we say we are.

We name files and folders in our computers; we can also rename them as needed. Naming is one of the first things we do when a baby is born or a pet is chosen. Naming is a way to form an attachment to something or someone and a method to establish our way of understanding the essence of things. Naming is how we sort moments, thoughts, actions, people, and things. On a map we have street names and town names and names of nations and even bodies of water. Naming is a part of sorting. Naming is an activity of creating. Naming is also an activity we apply in Intentional Spiraling.

Since we all already know how to name things, it is a handy and immediately accessible ability we all have. The (W)hole Point Wisdom WAY model is based entirely on talents, skills, and capacities we all have right now. It is just a matter of putting it all together into one map. Sorting includes within it a recognition of the potency of naming. As I have said earlier, The Wisdom WAY awakens (W)holeness first by sorting and naming portions of our perceptions so as to reveal to ourselves all that is transpiring behind the scenes or outside our view of awareness.

At this point we have explored the act of identifying, sorting, and naming - the Horrible Truth, our OUCH, the Curb, our Meaning Maker, and Yuckies in our (w)holes. We sort by naming. We named something a feeling rather than a thought. We named an event current or past. We named our "Me" parts and our "Not Me" parts. When we name something, we are sorting. Without even realizing it, we were using this talent to name and thus sort things since we were born.

Now let's broaden the use of this ability to name.

As we engage in the Intentional Spiraling process, the courage to be what we are, the (w)hole creator, includes taking on the authority to name our parts. We have been using the power to name in every (w)hole. We name ourselves by saying "I am this, but I am not that." Daring to engage consciously with the capacity and power to name and re-name, we are also implicitly admitting to a (W)hole Truth: We are the creator of our world! Mind you, this is no small admission, for you can see immediately that if there is no one else to "blame" for what you and I alone have created for ourselves, then where can we hide from our own authorship in our lives? The (W)hole Truth is all about the bald, naked truth of the glory and power of our essence – even as we reveal our dark (w)hole creations to ourselves, we are revealing our (W)hole Power.

When folks are head first in a (w)hole, they feel powerless, without authority in their lives, and often lost and stuck. Just the act of courageously and consciously naming a part of ourselves shifts the internal landscape and begins to create movement in the psyche. In addition, by daring to name a part, we are re-establishing and re-owning our authority to create ourselves anew. Rather than feeling and believing we are a victim in a (w)hole, through the act of naming, we begin to shift our felt experience to "I am the authority of this (w)hole. I am the one who created this (w)hole! I did it to save my 'hope.' Now I can change my mind and reclaim what I had to push aside."

Naming the "Me" and "Not Me"

Naming is the action of declaring worth and ownership. Consider when we first name a pet. In that action it becomes officially ours. The name we bestow upon our new pet matters. Its significance is found in the meaning of the name to us. Only that pet with that name is our pet. Do you see? Now, let's meet these parts of ourselves by naming them.

Once we have sorted our Horrible Truth (yesterday) from our Curb (today), and our OUCH we dumped in the Spiral (feelings), and our Meaning Making plan (thoughts), we are ready to name each side of the (w)hole. The first line of our MM tells us the essence of our "Me" side of our (w)hole. Everything we must "get rid of" to *only* be this "Me" goes on the "Not Me" side of the (w)hole. The "Me" is on the left side of the (w)hole because it is what is left of us after we shatter ourselves. The "Not Me" is on the right side of the (w)hole because it is what our Meaning Maker decided was "right" to get rid of.

A (w)hole Play Opportunity for You

Look at the clump of all the qualities on the right side or "Not Allowed to be Me" side of your (w)hole study. If you met a person who was like that and **only** like that – and **always** like that – what might you name them? Make it a character or phrase; for example, "The Lame Duckling" or "The Raging Bully" or "The shy little mouse." Make sure that the name reflects and summarizes the essence of that side. Just take a quick guess, and then read on. Have some fun doing this. Be a bit silly about it. Silliness helps to open our inner wisdom and curiosity. Naming is an art, and it is play. Once you have named your "Not Me" side, apply your creative genius and name your "Me" side. Just take a running start at this. We will return to these names again.

Let us go back to the boy whose Horrible Truth was that his parents brought home a baby brother. Suddenly he felt a terrible pain in his heart that he named as unloved. His Meaning Maker sounded like this, "If I am big and do it all, they won't bring home any more kids. They'll get the big brother kid they want, and I'll be loved again." Sounds like a good strategy, doesn't it? So now, he had to put his strategy into action by tossing away to the far side of the (w)hole all those parts of him that would interfere with his plan, parts like being weak, being second best, being emotional, being dumb, and being tender and soft. The parts he kept were being the first and best, being tough, being serious, being in charge, and being unemotional. When it came time for him to name his "Me" side of the (w)hole, he named it "Oz," from the Wizard of Oz. His "Not Me" side he named the "The man behind the curtain." For him these two names captured, in a felt way, the essence of what each side of the (w)hole felt like to him. Oz was bigger than life, and "the man behind the curtain" was smaller than life. Can you feel the power of those names if this were a (w)hole of yours?

Naming, when done well, can be felt by your (w)hole witnesses, those with whom you share your (w)hole play. Remember, you are the expert of you. No one can name your pet for you, and no one can name your parts for you!

Here is another example. Let's say a "Not Me list" was: loud, proud, cherished, needy, bossy, truth speaker, and adored. I would say to myself, "If I was always and only loud, always proud, always cherished, always needy, always bossy, always a truth teller, and always adored, I would call myself 'the pushy brat,' or 'bossy britches,' or 'tattle tale.'" The point is the name must speak to your heart and capture the essence of that list of qualities and behaviors as if they stood alone. So if I were to "introduce" Bossy Britches to someone, they would have a general idea and a felt understanding of what this person would be like.

Naming Tips

- Names that are **not** names of real people work best. Fictional characters from books, movies, cartoons, and television programs work really well.

- Names that have a felt experience for others when you say them are helpful. For example, if you were to tell someone else the name you had chosen, they would be able to get a picture in their mind of what that would look like. From the example above, could you get a picture of what "Oz" or the "Tin Man" or "the Man behind the curtain" or "the wicked witch" would look like?

- Names that are of the same analogy on both sides of the (w)hole are helpful. If you use a gardening analogy, i.e., weeds and flowers, make an effort to name both sides of the (w)hole from the same genre.

- Names that make you smile because they are so "right on" and capture the exaggerated nature of each side of the (w)hole work the best.

Some examples of names are listed below. Read them as two sides of a (w)hole and imagine what the (w)hole might be pointing to. The names are a summary of what the (w)hole creators put on each side of their (w)hole. Remember, each side is meant to sound extreme because we are looking at someone who is *always* and *only* these things.

Suffering Susan	Happy Hannah
Dawn – just beginning	Sundown – over already
Peter Pan	Captain Hook
Two-star general	Lowly private
Wall flower	Wild flower
Stagnate Waters	Tidal Wave

Can you feel the tension between the opposites? Can you feel the extreme feeling of the two sides? Can you get a sense of what a person might put as a list of qualities on each side?

This "Not Me" part of you has been "orphaned" for a long time, wandering namelessly in the mysterious terrain of discarded parts. It has not been valued enough even to have a name. It has become somewhat distorted and grungy, as it has lived a homeless life. It is not cleaned and buffed up in its appearance or presentation. It hasn't had any practice expressing itself, and so it is a bit rough. The name you give this orphan, for it to be the (W)hole Truth, must reflect even the roughness and raggedness of it, which is the result of its orphan status.

Me   Not Me

Naming is an act of honoring, adopting, recognizing, and feeling the (W)hole Truth of "Yes, this too, is a part of me!" Make no mistake, when you name a part of you on either side of the (w)hole, in that act alone you are choosing to create greater motion in the (w)hole which will begin the collapsing effect. Naming is a big deal. Keep your eyes on the naming. The collapsing of a (w)hole is a felt sensation in our bodies, our minds, and our hearts all at once. Naming is an act of a Life Creator!

When naming any part of yourself, the "Me" side of a (w)hole or the "Not Me" side of a (w)hole, do this with the awareness that you are honoring yourself. Do this with joy, with creativity, with fun, with imagination, and with a sharp eye on the truth. You are choosing to move toward your (W)holeness by your own authority when you choose to name yourself again.

Naming also helps us to get to know "who" is on each side of the (w)hole. Remember, the "Not Me" has been ostracized and may very well feel like a stranger to you, even though it is a part of you, too! Intentional Spiraling is much like going to a gathering and introducing yourself to everyone there, only to find you have been simply meeting yourself.

When we are naming, you can use anything you like as inspiration when it comes to the name – a character from a book or a movie, an image – anything that sums up all of the characteristics of that side of the (w)hole in one or two words. The name is usually not a full phrase, as we are not looking for a description. Pick with care and also with creative thought.

Everything about naming applies to both the "Me" and the "Not Me" sides of your (w)hole. We name both sides of the (w)hole to honor them as parts of our (W)holeness.

A (w)hole Play Opportunity for You

Take a look at the "Me" side and your "Not Me" side of your (w)hole. Now that you have heard more examples, look again at your names. Are you happy with them? Have they captured the essence of each side?

When we are naming the two sides of the (w)hole, we are looking at each side separately and distinctly. So, when you are naming your "Not Me" side as someone who is always and only these parts, you are simply looking at this side on it's own, separated temporarily from the Meaning Maker and the "Me" side of the (w)hole so that you can get a better look at it, to see what it really is.

The simpler the name, the better it is because the name is meant to stand on its own without explanation. It is like a felt "picture" that captures the essence of only this bit of you when listed separately from all the rest of you. It is a snapshot of a part of you, and only you can pick the frame. A key is that the name will capture a clear feeling and image for you, and ideally anyone hearing it would "get the feel of it."

You can always ask for help with naming. You can read the list of qualities and ask someone for suggested names. Of course, only you can choose the name that fits exactly right for you because these are your parts, your (w)hole, and your (W)holeness.

Naming the (w)hole

Name your entire (w)hole as a way to honor its existence and impact on your life. It is also helpful to name the (w)hole itself because this offers easy reference as you discover (w)holes, and it again establishes you as the creator of all of them. As the owner you get to name them! You can name a (w)hole anyway that makes sense to you. There are no rules about (w)hole naming. The names are for the sole purpose of reminding you of that particular messy experience.

Here is an abbreviated list of some of my own (w)holes.

Father's suicide (w)hole
Step-family (w)hole
Still single at 30 (w)hole
Marriage (w)hole
Divorce (w)hole
Choosing to re-marry Terror (w)hole
Being fired from a job (w)hole

Why is God doing this to me? (w)hole
When will I ever be good enough? (w)hole
I hate my job (w)hole
I can't write (w)hole

When we name a (w)hole, it can be anything at all. After all, it is your (w)hole!

A (w)hole Play Opportunity for You

Take a moment to write a name for your (w)hole. You can write it right it in the middle of the oval or space between the two sides of the (w)hole, or you can write it at the top of your paper. If you wish, you can take another moment now and make a list of your (w)holes – just go back to your page of concerns. It is a (w)hole list!

Have you noticed that there is a distortion on both sides of any (w)hole? No one could be *just* this and *never* that! It just isn't humanly possible. Remember, we create our (w)holes when we believe that by hiding a portion of ourselves, we will be "safer" from a repeat of the Horrible Truth. Our (w)holes are disguises for (W)holeness in that moment. What occurs when we make (w)holes is a distortion or a warping of our (W)holeness. Each side of a (w)hole is an extreme and an exaggeration of that particular expression. Each side is an opposite of the other. Each side contains distortion and truth. The distortion effect is one of the reasons that our issues seem so complicated to us. The "Me" and the "Not Me" sides are out of focus and skewed. No wonder we are confusing to ourselves!

Chapter 11: Waking Up to the Distortion Effect

It's important to understand that when we cut off an aspect of our (W)holeness (make a "Not Me"), what is left is an exaggerated expression of its opposite ("Me"). (W)holeness broken into pieces results in each piece becoming more extreme in some way, a distortion of the (W)hole Truth. Both parts (the "Me" and the "Not Me") become exaggerated and distorted because they are kept separate; they are no longer part of the (W)hole. Yes, there is still truth in each of them, and at the same time each of them becomes distorted or skewed.

When we split qualities and keep one-half of an expression or a quality separate from its opposite, both sides of the expression became distorted or warped or twisted. This Distortion Effect happens to **both** sides of any (w)hole. This effect is not something we can prevent, nor is it something we cause. It is an inherent effect of shattering our (W)holeness. This is important to understand, so I will say it again, *both* sides of the (w)hole become distorted. It is not just the "Not Me" side; it is also the "Me" side that becomes distorted as well.

The Distortion Effect is due to a subtle psychological, spiritual, and physical fact. You cannot have only half of something. There is actually no way to have half of a living body or half of a healthy psyche or half of an authentic feeling. In the case of the first two, there is death or insanity. In the case of feelings, one either has access to a full range of a feeling expression (sad-happy) and all that is in between, or there is a (w)hole. If one has pushed away one half of the feeling spectrum (let's say it is sad), a person is left with a distortion of the remaining feeling expression (happy all the time). Obviously, a human being isn't happy all the time.

We've all heard the saying, "Nature abhors a vacuum." So, too, do (w)holes! In nature, the concept behind this expression is that empty or unfilled spaces are unnatural. They go against the laws of nature and physics. Nature will step in to fill the empty space. The same thing happens in our (w)holes. When we shatter our (W)holeness into bits and pieces and separate them by putting some of the pieces on the "Me" side and some of the pieces on the "Not Me" side, the laws of nature and physics step in. The empty space of one of our parts will be filled in with distortion so that it is no longer a half of something. For example, if being "quiet" is on my "Me" side and being "loud" is on my "Not Me" side, you can see that these are two opposites of one quality. One half of the quality is "quiet," and the other half is "loud." Because there is only half of the quality on each side of the (w)hole, the empty spaces will be filled with distortion. On the "Me" side, the empty half of the "quiet" part will be filled with more of the same so that "quiet" becomes distorted into "mute." The same will happen with the "loud" part. The empty part will be filled with more of the same so that "loud" becomes distorted into "deafening."

So, stop, and take a moment. Can you **feel** how the distortion effect operates?

Having access to the full spectrum of any feeling expression doesn't mean you must always express all feelings. It simply means you can and could feel the entire range of any feeling spectrum. Feeling a feeling does not mean one must *act* on a feeling. To feel is to feel, period. In our example above, the person who is "Happy all the time" is clearly unable to access the remainder of the feeling spectrum of happy all the way to sad.

If you cut open a cantaloupe and leave each section out on the counter, after a while both sides begin to rot. If the cantaloupe is stored (W)hole, it will last far longer. This is also true of people. Cut them into parts and pieces, and they will begin to get moldy quite rapidly.

How Does This Distortion Effect Show Up?

When the "Not Me" part of us does sneak out, and it will occasionally (even though the purpose of a (w)hole is to keep it hidden away), its expression will be distorted or exaggerated or twisted in some way. The "Not Me" parts are behaviors or expressions of our feelings. When we act, express, or behave in ways we have promised ourselves that we would never ever do or express, there is a dreadfulness about these moments. We may find ourselves overreacting, or our expressions may be more forceful or exaggerated. This is because we have had no access to these parts on a regular basis. We don't know how to use them, so we muck it up a little. In a sense we are living right there in the moment, the felt experience of the Distortion Effect.

It is also in these moments when we know we are head first in a (w)hole. Just as if you tripped on a Curb and fell into a pothole, we do the same thing with Life (w)holes. Either way we fall head first and upside down! Inevitably, we will act out the "Not Me" because we are so disoriented by the failure of our Meaning Maker strategy. These strategies will fail and do fail because they were created by a child with a child's limited and magical understanding of the world. They simply do not work in an adult's life.

How do we recognize the MM strategy has failed? When we are head first in a (w)hole. Instead of feeling "relieved," we feel worse. Instead of being securely the "Me" we would prefer to be, we discover ourselves behaving or feeling or reacting in ways that do not serve us or worse, do damage to our situations. At these moments it is clear the Meaning Making "plan" of managing life is not working. The truth is we can't manage life! However, children believe that they can.

We are also feeling our Yuckies breathing down our necks, pressuring us to do whatever we have to do to make this MM strategy be effective. Our Yuckies rise up because when we fall in a (w)hole, we are being or expressing a "Not Me" part. Being the disallowed part violates our Meaning Maker strategy. We have broken our own life-saving Meaning Making "rules," and thus, we have betrayed ourselves without knowing or choosing consciously to do so. Consciously or not, we can feel our self-betrayal. No wonder our (w)hole moments are so challenging. We have put our selves at risk. We have violated our MM plan. We are being a way we have named as "Not Allowed," while shockingly not being who we think we are or should be.

Consider this example. If I am only quiet and I am never, ever loud and boisterous, when I do occasionally express my loud and boisterous self, my expression of loud is messy and awkward and sometimes even a bit out of control. We lack the skills and finesse of expressing that part we pushed to the far side. This is also true in a different way for the "Me" side of the (w)hole. This is because when we express either side by itself and as an un-integrated position, the appearance will also be distorted. We simply are messier, more exaggerated, or awkward, just like a child who is first learning to eat will spill food all over the place. Whether we are expressing "quiet" or "loud," neither will be free of the distortion, and both will be somewhat true. In this example, "quiet" would be noticeably, extremely quiet, even withdrawn, while "loud" might be intrusive and pushy.

So, when I am only quiet, which is the comfortable "Me" side of this (w)hole, I may seem mousy, shy, and insecure to others. This is not just "quiet," it is a distorted expression of quiet. I may be aware of only being "quiet." Others often will see the Distortion Effect long before we do.

Let's take two more (w)hole studies and look only at the two sides of the (w)hole just to be sure you have a sense of what and how the Distortion Effect operates.

If "I must always be nice" is on the "Me" side, and "I must never be angry" is the "Not Me" side, then "nice" might become doormat-like or wimpy or indecisive, and the "angry" might become abusive or out of control. The word "always" is placed in front of the "Me" qualities, while the word "never" is placed in front of the "Not Me" qualities. This is an effective way to check if your (w)hole study is on track and feeling true to you. The "always list" will feel familiar, and the "never list" will feel absolutely impossible, either because it is "bad" or "wrong" or it is "unquestionably out of reach" for you.

Here is another example. If "I must always be helpful" is on the "Me" side, and "I must never, ever be selfish" is on the "Not Me" side of the (w)hole, then "helpful" might become a slave to others, a "do-gooder," or extremely independent, while "selfish" might become self-centered, bossy, demanding, and arrogant.

The bald naked truth is that both sides of any (w)hole are distorted expressions of you. Being able to notice the Distortion Effect is quite helpful in (w)hole identification and sorting.

As an adult, we may try to edit ourselves when we're figuring out each side of a (w)hole because somewhere in our head-logic, we *know* that we cannot *always* be something or *always* feel some way. And we know logically that we cannot *never* be something or never feel some way. But remember, we made most of these (w)holes back when we were little kids.

Little kids use the words "always" and "never," and they use them a lot. If you have the chance to listen to a child between the ages of five and eight, you'll notice that they say these words, and you may laugh to yourself as you hear them now that you're a (w)hole expert. "You never let me have any fun." "You always get to go first down the slide." "You always say that." Sound familiar? Can you remember when you were this young and said these things? We really did think and talk and act this way, and we really did make (w)holes using the basis of "always" and "never."

A (w)hole Play Opportunity for You

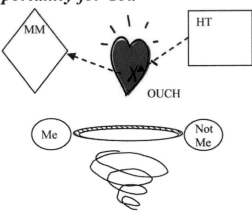

Look at your (w)hole study notes. If you look at the "Me" list of your (w)hole and apply the word "always" to each word on the list, you will see some surprising things very quickly about yourself, and you sort out more of the mystery of you. Review the following points to help you further sort through the "Me" and the "Not Me" descriptions. Look at each list, and ask these questions of anything you have written down on that one side.

Sometimes, after beginning a (w)hole study we find we are shifting and sorting things from one side to another. This is fine.

• Is this something you **always** believe you ought to, have to, should be, or do or act like or feel? Then it is in the correct pile of parts if it is on the "Me" side.

• Is this something you long to be but **never, ever** dare to be, are, or can do? If yes, then it belongs on the other side, the "Not Me" side.

• Is it a feeling such as sad, hurt, scared, angry, frustrated, or vulnerable? If yes, then move it to the middle of the Spiral area of your (w)hole. This is where we have dumped the feeling experiences that hurt so horribly. Sometimes we also have feelings on either side of the (w)hole; however, listing only behaviors or qualities under the list of "Me" and "Not Me" make it clearer.

• Now, read the list on the left side or "Me" side of the (w)hole one word or phrase at a time, and say before each word or phrase, "I am **always**_____." What do you feel? What do you think? What do you notice?

• Now, apply the word "**never**" to the "Not Me" side of the (w)hole. Again, you will begin to reveal to yourself what expressions you have disallowed in your life by your own choice, albeit unconsciously. Read them one at a time, adding the word "never" in front of each one. Again, what do you feel? What do you think? What do you notice? Is this something you never, ever are? Is this something you were never, ever allowed to be? Is this a quality or behavior that you totally know is bad, wrong, dangerous, or scary to be? If so, very good; it is in the correct pile.

• Is this something that you have longed to do, be, or express but it simply wasn't done in your family? It is a "Not Me."

- Is this something that feels risky to even consider might be a part of you? It is a "Not Me."

- If any of these qualities or behaviors feels "off" somehow, consider moving it to the other side of the (w)hole, and see if it feels more true to you. Remember, you are the expert of you. You are the only one who knows.

Now, take a moment to check the names you've given to each side of the (w)hole. Ideally, these names have captured the exaggerated elements of each side. Can you feel the Distortion Effect in the names? If you can, great job! If you can't quite feel it, try giving them another name. If you cannot feel the Distortion Effect on both sides of the (w)hole, you won't be able to properly introduce each side to yourself. You won't get the full effect of who these parts are.

As we are repeatedly creating (w)holes and since both sides of all our (w)hole creations are distorted, we end up feeling "broken down by life." We experience ourselves as NUBs – just little bits of ourselves that we still allow ourselves to be.

Chapter 12: Waking Up to Being a NUB

NUB stands for "Not enough of U to B."

Let me begin with a (W)hole Truth. Once we have created a (w)hole, we are guaranteed to keep falling into that (w)hole until we collapse it. I am sure you have figured this out by now. Before we can move into the final steps of collapsing a (w)hole, there are a few more aspects to (w)hole creation and (w)hole discovery that are helpful to learn. Life will continue to happen and so, too, will your (w)hole play experiences until you have a full grasp of the Wisdom WAY model.

It's pretty difficult to know ourselves as (W)hole if we've flung parts of ourselves into one (w)hole after another (w)hole. With each (w)hole we have created, we have named another part of ourselves an orphan. There are only so many parts of us that we can orphan until there is little left of us. And all these parts of us are calling to us saying, "Please, please may I come home?" We are feeling their pleading, their longing to come home whenever we fall into a (w)hole.

Just as (w)holes happen in our hearts, so, too, does (W)holeness happen in our hearts. Both are feeling experiences; we cannot "think" our way to (W)holeness. However, we can invite our minds to be curious about our (w)holes. It is the activity of curiosity without judgment that most profoundly creates the movements that bring us to the points of (w)hole healing.

We start off by making our first (w)hole. How clever of us! We found a way to avoid or at least manage the HT. We found a way to save our life. And since it worked so well the first time, we do it again and again and again, always placing more parts of ourselves onto the "Not Me" side of another (w)hole. After a while of doing this, all that is left of us is what I call a **NUB.**

With each (w)hole creation, we push to the "Not Me" side just a bit more of us until all that is left is just a tiny little bit of our huge, wonderful, original (W)hole self. With each (w)hole we create, we set aside another aspect or expression of ourselves until there is little wonder that many of us feel dry and dusty in life, all used up and sick and tired. This is how life as a NUB feels.

Imagine yourself taking slices out of a whole pie. Eventually, there would be just a sliver left. Imagine if you were given an ocean of life to explore and then kept excluding areas of the ocean from your allowed explorations charts until all you were permitted was a small pond of life to explore and then a bowl and then a tea cup and then only a teaspoon. Imagine you keep avoiding the streets that have potholes in them; eventually there would be no place left to drive, or walk.

Here is a (W)hole Truth.

With every bit of us we push away into the "Not Allowed" pile, we also push away a bit of our (W)hole life force. The sad fact is that most of us spend our lives living from the resources of just that sliver of ourselves, from just the few "Allowed Me" parts that we haven't yet thrown aside. This is being a NUB. It's exhausting. It's not very much fun, and it often is very frustrating.

What we long for and what motivates all forms of self-growth, self-development, and healing therapies is to once again live from the (W)hole of ourselves with all of our life force flowing fully and vitally within us. This is what (W)holeness is. **From NUB to (W)holeness is the WAY of Wisdom**. To live a (W)hole life, we just choose to Intentionally Spiral every (w)hole we have a chance to find. This reveals and frees up more of our own (W)holeness.

When we feel our own life force flowing and vital and wholly allowed in each moment – we are being who we were born to be: Ourselves, **boldly!** I call this "**Radiance**." It is our choice to live as a NUB or as a (W)hole Radiantly alive being.

(W)hole & Radiant

Not Allowed

A Nub longing for or judging all the "Not Allowed" parts

The Consequence of Being a NUB

We live as NUB's with less and less of ourselves available for the joy of life. Consider how small a NUB is. Maybe a NUB is as small as a crumb of bread or a small seed or a grain of sand. A NUB is very, very small. After a while, we end up becoming the emotional and spiritual size of a NUB as well, and then we wonder why living seems to have little value except to "bring home the bacon" or "take care of the house and the kids" or "get a better job" or "continue on the same old rat race."

I sit in my office and hear person after person tell me about how small they feel or how dissatisfied they feel with life or with themselves. I hear them tell me how much pain they are in or how frustrated they are that they do not feel happier after all this self-growth work. They are describing their very own personal experience of being a NUB. Whether the symptom of our NUB-ness is depression or anxiety or marital disharmony or ulcers or panic attacks or just a general sadness or a sense of wanting more, it is still all about being a NUB. After we make enough (w)holes, we *all* end up feeling like a NUB. It is the inevitable result of multiple (w)holes!

No wonder so many of us keep reading self-help books and attending life enrichment seminars, because to stop is to give up hope for something more, for something to help us. The great fear is that if we stop and really feel what is happening, there will be no hope left, that all there will ever be is NUB-ness! So, we keep on trying to get beyond our condition of NUB-ness without ever really understanding how we got to this state or what has occurred.

So, we persist, but we do so blindly because we haven't understood the essential difficulty. It is not your particular dysfunctions or issues that are the real concern. It is that we are and always have been creating (w)holes unconsciously and automatically for so long that there is little left of us. The real point here is we didn't realize what we were doing! We are all unconscious (w)hole creators. The secret is to become conscious (w)hole explorers!

I realize that this may sound like a great deal of work or just really bad news. However, there is good news. We are not stuck with our (w)holes. We are not powerless in our (w)holes. We can come to know the (W)hole Truth in particular in our (w)holes, and be empowered beyond our wildest dreams. I have watched it happen in my office and in my workshops over and over again. In a flash of a moment, the light comes on and (W)holeness returns!

More good news! We don't have to work at locating our (w)holes! Everyone and everything around us will offer assistance in locating our own particular (w)holes. Anything and anyone who creates "agitation," "pain," or "annoyance" in our lives is helping us by creating a felt-moment in today (a Curb) which trips us head first into another (w)hole. All we have to do is walk through our day, and someone or something will show up and gift us with the identification of a (w)hole. Typically, we have blamed these people or events for our troubles, but the (W)hole Truth is that they are precious teachers and guides.

No, we are not stuck with our condition of NUB-ness, unless we so choose.

Chapter 13: Waking Up to (w)Hole Helpers (HH)

Another reason that our experience of (w)holes is so consistent is that other people will continually bump up against us, shoving us right smack dab into one of our (w)holes. I call these people **(w)Hole Helpers (HH)**. (w)Hole Helpers are those people, events, moments, thoughts, feelings, and conditions that push us into a (w)hole. Just being alive means that, repeatedly, we will be asked directly or indirectly to access a "Not Me" part of ourselves. These invitations will "help us" into a (w)hole. They are (w)Hole Helpers. (w)Hole Helpers hang out at the Curb. We cannot collapse a (w)hole if we don't know it is there, so all those folks and situations that you have been blaming or feeling victimized by or resenting or avoiding or longing for are most likely (w)Hole Helpers for you.

(w)Hole Helpers usually do not know that they've pushed you into a (w)hole. They are not the enemy, although it sometimes does feel like they are! Hating them or resenting them serves no purpose and just uses up a lot of energy. All HH's have a secret mission, and it's so secret that they don't even know about it. Their mission: to plop you into a (w)hole so that you'll look around and notice there is a (w)hole here. A (w)Hole Helper's job is done once you've fallen into the (w)hole. They are offering you an invitation to discover and reclaim your disallowed parts. They are really the good guys because they are giving us an opportunity to reveal our Radiance, our (W)holeness consciously owned. These invitations are the guaranteed upside to the moments of feeling shattered by what another has done, said, not done, or not said. Of course, I would hope that the (w)Hole Helper also is attending to their own (w)holes, for any time we are a HH to another, we are also revealing something to ourselves about ourselves.

Part of what I hold as quite sacred about the Wisdom WAY approach, is that nothing is lost, nothing is wasted, and nothing is "bad." Every part, every feeling, every reaction gifts you a portion of your (W)holeness, if you choose to receive it. Our focus is the process of revealing all of ourselves to ourselves. The vast amounts of energy that become available to us is astonishing as our (W)holeness is awakened and empowered by revelation alone. (w)Hole Helpers are precious when you know about the Wisdom WAY map and methods.

A (w)hole Play Opportunity for You

Take a blank piece of paper, and just jot down all the folks and situations you find "obnoxious," "irritating," "bothersome," "hurtful," or "frustrating." (w)Hole Helpers are anyone and anything that seems to cause a reaction in you. Remember, this is not about judgments – you are just making a list.

After you have done this, pause, and breathe. Now, you are open to the invitation that each of these (w)Hole Helpers is offering to you … or not! Each HH is pointing to a (w)hole. Some HH's may be pointing to the same (w)hole; some HH's may be indicating other (w)holes. Every (w)Hole Helper is a Curb indicator. Don't miss the gift of your Radiance. Sometimes a (w)Hole Helper can help us notice a Curb that we never knew existed. If you notice as you're identifying your (w)Hole Helpers that you've come across a new Curb, simply write it down on your paper for later spiraling.

Set this paper aside for a time. It is a big step to understand and accept that there is no one to blame for the (w)holes we have created. This would be a good time to do a Good for Me Mudra!

Chapter 14: Waking Up to the Shattering of Our (W)holeness

The effect and process of making (w)holes is called **Shattering**. When we shatter, we push away or disallow certain expressions of ourselves. We create a space between me and the pushed away parts of me. This is a (w)hole. When we create a (w)hole:

> We shatter our life energy or vital (W)holeness.
> We shatter our authentic presence.
> We shatter our self-appreciation and pleasure of being who we are.
> We shatter our perception of ourselves.
> We shatter our capacity to see what the Truth is of any situation.
> We shatter our ability to receive and give love – without condition.
> We shatter our beingness.

Shattering breaks apart our original (W)holeness into bits and pieces to save our lives and preserve "hope." We shatter like fine crystal dropped on a hard surface – into a zillion pieces, or so it seems. It's no wonder life begins to feel overwhelming and difficult and sometimes nearly impossible. We only allow ourselves access to bits and pieces and shards of ourselves due to our (w)hole creations.

We have all shattered over and over again. When we shatter, we are breaking apart the (W)holeness we are, and it feels like it is really occurring physically. In fact, we are usually

Us - in pieces

quite sure about how horrible it feels to shatter. It is important to note that **it is our awareness** that shatters. The felt awareness of being (W)hole breaks into a zillion pieces. An infant is just being wholly who they are. Then stuff happens (HT), and the felt (W)holeness is broken into bits and pieces by our Meaning Maker in a valiant effort to stop the pain, prevent any reoccurrence, and establish a bit of hope. It is not that we literally, physically are cutting off parts of ourselves; rather we are "cutting off access or permission to be" **that** part. Our (w)holes are gaps in our permission to be wholly ourselves.

Our (w)hole creation motivation: to be loved – at whatever the cost

We create (w)holes from one motivation only – to be loved and accepted – no matter how much of ourselves we have to "get rid of." Since the experience of Horrible Truths proves to us that love is conditional upon our adjusting to the other, what choices do we have? We can adjust and be loved or rebel and be alone. Simply put, creating (w)holes really isn't optional. Creating (w)holes is how we make these life-saving adjustments.

The (W)hole Truth is that collapsing (w)holes **is** truly our only life-giving option. However, you get to choose! **This is the (W)hole Point of this book**: to share with you the Wisdom map and the tools so you, too, can choose between a life of (w)holes or an empowered life of (W)holeness. What will you choose?

Hidden in every (w)hole is an essential confusion between feelings, sensations, and behaviors of ours and others. Let's look back even further to establish the broadest framework possible. Let's go deeper.

Innocent Unity

In the beginning of our lives, we experience our feelings, bodily sensations, and behaviors as one element. We are (W)hole and unconscious. There is no distinction between our feelings, sensations, and behavior responses and those of other people. The world is one, and we are at peace with the world. We live and breathe every experience with all of our parts as it is happening. We participate in the experience of each moment. We are (W)hole, but we are not aware of this (W)holeness. Even the idea that there is another person isn't part of our original experience. This is a "Unity" born in Innocence. There is no concept of worth or value, since this already presumes a "standard" outside of the self. We just are. We are not "separate from." We are "all that is." We are one.

Then surprisingly there is the experience of "separate from" which we discover because there are other beings around us. This includes "all the others." How *they* responded to our behaviors, feelings, and expressions tells us how they perceived us. **How they received our expressions "equals," in our inner feeling selves, our worth, our goodness, our value, our very right to exist!** Since we are born into this state of Innocent Unity or (W)holeness, we haven't sorted any part of us from any other part of us. In our beginning (W)holeness, all we are is one (W)hole being. We also have not sorted out US from THEM.

When they are loving towards us, then we are loving towards us, and we are OK. When they are judging towards us, we are judging towards us, and we are less than OK. We want to be loved, to be OK, so we adjust who we are to "keep that love feeling going." Do you see? The process of (w)hole creation begins very early and beneath consciousness. In fact, it is actually cellular and limbic. Many of our (w)hole creations are based on original limbic adjustments to "keep the love feeling" and are then later reinforced with more sophisticated Meaning Making strategies! It's no wonder that our (w)holes are so embedded in our way of being!

Innocent Unity is precious. Each of us is a bundle of (W)hole experience moments happening over and over again. The reception we receive from the moment we are born operates like a constant stream of sorting and censoring messages. Each response of the other towards us tells us what parts of us are OK and what parts of us are Not Allowed. It is inevitable that this innocent (W)holeness is lost in the process of growing up. You can see and feel the innocent (W)holeness in the eyes of infants. You can see and feel the loss of it in the eyes of adults.

Radiance, however, is what you see in the eyes of adults who have been collapsing (w)holes and are receiving their orphaned parts home again. Radiance is conscious (W)holeness, chosen (W)holeness, ripened (W)holeness, empowered (W)holeness, and embodied (W)holeness. Radiance is cellular and limbic as well!

The Fusion Effect

The Fusion Effect occurs because of our being born in (W)holeness, regardless of our form. We are (W)hole. Nothing of our direct experience is distinct or separate from us. We are the world, and the world is us. This is a limbic orientation. What we feel is what all the world feels. The world and us are the same. The experience of "separate from" is new from the moment we are outside the womb! From this first moment of being "distinct from," each of us is exploring the experience of what it feels like and looks like to encounter others who are separate from us. Gradually, as we grow up into adulthood, we come to realize that "Oh, I am not the same as them. There is something more going on here." However, as children we often are unwittingly confused between their behavior and ours, our feelings and their feelings and what caused the behavior to occur. Who is doing what?

We're born in Innocent Unity, which is our unconscious orientation, and the Fusion Effect is the result of that orientation. For example, when dad yells at us (a behavior outside of us) for showing our joy (an interior feeling and an outer behavior) and we feel scared (an inner feeling), the outer and inner merge and become united in our felt understanding. The child believes that apparently expressing joy seems to simultaneously cause yelling and a feeling of fear. There is no distinction between outer yelling and inner joy and fear. The child concludes that showing his joy is a bad or dangerous thing to do. There is a fusion within the child's awareness between the behavior of the other (dad) and the felt conclusion about the child's worth. The child will feel that showing joy is not allowed. The child then sorts out what part of him (behavior or feeling or both) must be censored.

This **Fusion Effect,** rooted in our Innocent Unity**,** results in a cellular-felt conviction that their behavior, their feelings, and their words are all true statements about us. Innocent Unity is an orientation that "everything is about us." The fact of separation is not yet integrated into our awareness. Therefore, there is a confusion of what and who anything is about. Take the example, "Dad yelled" (because of me). The "because of me" is a given premise due to the Fusion Effect.

The (W)hole Truth, however, is that dad chose to yell, which is a behavior choice of *his*. This behavior choice was stimulated by what he was feeling inside himself. His behavior was independent of anything that the child was doing. To say it a different way, a child cannot make, coerce, or cause an adult to do anything! This is very important to grasp. Children do not have this power, and, in fact, no person has that power over another, regardless of what the situation is. Even held at gunpoint, we have choices. I have no doubt that any number of readers will want to make a case that "If the kid hadn't done blah blah, then I wouldn't have had to lah lah" and so forth. Look closely. Do you see how easily we adults can hand off our responsibility, our choices to the other, to the child? Can you see how easily we adults *want* to hand off our free will choices and sidestep accountability? The small people in the world, called children, are the ones most often left to carry the blame because they are so ready to do it anyway, given the Fusion Effect.

If we look at this from the Wisdom WAY point of view, we, as adults, are walking around in life with a bunch of (w)holes that we are not aware of. We ourselves are confused between feelings and thoughts and behaviors. Until we consciously "deal with" our (w)holes by sorting through them, exploring them, and collapsing them, we are destined to pass the "gift" of (w)hole creation to the next generation, and on and on it will go. I often say, "It really matters what we do with our (w)holes. It matters to the (W)hole world." Can you see how this is true? Can you imagine how different the world might be if we all did our (w)hole play?

Intentional Spiraling is all about choosing. Intentional Spiraling is all about full ownership of our power as creator beings. There is no room for dodging our responsibility.

The Fusion Effect stimulates and underlies the automatic Meaning Maker strategic response of (w)hole creation. Because of the Innocent Unity we are born with combined with the Fusion Effect, each of us automatically shifts the "Power Point Location Shift" from them to us. The child is left with only one solution – to eliminate the cause of the response, which is a bit of himself. And then we have, yes, a (w)hole!

Now look again, an additional (W)hole Truth is embedded in the Fusion Effect. Because "they" are big and our lives are literally in their hands, their judgments and reactions to us carry far more weight than our own. If "they" say "_____" about us, it is as if "God" has spoken. Sometimes folks will rebel against "them," and sometimes folks acquiesce; yet, in either case it is *they* who are dictating the necessity of an adjustment. This is the reason we shift the entire responsibility to our shoulders – "they" said (directly or indirectly) that parts of us were "bad," so it must be true!

How very potent (w)hole creations are! All (w)holes are rooted cellularly in Innocent Unity, which results in a Fusion Effect and thus disempowers the (w)hole creator even in the moment of the first shattering. A first shattering is inevitable and not necessarily brutal. Everyone must discover that they are separate beings from all the others. The Innocent Unity *will* shatter; however, *how* this occurs is of paramount significance.

Let's look again at an example. If an adult stops and explains to the child when and how to show joy so it would or could be received, if the adult stops and explains that the context affects how joy might be expressed, then there would be no reason to deny that part of ourselves. Instead, we would just learn and evolve. We wouldn't need to create (w)holes. This sounds so simple, but remember, even the most aware parenting figures are people full of (w)holes, too. The are just doing their level best, just as we are.

My sister, who also has an MSW (Masters in Social Work), is the most skilled person I have ever witnessed as an advocate of children. As I have mentioned earlier, she is a co-creator of Conscious Intentional Parenting, a program for teaching parents how to receive their children consciously. (If you wish to know more about CIP, contact me through my website and I will forward your request). I have learned a great deal from her. I recall one time when one of her children, who was maybe four years old at the time, was having a very frustrating time. She took the child aside, and I overheard her explaining in very simple language that "there are times when one can run around, and there are times when big people want us to sit still even when that isn't what we feel like doing." She said, "Nothing is wrong with you for wanting to run around. Let's go find a place for you to do this." What a gift! The child knew he was OK, his desires were OK, and there was a big person helping him manage what felt frustrating and understand what was happening without asking him to give up who he was.

Sadly, most of us were not parented in this way because our parents themselves were not parented this way, and back through the generations it goes. It is not that our parents are "bad" or to "blame" but rather that everyone, even our parents, even the Big People have and had (w)holes. Our parents and their parents before them created (w)holes for the very same reasons and because of the very same confusions that we have created our (w)holes. The only difference is the particular meanings we have made and the events we have felt that were horrible enough to be called our Horrible Truths. Our (w)holes are particular, even across the generations.

The anatomy of a (w)hole is the same for us all. There is our Innocent Unity, Horrible Truths happen, OUCHes happen, shattering happens, Meaning Making happens, and a (w)hole is created to save our lives and preserve "hope." What is at the bottom of every (w)hole? A doorway, a portal, a revelatory potentiality, an invitation to see, know, and be all of ourselves once again by our own authority. However, cognitive decisions alone will not stimulate this empowering transformational awakening of our (W)holeness. More is asked of us.

This "more" is the willingness to soften towards ourselves, to be gentle, curious, and to drop judgments. When we do this, the impact is to soften the tension between the two sides of any (w)hole. This softening is *not* mental alone but is a visceral emotional and spiritual opening. Through the sorting and naming process, this softening is invoked without effort. As we are curious without judgment about the parts of ourselves we have previously judged, the parts of ourselves we have clung to, and the parts of ourselves that have been hurting for so long, we soften. We are curious without judgment when we sort. Softening is the beginning of (w)hole collapse and (W)holeness awakened.

The beginning signal of this softening is when folks notice and admit that, "Yes, sometimes I am this "Me" side of the (w)hole, and yes, sometimes I am that "Not Me" side of the (w)hole. The word "**sometimes**" is an indication that a shift is happening! We see the potential of embracing more of our "Not Me" parts. We begin to feel the two sides of a (w)hole introducing themselves to one another as two parts of one person! This introduction sounds like, "**Yes, sometimes I am this *and* that!**" Once begun, this awareness does not stop unless you actively choose to stop it for fear of your own radiant (W)holeness.

Getting Closer to the (W)hole Truth

As we are naming, sorting, and remaining curious without judgment about one (w)hole after another, there is a movement towards truth. In fact, we never completely forget who we are – even when it feels like we have. As we persist in our sorting, a softening begins to gently move through our being, much like a person slowly waking up. In fact, this is exactly what is happening.

One indication of our awakening (W)holeness is that we begin to recognize the Distortion Effect that happens on both sides of the (w)hole. This recognition is not just cognitive. It is physically, mentally, spiritually, and emotionally felt. This is the softening as you awaken to yourself.

This softening is often noticed when a person begins to say, "But wait! Sometimes I am this, and sometimes I am that. Sometimes I *am* both sides of this (w)hole!" There will be a bit of an inner objection to the absolutes. This interior subtle objection to the absolute of **always** and **never** will rise up without effort because we actually never totally "forget" the (W)hole Truth of who we are. Every (w)hole is our (W)hole Truth waiting to be revealed and welcomed as truth – no matter what *their* reactions might have been in the past or are today.

This softening is a very potent and precious experience. It's (W)holeness waking up to itself. This is Intentional Spiraling happening within you. There is no way to avoid our own awakening if we continue to sort, name, stay curious, drop judgment, and engage with our precious (w)holes, for they are our stepping stones home, unless, of course, we allow the Distortion Effects to keep us from moving forward or we contract in judgment or we stop sorting and start blaming. The point is – the choice is ours. Sometimes the distortions are so familiar we don't see them immediately.

Initially, the Distortion Effect causes us to believe in our (w)hole creations (i.e., **Obviously** this way is "good" and that way of being is "bad"). We are the true believers that our (w)holes are "facts" about who and how we are. We have come to know that we are "never" the "Not Me's" and "always" the "Me's," and it may be quite shocking to realize we are both our "Me's" and our "Not Me's!" Influenced by the Distortion Effect, our entire world is turned around as we sort, name, and claim our own (w)hole creations.

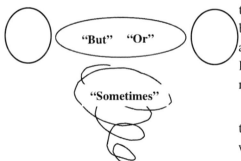

It is important to notice that as we begin to be able to say, "Sometimes I am this and sometimes that," we are acknowledging to ourselves that there is a bit of the truth of us on both sides of every (w)hole. Every side of every (w)hole is somewhat distorted by the absolutes; yet, each side also contains truths about us.

It's All About Creating Motion

As we Intentionally Spiral and apply curiosity without judgment, we begin to feel and actually sense the presence of both the truth of us and the distortion of us on both sides of the (w)hole. The places of distortion are places of frozen or stuck energy. Emotions are actually "energy in motion." Our (w)holes are internal spaces where we have frozen ourselves in "kid-time." The Meaning Making systems are creations of another time; yet, we are still living them today. Our Meaning Making dictates where and how we are allowed to have our emotions and life expressions flow. The Meaning Maker is the boss of our life expressions. Our particular emotions are our particular life energy in motion or not. As we Intentionally Spiral (i.e., go into the (w)hole on purpose to sort, sift and be curious) what has been frozen within us begins first to heat up, then melt, and then to flow! This is the slow motion description of waking up our (W)hole Life!

The progression of these motions or movements of awakening are: First, curiosity without judgment – noticing a (w)hole. This first step creates an interior "heat." Assuming we continue, there begins to be an increasing movement. We call this oscillation – moving back and forth between the sides of a (w)hole. This sounds like, "I am this side OR that side of this (w)hole." It can also sound like, "I am this side but not that side of this (w)hole." Oscillation creates a gentle momentum, like rocking back and forth." By the way, it is not uncommon for folks to actually physically begin to rock back and forth as they say, "I am this 'Me'" or "I am that 'Not Me.'" In oscillation we begin to recognize that both sides of the (w)hole are parts of our (W)holeness.

Then as we add direction and our intention to the movement (i.e., towards the bottom of the (w)hole on purpose) the motion changes to a pattern of pulsation. This may sound like, "I am this 'Me,' and *sometimes* I am that 'Not Me.'" At this point it is quite useful to stand up and rock from one foot to the other so your entire being joins in the pulsation. We can even allow the phrasing to soften into "Sometimes I'm this and sometimes I'm that."

Finally, as the rate of the pulsation increases, it naturally transforms into a vibration, a "hum." It may sound like this, "I am this and that and this and that and … and…and…and." Much as a string on a musical instrument when plucked will vibrate and then settle into a particular single tone, the same thing occurs in our being. The two separate "Me's" (i.e., one from each side) blend into one sound, feeling, and sensation. Our vibration becomes a sensation cascade into a (W)holeness recognition. This cascade is a felt effect, not a thinking thing. A sensation, a "whoosh," a "warmth," a "softening" – these are the type of words folks have used to try to capture the experience. The truth is that it is the mysterious process of awakening (W)holeness and cannot be captured in words. It can only be experienced. You, too, will experience this – it will inevitably occur if you just keep sorting and Intentionally Spiraling.

Once folks have the sensation or feeling experience of revealing their (W)holeness to themselves just one time, they have a growing hunger to know "more" of themselves until ultimately, the Power Point shifts from an external focus of "keeping them – the outer people – appeased or pleased" to an internal focus of "enjoying being really me without restraint." Sometimes there may be an initial inner resistance to Radiance, due to the Yuckies moving in to maintain the (w)hole structure. However, if one persists, the Yuckies will cease to clamor and a gently awakening freedom to BE arises from within. Radiant conscious (W)holeness is a return to our original unity of self, while maintaining all the gifts, comprehensions, and wisdom gained from our precious (w)holes.

(W)holeness vibrating as us once again is the (W)hole point of (w)holes

When our focus shifts to living as Radiance – conscious life force in flow – we wake up to our (W)hole Life. The "How-To's" of this are universally simple and are challenging in particular:

- Identifying your (w)hole – it doesn't matter which one you begin with.
- Deciding to go into your (w)hole on purpose with curiosity and dropping all judgments
- Sorting until you can name both sides of the (w)hole
- Creating motion in that particular cold and frozen (w)hole by admitting, "Yes, I am this *and* that."
- Then there is the surprise! YOU waking up in your (W)hole Life.

Every student and client who has dared to persist with this process has come to a moment of surprise. The surprise is how much pleasure there is in simply being themselves for no other purpose than to be who they are. The pay-off of Intentional Spiraling is the simple, profound pleasure of being. The path to this experience is found in our (w)holes.

On this path we are, consciously or unconsciously, asking the questions, "Do I dare to be this alive now?" "Do I choose to wake up to more of me now?" "Will I allow this orphaned part and that orphaned part to come home, now?" "How big do I dare to be?" "How alive?" "How (W)hole?" "What about right NOW?"

If you say, "No, not today," so be it. You may hold onto your (w)holes for as long as you wish, and there is no judgment in this. If you say, "Yes, today I will look. Yes, today I choose to say 'sometimes I am'" and drop your judgments of good and bad, right and wrong, then you create movement. Movement – first oscillation, then pulsation, and then vibration – leads to (W)holeness recognition and ultimately to the collapse of a (w)hole, the embrace of more of your life force and the revelation of more of you.

This is the (W)hole point of every (w)hole you fall into, to wake up and be alive as you.

Who are you? You are a "Radiant Pulsating Being of Light" right now! Yes, even with all your (w)holes, you are a "Radiant Pulsating Being of Light." All that (w)holes do is invite us to believe that we are "less than." Being frozen in time is another way of saying "I am less than." When we were little and they were big, we did feel small, less, and little. The way *you* feel "less than" is different from how another person might feel "less than." Every (w)hole is how each person has designed their "less than-ness." The (W)hole Truth never changes: we were born (W)hole and unconscious with great big hearts! The only thing that changes is what we agree to believe about who we are. The only thing that changes is what we allow ourselves to express of ourselves.

What We Know So Far

I am sure that you know by now that the point of (w)holes is **not** to scramble or claw our way back out of them, avoid them, or judge them. Falling into our life (w)holes is actually our psyche's way of pointing us towards the orphaned parts of ourselves which we have lost touch with or abandoned.

Our Radiance, which is a bit of our life force or (W)holeness, calls to us. It calls to us from the bottom of every (w)hole, offering us an invitation to welcome back a bit more of ourselves. We can say "Yes," and we can say "No, maybe later." What is essentially not possible is to say, "Never." The radiance we are will simply return another day and knock again, asking if today is the day it will be received. We will recognize the return in one very simple way; we will be head first in a (w)hole again! The only question is *when* will you wake up to the (W)hole point of (w)holes and begin your Wisdom walk? When will you choose to be (W)hole?

When we fall into a (w)hole, we are being shown where we, in particular, shattered our (W)holeness and what parts of ourselves we have pushed away. We can consider (w)holes as a way of introducing ourselves to our orphaned parts. Do not be dismayed if you begin to recognize that you have an entire orphanage waiting at your heart's door. Just meet, greet, and embrace them one at a time by being curious about whatever (w)hole you find yourself in that day.

The key is to know how to sort through the information you are being given as you fall in. At this point you know a great deal about the anatomy of a (w)hole. They always have two sides: the "Allowed to be expressed Me" ("Me") side and the "Not Allowed to be expressed Me" ("Not Me") side. These two sides are opposites of each other. There is a Horrible Truth (HT) and the OUCH. The OUCH was so painful it required a preventative solution to ward off the Horrible Truth. A Meaning Making (MM) strategy is then formulated for each HT. There are a bunch of feelings you have dumped into the middle of the black pit of the (w)hole, into the Spiral. There is the Curb, which is the today event that tripped you into the already established (w)hole. There are the Yuckies who keep us away from those "Not Allowed" parts. And, there are our friendly (w)Hole Helpers (HH's) who give us a shove.

Chapter 15: Waking Up to Our (w)hole Management Systems

All Our (w)holes Together

Our **(w)hole Management System (WMS)** is our unique approach to how we try to avoid all of our (w)holes at the same time. This is what our life has become: managing, avoiding, leaping out of, and fleeing from (w)holes! It's the life of a NUB! No wonder we have such little energy, such little creativity, such fatigue at the end of the day! A great deal of our life energy is spent in our particular forms of (w)hole Management.

You can think of the entire set of your different Meaning Making strategies as being your own personal (w)hole Management System (WMS). It is designed to keep you away from the (w)holes, to keep you numb, and to prevent any accidental expressions of your "Not Me's." Additionally, a WMS *may* also integrate what have been called "self-help" tips, which may actually help in keeping us away from experiencing and embracing parts of ourselves. Affirmations, assertiveness skills, relaxation strategies, stress management techniques, mediation, yoga, and exercise can all be used to keep us from facing and feeling our precious (w)holes. Any technique or approach can be co-opted by our Meaning Maker to prevent any encounter with our (w)holes and thus, our "Not Me's! They *can* operate like band-aids over a wound or as a lid over the (w)hole or as a barricade against active investigation, meanwhile, the (w)hole is still there. Our WMS is *anything* we are using as an "excuse" to not go into the darkness and look around. I call these "**by-passing" strategies**.

Our "by-pass" strategies can also include food, drugs, alcohol, work, violence, exercise, television, isolation, sex, computers, self-development addiction, spiritual flight, confusion, overwhelming ourselves with activities, and even shopping until we drop. We get busy filling our lives with work and activities so that we simply don't have time to look. We overeat, over-shop, overwork, oversleep, drink excessive amounts of caffeine, gamble, smoke, complain, blame, shame ourselves, act out our feelings, and even just plainly refuse to look. I hope you are seeing that *anything* can be used to avoid our (w)holes. In fact, *everything* (i.e., the "good" stuff and the "bad" stuff) has been used by someone for this exact purpose of **(w)hole flight**! In fact, we all are in (w)hole flight until we stop and turn around. This is not our fault! No one has ever told us before that the (W)hole Point of (w)holes is to go into them, not to climb out of them!

None of the self-help strategies and techniques are wrong! They often have taken us quite a distance in our awareness journey. They are useful practices when we use them *to take care of ourselves*. Each of these techniques can support us in our journey. However, if they are used to help us keep our (W)holeness a secret, then they are no longer helpful. You alone know the truth of this. When and if we are using anything to *avoid* the (w)holes or *manage* the (w)holes or *cover up* (w)holes, then these techniques are now part of our very own (w)hole Management System. What can be particularly confusing is that often when we apply these techniques in response to our falling into a (w)hole, there is relief at first, so it appears the "problem is solved." The key question to ask is, "Is this helping me go into the (w)hole, or is this helping me to avoid my (w)hole?"

So where are we with these (w)holes of ours?

We all have (w)holes.

We will keep falling into the same (w)holes until we collapse them. Our (w)holes can-not be collapsed by avoiding them, filling them up with food (or whatever else), studying them theoretically, covering them up, or copying someone else's way. All (w)holes are col-lapsed through a feeling journey only – thinking alone will not take us there.

We created these (w)holes all by ourselves for the purpose of self-preservation.

We sorted and censored ourselves after we shifted the Point of Power from them to us.

At the bottom of every life (w)hole is a bit of our life force. This is called Radiance or awakened (W)holeness or a bit of wild Life Force.

The key to (W)holeness is to collapse the (w)holes.

Our (w)holes are a Spiral path uniquely created for us and by us. Our Spiral WAY is laid out by following our particular wisdom to return us to and reveal to us our (W)holeness consciously. No one else's WAY will take us home to our (W)holeness. No one else's WAY will mirror back to us the greatest secret of all.

The Great Secret of our (w)holes is that our holey selves lead us to our (W)hole Selves which is our Holy state of being.

The WAY to wake up your (W)hole life is through Intentional Spiraling. The primary skill of Intentional Spiraling is curiosity without judgment through the practice of sorting.

There is only one thing to do when you fall in a (w)hole: GET TO THE BOTTOM OF IT!

What the World Tell Us About (w)holes

We hear it all the time from our family or our friends, or even ourselves. "Snap out of it." "You're just in a slump, a funk; it'll pass." "What is wrong with you? Your life is fine!" "When are you going to let go of the past and get on with your life?" "You are just going to have to live with it!" "Drink something; eat something, do something to get your mind off your troubles." "You are making too much of these little things!" "Just grow up!" "Just relax!" "Pray harder" "No one has it easy; just get over yourself!" "Life is tough – toughen up." "This is just how life is. Get used to it." What have you heard?

Life (w)holes are where all the pain is, so why would anyone want to go there on purpose? Well, you now know the answer. The only way to conscious (W)holeness is found *inside* of the (w)hole. The only, absolute WAY to wake up to who we really are, is to go into the (w)hole to embrace all the discarded parts of ourselves. To wake up to our (W)hole life is totally possible. We just simply go *into* our (w)holes so we can follow the path.

I also know that some of you may be impatient. What I have found is that most folks who are interested in (W)holeness "get" all of this theoretically, but the actual "Hands & Feet" of the process, the "how-to's," have evaded them. Many students and clients say "OK. OK. I get it, but how do I do this?" If you don't know the particular steps to take to walk your Wisdom WAY, I assure you that all the good intentions in the world will not bring you into the awakening moments you are wanting. Unfolding the Wisdom WAY map in a step-by-step manner is the only way I know how to insure that YOU have the "Hands & Feet," the practical "How-to-do-its" that so many others celebrate having. Once the map is fully revealed, you, too, will be able to wake up NOW to your (W)hole Life.

We don't have to stay a NUB! No matter what the Horrible Truth was, we can come back to life. This Radiance isn't just admitting to the truth that the "Not Me" is really a part of us. This Radiance isn't about being "happy, happy" all the time. That isn't real or authentic. Radiance is you being really you, being *all of who you are* without apology and by your informed authority and conscious choice. All (w)holes undermine our clarity, reduce our aliveness, and keep us in a "less than all of me" state. This isn't just a theory. The (W)hole Point Wisdom WAY is an empowering practical "Hands & Feet" map to your own magnificent awakening. The foundational promise of the Wisdom WAY is to put the power of your life back in your hands in such a way that it becomes particular and do-able for YOU in your life.

How could this be true? So many of my students and clients say, "It couldn't be that easy!" "Don't we just have to settle for how things are and who we are; after all, we can't change what has happened in our lives?" Yes, it is true that we cannot change what has happened; however, we can wake up to the power we are and to the power we have. The (w)holes we have created demonstrate our power as creators. Now, we can wake up to the clues of who we really are by using the (w)holes we have left for ourselves. We do this by collapsing the (w)holes we created in response to our Horrible Truths. We can do this because we are the creator. We have the power to choose what we want to do next. Your Radiance can only be revealed by your choice; it will never be forced upon you!

Enlightenment, "letting the light in," is a lived, walked, felt, being experience one (w)hole at a time. It is not a static state, nor is it a goal, nor is it a one-time event. To let light in or to open the Spiral path and engage in your walk of Wisdom is an invitation to come alive to your own life. Many are "seeking" enlightenment while having little idea of the "Hands & Feet" or the "How-to's." The steps you have been given so far are some of them.

Once we have identified a (w)hole, sorted through all our wisdom elements (HT, ,MM, Curb, OUCH, Me, Not Me, Spiral of feelings), we come to The Portal where (w)holes collapse into (W)holeness.

Chapter 16: Waking Up to Collapsing a (w)hole

What do we feel as we collapse a (w)hole? First, we feel impatient – then **Alive**!

When we collapse any (w)hole, mysteriously, alchemically that bit of Radiance is ours again. We free more Life Force so that it now becomes available to empower our lives. When this happens, we can feel its return. Some of my students say, "I feel fuller." "I feel bigger." "I feel lighter." "I feel more fluid and softer." Some say, "I feel warm or pulsing or vital." Some say "Wow, I sure feel warm!" I wonder what you will feel when you collapse your first (w)hole?

Each time we collapse a (w)hole, we are more free to be alive, more fluidly awake, more naturally vital, more authentically empowered. No one can fake Radiance. You, too, will feel it happen.

By now, I hope you are impatiently waiting to find out the final steps to collapsing your own (w)holes. This impatience is an openness and a willingness to really allow the (W)hole Truth to reach in and touch you with the mystery of your own being. I hope by now you are eager to learn the art of consciously knowing yourself as a Radiant Pulsating Being of Light. This is good! It takes enthusiasm for our own (W)holeness for us to dare to dive deeply into our (w)holes. After all, we have been fleeing from them for years! It takes courage just to stop and turn around, much less dive into those dark spaces on purpose! When we have a sense of impatience, it suggests we are ready, we are willing, and we are able to take the next step, which is a leap into our (W)holeness.

When a student or client first comes to see me, I ask them if they really, really want their lives to be different. I ask this because things will be radically different after they begin walking this WAY. The impact of Intentional Spiraling cannot be predicted. I do not know what parts of themselves they have pushed away to the far side of the (w)holes and neither do they! After the first session, I tell them I will not accept their decision to work with me for three days. I tell them that I, too, will take that time to decide if I will work with them. They usually want to set up their next appointment right then. I won't do that. Here is the reason. Revealing (W)holeness, "awakening," or as some call it "healing," can only really happen when we are hungry for it. Only when we are ready to face our biggest terrors, our most secret selves, and most of all, to be totally surprised – only then are folks ready, or as I say "ripe," for awakening. It takes courage to come alive again. It takes persistence to walk around in those dark places. This is not for the faint of heart or soul!

A Portal or doorway is found at the bottom of every life (w)hole you have ever created! It is only revealed after you have sorted, after you have named your "Me" and your "Not Me," and only when you are in motion. Then and only then is this doorway at the bottom of YOUR (w)hole activated and revealed to YOU. No one can make it happen, and no one can tell you the particulars of your Holy Portal of (W)holeness! Remember, you are the expert of you!

Impatient to know how? This is what the hunger to wake up feels like. It is when we are willing to risk it all to really know ourselves as (W)hole. I hope you are feeling it right now! Hunger for our (W)holeness is a potent energy. Remember this feeling! It supports us as we move through the Portal.

A BIG (w)hole Play Opportunity For You

Let's get right down to the bottom of a (w)hole right now, down to the Portal. Let's do this by using a (w)hole of yours! Sure, right now! There is no need to wait any longer for your (W)holeness. You know all you need to know right now. Besides, let's be really honest. Your (w)holes are the reason you are reading this, so even if it is nice that someone else can collapse their (w)holes, it is yours that really are important to you. It is for YOU that I have written this book! The Wisdom WAY is all about YOU and your empowerment now!

As we move through your (w)hole, you will see a picture of your personal strategy for avoiding life's pain unfolding by your own hand. The path to your own Radiance will reveal itself to you. Remember, we do one (w)hole at a time. The next step will be your choice. Watch carefully as the mystery of you unfolds before you.

First, get a blank piece of paper. All of your previous (w)hole play opportunities have been readying you for this first (w)hole experience. Yes, you are ready! Remember, there is no way to fail because your (W)holeness is already present. Engaging in (w)hole play is not about fixing you! It is about revealing all of you to you – one (w)hole at a time.

Take a few moments to breathe deeply (really deeply) three times, and then read on.

To collapse a (w)hole, first you must pick a (w)hole. And guess what? There are no "right" or "wrong" (w)holes. Just pick one. The truth is that it doesn't matter. Any (w)hole will work as long as you can feel the "ouch" of it. It is easiest to pick a (w)hole you are currently feeling. To pick a (w)hole, think of a place where you hurt or where your life feels messed up. This might be clear to you by looking at areas in your life where you are not satisfied. You might also look back on some of your previous (w)hole play sheets you created. Pick your (w)hole.

Shift your viewpoint – step into "Curiosity without Judgment." We are standing back and looking at or exploring this space of discomfort. Intentional Spiraling is about staying curious, sorting, and feeling your way in the dark until we find the light switch. All we will do is follow the Wisdom WAY map, which you now know.

We will do this by **sorting** one wisdom element at a time.

You may use this roughed out image of The Wisdom WAY map, as your life line. I suggest you draw it on a blank paper an element at a time by following the instructions below.

The one new image we will add to the Wisdom WAY map is the Portal shape at the bottom of the (w)hole. This shape is the Omega sign, representing the end of a (w)hole and the beginning of your (W)hole Life. At this point you do not need to know anything more about it.

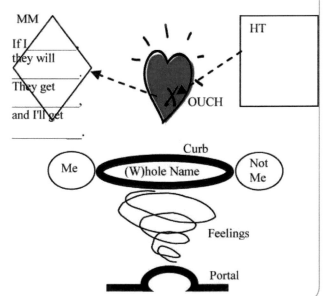

Begin Sorting:

Identify the Curb. One of the most common and easiest places to start is the Curb. Later as you've practiced using the Wisdom WAY map, you may develop your own preferences as to where to start sorting. For now, let's start with the Curb. The Curb is often the first idea or clue that we have a (w)hole. It is usually the "thing" we blame for "feeling icky." The Curb is simply the event of today that seems to have caused you to feel the discomfort you are feeling. The Curb is an important element of any (w)hole. It is whatever just happened or didn't happen that left you feeling "in the pits." The simplest description is the most helpful. Remember, the Curb is not the same thing as the Horrible Truth, although they feel similar. There is no need to describe it in detail. You already know what happened as it happened to you.

Remember: The Curb is about today. The Horrible Truth is all about long ago history. Draw an oval in the center of your paper, and make the edge of it darker to represent your Curb. If you are clear about your Curb, write it on the edge of the oval. Just write enough for you to know what you mean, and remember to be particular. If you are not sure, skip this step and move on. Sometimes the Curb gets clearer as you move through and around and in your (w)hole. You can always come back to this step later.

An important point here is that if you feel stuck on a particular step, move on to another step and go back to that step later. Motion inside a (w)hole is crucial, as you know. Sorting and exploring your (w)hole in a particular sequence is not crucial. However, I will say that the **first three elements (the Curb, the HT, and your Feelings in the Spiral)** are the triad for the easiest approach to a (w)hole study. This is based on years of (w)hole play and is the reason I am taking you through this in this order. These first three wisdom elements may be written down in any order.

Simply start with whatever you know.

Name The Horrible Truth. What is your Horrible Truth for this particular (w)hole? The Horrible Truth is written in the top right corner of your paper. After you have written it down, draw a square box around it. The HT box is a visual reminder that the HT is a fact. It is also a reminder that once written, you may close the lid on the box since it is a past event over which you have no control.

To clarify the Horrible Truth, ask yourself questions. What was happening the first time, the earliest time you can remember ever feeling this clump of feelings? How would you describe your experiences as a child? As an adolescent? As a young adult? What does the Curb remind you of from when you were little? Remember, the Horrible Truth is about others, not you, and the Horrible Truth is about yesterday, not today.

Sometimes the HT is hard to name, and sometimes it is easier than any other part of the (w)hole. Just stay steady, curious, and gentle with yourself. Remember, the Horrible Truth can be a big obvious one-time event, a series of small horrible moments, or any combination. The key is you experienced it as so painful that it is still alive today inside of you.

The HT is ideally one sentence (at most) or a short phrase written like a news bulletin in a very matter-of-fact way. If your name is in it, change it to "the kid" or "the child." It is fine to just take a few guesses to start. Sometimes we don't always remember right away particular things that happened so long ago. So just write the earliest thing you can remember; you can always change it later. The HT is also written in the past tense since it has already happened. This, too, will help with the sorting. Write your best guess of the HT that relates directly to the Curb (if you know it). Do your best to use little kid language for the HT, since the HT was an event/experience from when you were littler than you are now!

Name all your feelings. How do you feel when you fall into this (w)hole? Draw the Spiral area from the oval downwards so that the top of the spiral near the Curb is the widest and the bottom of the Spiral is the smallest part. Whatever feelings come to mind, write them in the Spiral. Whatever you feel is the correct answer. You are the expert of your own experience. Just write what is true for you. This may be the feelings you are having now and/or the feelings you had when the Curb happened. These are the "icky" feelings that we don't want to feel. Usually there are many feelings we have when we fall into a (w)hole. List them ALL. The order does not matter.

Name the (w)hole. What would you like to name your (w)hole? We name the (w)hole as a way to say, "Yes, I choose to meet all the parts of me that are here in this particular dark place, whatever they are." Naming our (w)hole is a way to increase our focus and choose to own this as our own creation. There are no wrong names. The only requirement is that the name makes sense to you. Write the name you have chosen for your (w)hole in the center of the oval that you have drawn on your paper. You may want to change it later, so write it so you can erase it. Changing the name of a (w)hole is fine and can happen anytime in the process. After all, you created it; you can name it as many different times as you want. By naming it you are owning it as your own personal and particular creation, and you are shifting your relationship to it from one of animosity to one of curiosity. After all, wouldn't you like to know more about YOUR creation?

Name The OUCH. Identify the OUCH feeling. What did you feel when the Horrible Truth first happened? What was the OUCH? Write your word or phrase on the heart with the big "X." The OUCH is from a kid's viewpoint and is a feeling. Sometimes a feeling can be best said in a kid-type phrase. If you are uncertain, look at your entire list of feelings and circle three that you feel most deeply. Pause, and then ask yourself if there is a feeling word that captures the essence of these three. Sometimes we have the OUCH word already in our feeling list. This is fine; just write it again on the "X."

Take a walk down Memory Lane. Do a heart and head scan. Run your finger from the Curb to the feelings to the Horrible Truth. See if you can feel the trip down Memory Lane. Do the Curb and the Horrible Truth feel similar? Memory Lane is clear when you can feel how the Curb and the HT touch you the same way. It sounds like, "Wow! They seem so alike it's no wonder I reacted!" If you can feel the similarity between the Curb and the Horrible Truth, move on to the next step. If you cannot feel the connection, take another look at your Curb or your Horrible Truth. Ask yourself more questions about what happened "today" or "yesterday" and what does each remind you of? Remember to be gentle with yourself!

Identify The Meaning Making. What is your Meaning Making strategy for preventing that Horrible Truth from reoccurring? How did you censor yourself to appease the "Big" people in your life? What parts of you did you decide were Not Allowed? Do not list your "Nor Allowed Me" parts yet. It's only that it's sometimes helpful in revealing what our MM strategy is if we know what was no longer allowed. Remember, we are only looking to name the MM for this (w)hole right now. Look at your particular HT. Feel the OUCH. What did you do to make sure you never, ever felt that way again?

The Meaning Maker is written in the upper left corner of your paper. After you have written your first attempt, draw a diamond shape around it. Be sure to use the MM formula:

If I _____(only do/be this)
Then they will _____ (change this way, be the way I want them to be).
They get _____(what I think/imagine they want),
And I will get _____(what I want from them).

Remember, simpler is better. If you aren't sure, just take a guess.

Note: Guessing is important for one very key reason. Guessing helps us open up and access our inner wisdom. Guessing creates movement. Intentional Spiraling is all about creating motion, so take a guess, take lots of guesses. This invites your (w)hole truth to emerge!

Identify and list the qualities for both sides of the (w)hole: The "Me" and The "Not Me." What are your "Me" and your "Not Allowed to be Me" parts in this particular (w)hole? The essence of this part of sorting is to follow the directions of your

Meaning Making strategy. The first line of your MM will tell you about the "Me" you are **supposed to be** according to the strategy. You are simply following your own directions. Make a list of all the expressions and qualities of the "Me." The "Me" parts are listed on the left side of the (w)hole, and the "Not Allowed Me" parts are listed on the right side. You may ask yourself this question, "If I were following the directions of my MM plan, what would I totally, absolutely need to be?" This is the "Me."

After you have listed all the things you can think of for the "Me" side, stop and consider what are the **opposite qualities or expressions**? These are the "Not Me's." "If I were following the directions of my MM plan, what can I never, ever be?" This is the "Not Me." After you have two lists, (even if you are guessing), look at each side and think in terms of opposites (i.e., if "quiet" is on one side … maybe "loud" would fit on the other side). If, after doing this, more qualities come to mind, write them down on their respective "Me" or "Not Me" sides. Take your time. Sometimes the two sides of the (w)hole reveal themselves right away or over a day or two. There is no reason to hurry, and besides even hurrying is a (w)hole.

Name The "Me" and The "Not Me." The next step is to give each side of the (w)hole a name to bring this part of you alive so you can feel and see and meet that part of yourself face-to-face. The key here is to read to yourself out loud the list on one side of the (w)hole. Pick one side of your (w)hole to start with. It doesn't matter if you start with the "Me" side or the "Not Me" side. Next, ask yourself this question: "If a person were *only* this set of qualities, *only* and *always* and *nothing but* these traits, what would I name them?" Remember, be creative. It helps sometimes to list three or four choices in names before selecting your chosen name. Once you have a name for this side, now go to the other side of the (w)hole and repeat the same process!

When you have names for both sides, write your chosen name for the "Me" side in the circle on the left side of the oval (w)hole. Then write the name of the "Not Me" side in the circle on the right side of the (w)hole. You can always change your mind. Remember, it is helpful to think again in terms of opposites for the names as well as the qualities.

Check your Heart-Logic. Run your finger from the Horrible Truth to the OUCH to the Meaning Maker, and see if you can feel the heart-logic of your (w)hole. It is a way to check the felt truth of what you have written there. If it is very simple and clear enough so that others will be able to feel your heart-logic as well, then you have it. The **Heart-Logic** is present when you can say to yourself, very honestly, "I sure do make sense to myself that I created that Meaning Maker!"

Scan for The Distortions. Do a distortion check. Have you made the distortion and truth of both the "Me" and the "Not Me" obvious? This is clear when both sides of the (w)hole are an obvious exaggeration or are "more of the same of" or are an extreme set of qualities. This is true for BOTH sides of the (w)hole. Check one side and then the other to be sure that you can see, feel, and almost laugh at the exaggeration of the descriptions. Be sure the lists on both sides demonstrate the distortion effect.

Scan your Names. Take a moment and honestly check and see if you still feel right about the names you gave to both sides of your (w)hole. These names matter. It is not uncommon for the names of the "Me" and the "Not Me" to not quite fit as you gather more insights into your own (w)hole creation. Adjust them now, if you wish. Finally, look again at the name you gave to the (w)hole itself to see if it still fits and feels right to you. You have now brought yourself to the Portal! Good for you!

At this point we must stop and learn about the Portal which is at the bottom of every (w)hole, including this one. **The Portal is the doorway we pass through when we collapse a (w)hole.** Be sure to keep your paper nearby. As we discuss this next step, you may find you wish to stop and make adjustments to what you already have listed. This is fine.

The Portal: A Doorway to Your (W)hole Life

There is a Portal, a doorway, at the bottom of every (w)hole. It is found at the smallest point of the Spiral of feelings. Arriving at the Portal moment is a signal that the moment of choice has arrived. We begin our (w)holes knowing we can be this *but* not that. As we Intentionally Spiral through our holes down the Spiral, we come to know in a felt way that we are *sometimes* the "Me" side and sometimes the "Not Me" side. It's no longer either-or. It has changed to "sometimes." We are approaching being both sides. This is the softening effect of Intentional Spiraling or being with ourselves in particular. Now, we come to the moment of "AND."

At the Portal there are two heart-felt choices to be made. No one can make them for us. We can't choose just in our heads or just in our hearts or just in our bodies. All of us is invited and required to the choosing! (W)holeness is just that – all of us included in the choice of the moment. In this case it is the choice at the Portal. Each Portal is particular to each (w)hole and each person. This is one of the reasons that no one can do this for you, tell you the answers, or collapse the (w)hole for you. The other reason is the Portal Passage is all about feelings – YOUR feelings. The Portal Passage is all about free will choice, YOUR free will choice and decision. The Portal Passage is where you get to choose your (W)hole Life or not.

Two Activities of the Portal

Portals invite us to "let go" of the kid-magic (our stories, the Meaning Maker, the Fusion Effect) and to "embrace" the "Unknown AND" of ourselves. We do this with no conditions attached, meaning we embrace the truth of our parts not knowing whether or not our true self will be loved and accepted by them! This is, in essence, the correction of the Power Point Location  shift. As you recall, this Power Point shift moved the focus from the action/words of the Horrible Truth and our experience of them to how we could change all that by changing ourselves. In essence, Portals ask us to undo the Power Point Location shift by our own choice so as to re-align us with the truth.

Remember the Power Point shift? We made it all about us and not at all about them. We did this to make sense of our world and to give us hope. At the Portal, we are now asked to come clean and take **ownership only** of ourselves, completely of ourselves, and independent of them. To create a (w)hole, we first have to mix up "us" and "them." At the Portal we correct this mix up – consciously, but not just logically.

As you know, the image of the Portal is the "Omega" symbol. It is helpful to place the activity of letting go on the left side of the Portal and the activity of embracing on the right side of the Portal. This is a part of the Wisdom WAY map. All (w)hole studies are written the same way for ease and consistency between different teachers, students, and apprentices.

Portal Passages Are All About "AND"

As I said before, each side of every (w)hole has important qualities (truths) or actual parts of ourselves, and each side has become somewhat "rotten" or warped or twisted because it has been held separate from its opposite. This is the **Distortion Effect** with which you are now familiar. We are all meant to be (W)hole in our awareness of ourselves. Our (w)holes cut our self-awareness into parts, bits, and pieces. We were meant to know ourselves as (W)hole and to love ourselves in our entirety. This is the (W)hole Point! Arriving at the Portal by your own authority is an indication that you are ready to drop the distortions and stand in your truth. Each (w)hole you trip into has this same invitation and potentiality at its core.

A Portal is a passageway you pass through to embrace a piece of your Radiance. Radiance is awakened, conscious (W)holeness. We draw the Portal at the base of the Spiral to indicate and remind ourselves that we have been pulsating back and forth between the "Me" and the

"Not Me" sides of the (w)hole, moving towards Radiance. We arrive at a particular Portal through sorting, sorting the HT from the Curb from the MM from the Yuckies without judgments.

To pass through the Portal, which has an effect of collapsing the (w)hole, there are two activities you are asked to do. Both of these actions are heart-felt admissions we make internally to ourselves. The effect is to say, "Enough is enough. I choose in my deepest places to stop struggling against being all of who I am!" These admissions can't be made cognitively alone. They require your entire heart and mind to be effective. The good news is that they are not complicated. The challenge is that there is just no way to hide from what you really are choosing! If you think or say "yes" but deep inside you still aren't ready, the (w)hole will not collapse. If this is the case, you can't hide from this truth either. In (w)hole play, the truth will always be revealed.

The other challenge is that in a Portal Passage there is no place to hide from the experience of being "loved for no reason." This can be as demanding and difficult as facing your (w)hole creations. How come? Our Meaning Maker presumes and assumes that it is **only** possible to be loved **for** a reason. How radical it is to bring ourselves to a point of asking ourselves to love, embrace, own, and welcome the "Not Me" parts of ourselves for no other reason than they are part of us, too! They are also part of our (W)hole Life. Our (w)holes are based on the conviction of heart and mind that it isn't possible to be loved, accepted, or wanted just for who we are, so we distort and contort ourselves all to get love.

(W)holeness is based on the conviction that *who* we are is lovable **period**. The difficulties all come from creating (w)holes and distorting our original Unity or Oneness or Wholeness.

Let's take a closer look at the anatomy of the Portal.

The Portal Passage Anatomy

Letting Go of your particular "magical idea," your Meaning Maker, is the first activity that happens at the Portal. What in particular are we invited to let go of? We are invited to let go of our magical belief that by changing, disallowing parts of ourselves, the other person will change. How do we let go of this? Look at your MM. There are four lines to the MM formula. Read to yourself or out loud the first line and the second line, skip the third line, and read the last line. Be sure to insert your particular content. It might sound like this, "**If I** _____(censor myself this way and only be this), **then they** will _____ (change this way), and I will get _____(loved, liked, wanted).

Stop and really look at what you have written. Know deep inside your heart that you have totally believed this up until this moment. It was a given. Now look again – does this *really* work? If I change me, then they *will* change and I will get what I want? The magical idea is hidden in plain view in your MM formula. It is the magical-logic linking lines one, two and four! The essential magic is first seen between line one and line two – If **I** change, then **they will** change. This is the Power Point Shift. Here is the truth: they will change *only* if **they** choose and for no other reason. They have Free Will and always will. It is this basic understanding that we have set aside in order to create our (w)holes.

At the Portal we are invited to begin to accept that, despite all our hoping and efforts and strategic planning, we can't coerce or contain another's behavior, words, or feelings. Yes, I know it may seem so obvious, and yet, I promise you that every (w)hole you trip into, every dark "pit" you sit in, is first and foremost founded upon this magical idea of a child. In our (w)holes the child who developed these survival strategies is still in charge! Can you identify your Power Point Shift? Can you identify the magical idea that is embedded in between the first and second line of your MM? Can you recognize that you are separate from them? Can you recognize that (w)holes are your way to try and make the other be different than who they are?

The first step in collapsing a (w)hole is to admit and feel the truth that the Horrible Truth is about one person – them. The Meaning Maker is about one person – you. The OUCH is about two people in a collision of pain. Do you dare to admit that, "Yeah, there were two people involved in the OUCH collision. One was Big, and one was Little?" Can you admit you were the little one, and you took on the impossible job of changing the big person by censoring yourself? Can you dare and bear to **let go** of the wish and longing for them to be different? Can you admit that you can't coerce someone to behave a certain way, no matter how much you wish they would change? Can you admit that you know more now than you did as a kid? Can you admit and appreciate that you did the best you could with what you knew then? Can you give up on your Meaning Making and admit that it is a strategy you have out-grown and one that no longer is working for you? Can you let go of the "fantasy protection" and "fantasy solution" of the Meaning Maker and stand naked in the face of Free Will of self and other?

The first part of a Portal Passage is about asking these question of yourself without judgment and with a complete commitment to your (W)hole Life, rather than preserving your (w)hole. Cognitive answers will not suffice. A Portal Passage occurs in our hearts, with our mind's support and our body's presence. All of us must move through the Portal, or we have not yet collapsed the (w)hole.

Embracing the (W)hole Truth that you are both this **AND** that, is the second activity that happens at the Portal. This embrace is independent of the other person's choices, preferences, behaviors, or reactions. By embrace, I mean that this step requires the willing, heart-felt step of admitting to yourself that both sides of the (w)hole are valuable parts of who you really are, in fact, to admit that you *are* both of these parts and have never not been. The only thing that has happened is that in a (w)hole we are pretending we can get rid of a part of our (W)holeness. It actually isn't possible. To Embrace is to admit, "I am that, too." This is an act of choosing to enter the "**Unknown AND**" of your own (W)holeness.

This embracing action includes also embracing the risk you have been avoiding by creating the (w)hole to begin with. It's the risk that they won't receive you the way you really are! Every (w)hole has this risk, as you, in particular would define it. This step is an admission and a willingness to risk what you are familiar with on behalf of your (W)holeness. One of our Apprentice Radiance Teachers said it this way, "Can I embrace this "Me" and this "Not Me," even in face of the Horrible Truth happening again?"

Understand that our embracing both parts of ourselves doesn't change the fact of the other's Free Will. The Horrible Truth can still happen. People will act as they choose to act. The difference is that you will be (W)hole, able to access all aspects of yourself so you can choose by YOUR Free Will how you will respond! When we're in a (w)hole, we're reacting. After we collapse a (w)hole, we can choose. Collapsing a (w)hole is all about acknowledging Free Will and giving up the fight to change this universal law of the Universe.

Let us look at these two activities in more detail. I hope you can now see that a Portal Passage requires all of you to show up and participate.

Letting Go of the MM "Magic."

What we are letting go of is the magical idea and belief that we can change them by changing ourselves. We are also letting go of the presumed ideas and understandings of a child. We do this by identifying the magic in each of our own Meaning Makers. We will find magical ideas and child-like beliefs in every MM strategy that we have ever designed. Often, we are so invested in our MM that, at first, we do not notice the magical idea or thinking. The Portal asks us to look at our (w)hole creations directly.

Right now, try a small experiment. Change your breathing to a different pace. Look around. Notice, did the chair change? Did your room change? Did your spouse change because you changed something in you? Obviously not. I have been known to pout hoping to change someone's decisions. I have heard of other people being very angry in the hope of changing people's behaviors. Do you remember ever holding your breath as a kid, trying to force someone to do something? Did it ever work?

When we are children in our Innocent Unity, we don't know that our changing something in ourselves will not alter the other's behavioral choices or expressions or ways of relating to us. This is what Innocent Unity means! Innocent Unity says, "I am the same as all that and all those around me. There is only one world and I am it! Change me-control the world!" So can you see the logic is simple: If I change me everything will change. In our (w)hole creations we have applied "unity" in a concrete, magical idea to eliminate Free Will of the Other.

The magical brilliant creator

All Meaning Making strategies are "bargains with the Universe" we've attempted to implement based on the Fusion Effect. These bargains are child-like manipulations to get the powerful folks in our lives to behave a certain way (the way we want them to or wish them to). In essence we are attempting to bargain away the Free Will of the Big people who have acted in a way that hurts us. What courage! Do you see your bargains?

Personally, one of my magical bargains hidden in my Meaning Maker sounded like this:

If I am "perfect" (i.e., never make a mistake, never be human, or never show flaws)

> **Then** my dad would come back to life (i.e. rise up from the dead,
>> which is what I wanted him to do and how I wanted him to change)
>
> **He** gets to live (I assumed and imagined that he would want this even
>> though he killed himself),

And then I get to have my dad back (i.e., loved by him again).

I wanted him back. His death was a Horrible Truth. The OUCH was being "left alone." So I made a secret bargain with the Universe that I would only be perfect and never, ever make a mistake. In exchange, I would get my dad back. It doesn't matter that this "deal" was impossible. It doesn't matter that my goodness or badness had nothing to do with his choice to die. Remember our Meaning Making plan isn't created from adult logic. The MM plan isn't about honoring their Free Will – it is all about making the pain stop. Our MM is the creation of the brilliant, outside-of-the-box thinking child.

Of course, I know as an adult that nothing I do or don't do can bring the dead back to life, but the kid of me didn't know this. It is the kid of me that created the Meaning Making "deal," a bargain I was unaware of for years, a deal which drove my life, just as your MM's have been driving your life. This example is a very dramatic one, which makes it easy to see the "magical idea;" however, the MM responds to any and all HT moments – big and little.

When we feel ourselves in the pits, we are feeling the failure of our particular bargains. One of our (w)hole secrets is that inevitably the deals (MM) will fail because they are fueled by a child's magical ideas rather than truth. When we feel "crazy" or "confused by our actions," we are noticing that we are acting from a Meaning Making position that isn't based in truth. No wonder we don't make sense to ourselves! Meaning Making is actually based in non-sense. However, do not make a judgment against the brilliant creator you are – all our MM strategies were the best we could construct at the time. When we fall into a (w)hole, we are experiencing the failure of our MM to keep us from the "Not Me." The Yuckies are yelling at us to get the MM system back on line, and we feel the terror that without the Meaning Making strategy, we are in lethal jeopardy.

As an adult we can choose to go into the (w)holes, to sort, identify, reveal, and then let go of the MM magic. To do this takes courage. To let go of our magical idea – in particular - is the bold choice to truly let others have the freedom to be them, to be as they are, and let ourselves have the freedom to be (W)hole, to be as we truly are. To let go of the magical idea is to stand "naked" in our experience of ourselves and the others. There is no way to cover up what really happened, how it felt, and who they are, and who we are. There is no more hiding when the magical bargain falls away.

A (w)hole Play Opportunity for You

Take a look at your Meaning Making. Write down the first two lines from your MM on the **left** horizontal side of the Portal, "If I_____, Then they will_____."

For example, I might write, "If I am good and perfect, then the dead would rise." Write yours now on your paper.

If I am good and
perfect, then the
dead would rise.

Now write: "I let go of this magical belief" under the left side line of the Portal and sign your name underneath. Do this only if you really can feel and know and are convinced that this MM no longer is something you believe in.

If you are not ready yet or it still seems true to you somehow, read it later on. In Intentional Spiraling, we do not push past what we are feeling! That would be making another (w)hole! Just sit with it until you see the magic.

Regardless, now is a good time to do a **Good for Me Mudra**! Put your hand on your heart, pat it three times and say, "Good for Me. Good for me. Good for me!" Good for you.

Now breathe and consider this. Is it really possible that if you change or adjust yourself in this particular way, they will *have* to comply? Really think about it! Of course not.

Free Will

These inner mysteries of ourselves hinge on the spiritual question of Free Will – theirs and ours. We have been in a great wrestling match with life and the universal law of Free Will expression. These Meaning Makings are temper tantrums against the actual facts of our direct life experiences. Each (w)hole contains a particular way you have limited your (W)holeness so as to affect, cause, or force another to change. In fact, we could say that every (w)hole is the exploration of Free Will – ours and theirs.

In every (w)hole we limit our own Free Will in an attempt to limit their Free Will. It's a secret interior agreement of the child which sounds like "I'll limit my Free Will if you'll limit yours.

While this may be simply stated, letting go of a magical thinking (MM) deal is not always an easy thing to do. First, we have to be able to see it. Secondly, we have to see through it. Because our lives have been lived based upon these ancient agreements, hidden even from ourselves, they are often slippery at first. Our Meaning Makers have been around for so long that recognizing them is tough. If you have trouble seeing through to your MM deal, read the first and second phrase of your MM to a friend and ask them to show it to you. Others often see it right away. When you are in your hidey (w)hole, you can be blinded.

We may see and feel the logic of letting go (of course, I know I can't raise the dead by getting an A on my report card), but at the same time, letting go of our strategy of hope can be heart-wrenching. We've been living with this strategy for forever. It really, truly seemed to have saved our lives. It can be quite unnerving to just let it go. How will we be? What will we do when we aren't following this plan anymore? Be gentle with yourself if you feel resistance to this important next step. Giving up our strategy of hope, no matter how ridiculous it may sound to us now, is not an easy step to take. We are asking ourselves to give up what we have believed saved our lives. It sometimes feels as big as risking death.

Breathe. Exhale. Breathe again, and this time as you exhale let go of your (w)hole MM magic. How? By admitting to yourself in the core of your being that it simply doesn't work. Acknowledge that it simply will never work! Every time you have fallen into this particular (w)hole, you have been showing yourself that it didn't work. Now, just let go of the magical idea that changing you can make them change.

Good for you. Pat your heart area three times. Now give yourself a Gold Star – it is a very big deal to let go of such a precious creation as our Meaning Making creation.

Embracing the "Unknown AND"

When we let go of something, we make a space for something else. You are halfway through the Portal. It is hard work to keep trying to make something work that won't ever work. This is what we have been doing all this time until now. Letting go of the **impossible mission** of controlling the others' Free Will frees up a great deal of energy and makes spaciousness inside of us. Folks have lots of sensations as they let go!

Into this new space we've created by letting go of our Meaning Making magic we are going to invite ourselves to reveal the **"Unknown AND"** of both sides of the (w)hole. This is an invitation we offer to ourselves. No one can make us say "yes" to this (W)holeness opportunity. The invitation is to admit to and embrace the truth that we are both sides of the (w)hole while letting the distortions of "always" and "never" fall away. You have already done some of this by saying earlier on, "Yes, sometimes I am this, and sometimes I am that." This served to create the pulsating motion in the Spiral that led you to this Portal.

To embrace the "Unknown AND" is to say, "If I am this **and** that, the "Me" and the "Not Me," who am I?" The global answer is the **"Unknown AND."** The answer, in particular, is for you alone to name. How does one do this? Begin by saying "If you are this "Me" and that "Not Me," who would I name myself to be?" Once again we return to the power of Naming!.

Turn to your personal (w)hole play sheet. You have already named both sides of your (w)hole. Now write the two names on the right side of the Portal at the bottom of the (w)hole.

For example, I had.   "Almighty Goodie Two Shoes" (Me)
"Pathetic Barefoot Orphan" (Not Allowed Me)

Almighty Goody Two Shoes
Pathetic Barefoot Orphan

Can you feel them? Can you imagine what they might look like? That is the litmus test for your names. Names that are alive with the felt-essence of either side of the (w)hole capture both the truth and the distortion. The truths are the gifts or skills or talents hidden in that part of us. The distortions are seen in the absolute limitations to be always this and never that, the exaggerated expressions of each part as it stands alone, and the opposing tension of opposites of either side.

The invitation is to step into the unknown of who we are if we are **both** identities at the same time. The (W)hole Truth is that you **are** both. You just forgot! **YOU do not know WHO you are and how you will be if you admit you really are both sides of this (w)hole!** Admit the truth to yourself – **you don't know.** Your (W)holeness is an unknown!

It is unknown because we have not ever *consciously* lived both of these sides at the same time, at least since the (w)hole was created. Surprise! Either we have pushed away the "Not Me," being only the "Me," or we have suddenly found ourselves being only the "Not Me" and then quickly fled back to the "Me" expression, following a Yuckie attack. Either way, the "AND" of our (W)holeness, in particular, is foreign, new, unknown, and a mystery. Since the formation of the (w)hole, our integrated (W)holeness in this portion of our lives became a foreign entity. Just as Captain Kirk goes "Where no man/woman has gone before," so too, at the Portal are you are asked to "go where you haven't consciously gone before!"

The "Unknown AND" or reunion of these parts is what you are daring to embrace. Because it is unknown, we can't predict all of its expressions, but at the same time we can begin to engage with this Radiant (W)hole expression by giving it a name. The "Unknown AND" is not known by definition, but you have already revealed its segmented elements. By your own authority to name, you are now ready to invoke the alchemical integration and revelation of your own (W)holeness. It sounds complicated, and yet, it is quite simple.

You already know all about naming; you have already been doing it. You also know that naming has the power to re-create and reveal while reaching deep into the cells, the psyche, the heart, and the mind. Naming establishes ownership. When we name this "Unknown AND," we establish ownership of our (W)holeness. When we name this third expression of us, we are establishing ownership of both parts and declaring their value, despite the judgments we previously made because of our Horrible Truth experience.

When we name, by our authority, what we will call this "Unknown AND," we bring it to life. This is inherent in the naming act. However, naming does not mean we "know it all." Naming is the declaration that we are ready to be introduced to ourselves by our own choice. Naming the "Unknown AND" is the act of throwing our arms wide and saying, "Yes, I am willing to be surprised by who I am." Naming does not make everything known. Just as we name a child and then the child reveals his own personality, so too, when we name the "Unknown AND," it then proceeds to unveil itself through participating in our daily lives as us.

Naming doesn't mean we immediately know what it will be like to be this (W)hole third thing; however, when we dare to name boldly and whole-heartedly, there is an immediate feeling of freedom, a lightness, an "aaahhh," a whatever you feel. Everyone has their own name for this moment's experience.

To open the door all the way and step through, you are going to access your authentic creative powers. You are going to name yourself again as this third thing; however, this time it will be consciously. At the time of our (w)hole creation, we unconsciously named ourselves the "Unreceived One" and then proceeded to create a Meaning Making plan to become acceptable. Now at the Portal you are empowering, by your authority, your capacity to name yourself again as (W)hole. This is a universal process. It is only alive when you add your particulars to the alchemy.

I call this process **Alchemical Righteousness**. Righteousness means "all parts welcome to the table." (Dr. Neil Douglas-Klotz) This is our part of the process: naming and welcoming the parts. Alchemy is the mystery of the Universe at work on our behalf. At the Portal, Alchemical Righteousness happens on our behalf and by our authority.

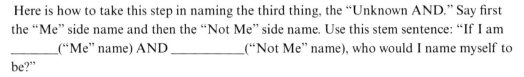

A (w)hole Play Opportunity for You

Here is how to take this step in naming the third thing, the "Unknown AND." Say first the "Me" side name and then the "Not Me" side name. Use this stem sentence: "If I am _____("Me" name) AND _____("Not Me" name), who would I name myself to be?"

Go back and forth between the names. Saying them out loud works especially well because you are asking your entire inner wisdom to engage with you in your new creation. Our inner creator (the part that created the (w)hole in the first place) totally loves doing this and is very good at it! Standing up and rocking back and forth while saying this is also helpful. Movement of any sort helps us soften into the new places and spaces of (W)holeness.

From my example I might say, "If I am Goodie Two Shoes AND Barefoot Orphan, who would I name myself to be? Who am I if I am both at the same time?" while I am rocking from one foot to the other.

Let your mind and heart free associate. The answer is already inside of you because it is you. Make a list of all the ideas for names that come. It helps if you keep the same analogies going, although this is not necessary. For example, I might be choosing images around shoes and feet and feelings of being wanted.

The moment you feel the truth of the name, you will have passed through your very first Portal! You alone can name this, and you alone will recognize the "right" name. No one else can do this for you, although they can offer suggestions if you get stuck. Trust yourself! You are an expert of this (w)hole and yourself! There is a feeling of "Yes, that is the name!"

In my example, if I am "Almighty Goodie Two Shoes" AND "Pathetic Barefoot Orphan" then who do I say I am? This piece of Radiance was called "Free Stepper." Other ideas offered to me were "Happy Feet," "Twinkle toes," "Freestyle Stepper," and "Wild Slides." However, I chose the name that touched my heart.

Write the name of your (W)holeness underneath the Portal on you paper. Take your time. Do not hurry, for that is just another (w)hole (I am here but not there – see the (w)hole?) Play with this without pressure. The "right" answer is whatever name you choose. Let it ripen if you are not sure yet. Whatever comes to you will have some

Free Stepper

element of truth, so you may simply list all the ideas that come and then let them move around inside of you.

Remember only the one whose (w)hole it is gets to decide on the name. The power to name is only in the hands of the (w)hole creator. No one else can do this for you, just as no one else can cause you to create a (w)hole.

Do you notice how the name of the third identity or (W)holeness has a totally different and new feel to it? Naming the third identity is not about just slapping oil and water together; it is about something new and (W)hole.

When you pass through the Portal, you will feel it. If you are only thinking your way there, there will not be body-emotion sensations. Yes, you will know it when you move through the Portal. The sensations are the experience of your (W)holeness coming alive!

You will have physical, emotional, and all-over-you sensations that are unique to you. They may come all at once. They may come slowly. They may come as a "whoosh" feeling. They may come as a "quiet relief." They may come as laughter; they may ripple through you as calm or even tears, but trust me … they will come. This experience is the felt experience of a piece of your Radiance returning to your being.

A great (W)hole Truth is that every "Not Me" and every "Me" part has only one desire – to be welcomed home! The only question is, "When will you open the door?" We keep falling into our (w)holes because our parts keep knocking on the door asking to come home to (W)holeness. Imagine an orphan who is standing at your door, knocking, hoping you will open the door and say, "Come on in! You are welcome too!" (W)holeness is like a huge orphanage where everyone is adopted back into their own family, and you are the head of this family.

Some Practical Tips

If you are stuck on your own (W)holeness name, ask some folks to give you ideas, or just simply sleep on it. Just stay with the simple question, "If I am _____ AND _____, who do I name myself to be?" The name will rise up, and you will feel it. If it still doesn't, go back and look again at your "Let go" step and your "Embrace" step. Are they clear enough for you to feel the admissions? If no name still surfaces, go to sleep saying softly in your mind, "If I am _____ AND _____, who do I name myself to be?" The Mystery will dance with you, and the Truth name will reveal itself.

One important thing to pay particularly close attention to as you Let Go and Embrace is to make sure you do not have any **Cherished Outcomes**.

Cherished Outcomes

When we have a **Cherished Outcome**, we are putting **a condition** on our passage through the Portal. We do this because we are attempting to avoid the vulnerability of being that "Unknown AND" or that third thing, as I sometimes refer to the (W)holeness. It's a scary thing we're being asked to do. We're dropping our magical thinking. We're embracing parts of us that we haven't really known for a very long time, and we're stepping into a (W)hole new way of being ourselves. This is not an easy walk in the park! So sometimes, we may unconsciously put a condition on our walk through the Portal. In essence, we're trying to make an unknown thing known when we have Cherished Outcomes. It may sound something like, "I'll only do this if they'll still love me afterwards." Can you see the bargaining again? Can you see how we're trying to make the unknown (will they love me?) a known thing?

A Cherish Outcome is like a huge bag of old hopes and wishes and conditions. It is so huge that you can't pass through the Portal while still carrying it. A Cherished Outcome is just what is sounds like: an outcome we are cherishing, clinging to, hoping for desperately. In (w)hole play, it sounds like, "I will admit I am both these parts only if they blah blah blah." The "Blah Blah" is the Cherished Outcome. It is also a definition for the unknown, unremembered (W)holeness of us.

A (w)hole Truth: We all pass through a Portal naked – save for our power to name.

We cannot pass through the Portal if we are carrying around bargains, deals, or conditions. It would be like an adult trying to walk through a child's dollhouse door. We can't fit through the door with all this baggage. Walking through the Portal is a bold step. It requires that we stand naked, naked in the sense that we do not exactly know what it will be like once we pass through. It's our first conscious step into our own (W)holeness, and we have no idea what that looks like.

So, if you're stuck at the Portal, which is where a lot of us can get stuck and hang around for a while, just relax and breathe. It's ok to sit there for a while. Remember, there's no room for judgments about yourself here. Simply acknowledging where you are, hanging around the Portal, is calming. The Portal isn't going anywhere. It simply awaits your choice to walk through, by dropping the Cherished Outcomes, Letting Go of the magical ideas, and Embracing the "Unknown AND."

Chapter 17: Waking Up to the Mystery at Work

"**Life awakening**" happens when we make space for something beyond the known and allow for the mystery to move through us without disengaging from ourselves. By renaming ourselves without knowing what it will all mean, we are invoking "**Mo-R-e**" of the greater life force we are to move in and play, to surprise us with even "Mo-R-e" of our (W)hole selves. I am spelling "more" in an odd way to indicate that it isn't just an addition of one plus one. The third thing, our (W)holeness, is greater than the sum of its parts. Collapsing a (w)hole is the alchemical effect of our choice to reveal ourselves to ourselves, dancing with the Mystery of Life, hence "Mo-R-e."

Do you feel the giggle, yet? The new bit of Life? The alchemical shift within? To declare our (W)holeness as valuable, independent of the other person, is to move into mature Free Will playing and living. To declare our (W)holeness worthy of our naming is the action of empowerment in particular. The name is no one's but ours! No one's name but ours will invoke the Mystery and breath life into our (W)holeness. The breath of life is ours!

What is the true magick here? We are daring to receive our own love. We are daring to receive our own embrace regardless of whether they love us or not! This is the foundation of true Free Will. When we accept our own self-love, then others are granted their freedom, and we have been granted our own freedom. Our (w)holes are our temper tantrum against their Free Will. Essentially we are in flight from their Free Will and resisting the responsibility of our own Free Will. When we collapse a (w)hole, we let go of a bit of our own resistance to being responsible for loving ourselves regardless of their conditional love.

What Are the Effects of (w)hole Collapsing?

When we collapse a (w)hole, we are freer to be more of who we really are. We are more of who we are by our own conscious choice rather than from our automatic (w)hole Meaning Making, which, by definition, reduces us. (W)holeness is conscious vitality. (W)holeness is being empowered. Our (W)holeness is embodied as us. Our (W)holeness is not a concept! It is not a theory! Moving through the Portal can only be a felt experience because as we admit the bald naked truth of ourselves to ourselves, we are saying, "Yes, this is who I **am**, no matter what anyone else thinks of me." What daring courage! What depth of heart this requires! This particular (W)holeness isn't real until and unless it can stand even in the face of that Horrible Truth happening again.

Only after making these honest admissions to ourselves can we truly release our efforts to keep these secrets from ourselves and keep the "Me" and "Not Me" segregated. It isn't the naming alone that effects a (w)hole collapse. It is also the heart-felt admission that loving ourselves is up to us, and the love of others is a free will gift. This, too, empowers the name with the (W)hole Truth which invokes the Great Mystery. This triad combination of admission, naming, and invoking the Mystery is what effects the deep interior shift within us. We cannot do all these three actions without opening up and being willing to reveal the secret of our (W)holeness.

We invoke the Mystery by admitting what happened (HT + MM) and Naming who we are, by our own authority. These two things added together equal the Mystery of Authentic Empowerment and Change. This alchemical formula cannot be effected by mere thought; it requires a deep engagement with ones' own (w)holes, profound courage, and a depth of heart-hunger for our own mysterious (W)holeness. Collapsing a (w)hole happens because we choose to sort AND because the Universe is in support our (W)holeness.

On the Other Side of Every Portal

The Portal of every (w)hole is a gift, a surprise, and a promise. You are absolutely guaranteed that each (w)hole will open you up to yourself, if you allow it. That is a **promise**! The **gift** is that you get freedom to choose to reveal yourself to yourself. The more of you that you embrace, the more alive, vital, and potent you will be in your life. It is that simple.

The **surprise** is just how amazing, brilliant, and alive your (W)holeness actually is. This is something we have forgotten since the very first (w)hole. Empowered living is the effect of collapsing a (w)hole and then another and another. Your empowered (W)holeness is the purpose of any (w)hole collapse. Waking up to Your (W)hole Life is the (W)hole Point.

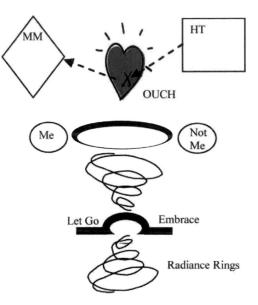

The symbol I use for this empowered (W)holeness or Radiance is the spiral that begins small on the other side of the Portal and expands into bigger and bigger spiral rings. **There is no end to the ever-expanding Spiral you are**! I call these ever-expanding rings of the spiral **Radiance Rings**. When we choose to collapse a (w)hole, we are choosing to let our Radiance ring out louder, richer, fuller, bolder, and brighter. We become like a call or a vibration rippling out into every space and place we are. This is the (W)hole Point of (w)holes. They are calling us to be an ever-expanding expression of ourselves by our own choice!

What is on the other side of every Portal? Radiance. Ever-expanding rings of Radiance. Awakened (W)holeness. Potent Aliveness. Embodied Empowerment. Your (W)hole Life. All these words mean the same thing. The point of (w)hole collapsing is to live your life with full empowerment, with awakened aliveness and embodied (W)holeness. The (W)hole point is you being **all** of you!

Remember the game of Hide-and-Seek many of us played as kids? One kid would cover his eyes (just as we have done in our (w)holes), while the others would run and hide (just as all our "Me's," our "Not Me's," our feelings, our HT, our MM, our Portals, and even our Radiance has been hidden from us by us). Then the one who had covered his eyes would uncover them and begin to look around. What was the point of the game? To find what was hidden. This is the (W)hole point of life. You now have the know-how to reveal yourself in all your hiding places. You now have the know-how to recognize your hidey (w)holes and turn the lights on – the Light of Enlightenment, the Light of (W)holeness, the Light of YOU being YOU. How rare it is for us to encounter an individual who is so at ease with himself that his inner Radiance shines forth without apology and without effort? You now have the "Hands & Feet" to shine forth as YOU.

A teacher of mine once said, "You will know you are awake when you could walk down the street, bump into yourself and recognize that person as YOU." How profound. Most of us have spent so long hiding from ourselves that if we bumped into ourselves on the street, we'd think it was a stranger!

At the end of the games we played as children, we would call ourselves back to "home" by singing out, "All-y, All-y In Come Free!" Now is the time to wake up, stop hiding, and step into your own (W)hole Life!

All-y, All-y In Come Free.

Understand that except for the Horrible Truth, every other part of the Wisdom WAY map points to a part or expression or an experience of you being you. Now the call has gone out: **"All-y, All-y In Come free."** This is the call echoing from the bottom of every (w)hole, from each and every one of your (w)holes, to all your parts. It is the call to be (W)hole now as you, with all of you boldly walking through each moment of your day.

Now, a (w)hole at a time you – yes, you – can reveal your own authentic (W)holeness to yourself. What this means is you really can come alive again. You are no longer a NUB, someone broken and in need of fixing. **You are consciously a "Radiant Pulsating Being of Light!"**

Now, we don't do this all at once; we do it one (w)hole at a time until quietly the cascade into our (W)holeness happens continuously. (W)holeness gradually becomes our way of being! This happens one (w)hole at a time until somehow – often it seems mysterious – we are simply being US. We didn't create a bunch of (w)holes all at once; we did this one (w)hole at a time. We didn't become a NUB all at once; we created our NUB-ness as we tossed aside parts of ourself, one (w)hole at a time. Digesting one hundred Thanksgiving dinners all at one sitting isn't possible. We would throw up! In the same manner, we collapse one precious (w)hole at a time. We couldn't possibly digest all of the information, all of the wisdom from all of our (w)holes in one fell swoop. We'd be overloaded and overwhelmed. Patience is crucial.

We embrace our Radiance one (w)hole at a time. And I am not saying we have to do "every (w)hole" because after a time, there is a cascade effect, and all the parts just start to come flying home. It is just that at first, one (w)hole at a time works the best. It's the easiest and gentlest manner.

All-y All-y In Come Free. Come home to BE! The call has now gone out to you – to all your parts, to all your wisdom, to all your feelings, to all your thoughts, to all your yesterdays, and to all your todays'! *How will you choose to answer this Holy Call to Life?*

Your New WAY

Now, when you fall into a (w)hole, you will gulp, breathe, soften, and say, "Good for me. I know this is a (w)hole, and I know the Spiral pathWAY!" Then name the Curb, the (w)hole, the HT, the feelings, the OUCH, the MM, the "Me's," and the "Not Me's." Notice the truth and distortion on each side of the (w)hole. Notice the MM magic and let it go. Then rename yourself more (W)hole than you were a moment before by embracing the "Unknown AND," as yet unlived, (W)holeness.

Do not make the mistake of thinking that you will and must do every (w)hole one step at a time for forever. We just move this way until we have this Wisdom WAY map deeply awake inside of us. Then it will become as easy as each breath you take. It is then that the cascade of orphans simply melts into your being. However, rather than make this a goal, just take one (w)hole at a time. The cascade will happen. You do not need to work at this. It will just happen.

After a time we come to focus on our (W)holeness rather than our (w)holes; however, be gentle and allow the ripening of your (W)hole self. You are right on time. As I like to say, "Hurrying is a (w)hole. I am here, not there." There is space between here and there, thus a (w)hole. So just let yourself take one (w)hole to start with, whichever one is feeling alive in the moment. Identify and Sort.

Lastly, here is a quick review of the **Intentional Spiraling sequence**:

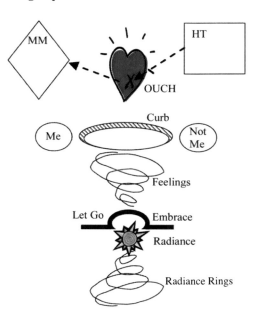

- Identify the Curb.
- Identify your feelings.
- Identify your Horrible Truth.
- Identify the OUCH.
- Identify your Meaning Making Strategy.
- List the "Allowed to be Me" parts.
- List the "Not Allowed to be Me" parts.
- Name the "Me" side of the (w)hole.
- Name the "Not Me" side of the (w)hole.
- Name the (w)hole sometime along the way.
- Name the magical ideas and beliefs and Cherished Outcomes if there are any.
- Let go of the magical thinking – admit that it doesn't work and it never will. Let go of your resistance to the Free Will of both you and them. Let go of hiding in your hidey (w)hole of "less than."
- Drop the distortions from both sides and embrace the truth by saying, "Sometimes I am this, and sometimes I am that."
- Name the "Unknown AND," in particular, and breathe life into your (W)holeness.
- Receive the timing and action of the Mystery of Life, be willing to be surprised.
- Embrace the (W)holeness of you. Receive the surprise of the "Mo-R-e" of you one (w)hole at a time.

The Basic Tools for Intentionally Spiraling one's (w)holes:

- Falling into your (w)holes - that's easy!
- Being curious without judgment.
- Trusting yourself as the expert.
- Being gentle with yourself.
- Choosing (W)holeness over (w)holes.
- Keeping the Wisdom WAY map clearly in mind, then add your own particulars to the Universal Story.
- Walking the Wisdom WAY Spiral path now laid out before you.

By choosing your (W)holeness over your (w)holes, you will inevitably reveal yourself as a "Radiant, Pulsating Being of Light," the one you were always meant to know yourself to be.

After a time you will be able to do this standing in front of the kitchen sink; you will be able to do this in your car, or while you are in a meeting until you are simply being (W)holeness rather than flailing around in (w)hole after (w)hole. You may want to refer to the (w)hole study examples in the appendix to offer yourself further understanding through examples. However, the best way to digest the Wisdom WAY is to Spiral every (w)hole of yours that you get tripped into until you can feel your way through the process. The best way to learn a map is to walk the paths sketched out upon it. The way to wake up to your (W)hole Life is by one (w)hole collapse at a time.

The Mystic Moment:

Following the Portal process of Letting Go and Embracing the "Unknown AND," you experience what I call a Mystic Moment. This moment is a still moment. The Mystic Moment is our first moment of emerging from a Portal. It is quiet, delicate, and very alive. In this moment, we are stepping into being something more than we were a moment ago. There is a still-vitality. There is the aliveness of a newborn, for this is exactly what you are. There is a felt awe of the wonder of you. There is whatever you feel when you have revealed "Mo-R-e" of your (W)holeness. The Mystic Moment is a felt-presence of the Mystery. Be present to these moments of new life – these are your true birth-days. Every (w)hole is an invitation to hold your own birth-day celebration.

A Mystic Moment occurs after every Portal. Sometimes it is very noticeable, and sometimes it is subtle. However, it is always there!

The Mystery is:

All of **YOU** is the answer to the question, "What is Radiance?"

You are the answer to the question, "What is (W)holeness?"

You are the answer to the call issued by every (w)hole you ever fall into.

You are the WAY to (W)holeness.

You are the Wisdom.

You are the emptiness of the (w)hole.

You are the richness of the (w)hole.

You are the embrace and the orphans and all that is between.

You are the (W)hole Point!

Yes, each one of us is the point. Each one of us is our WAY home. Each one of us has all we need right now to walk our Wisdom WAY until we reveal ourselves as (W)hole, (w)holey, and Holy.

I offer you this question as a "global summary" of The (W)hole Point Wisdom WAY of empowerment: "Who do you say you are?"

Chapter 18: "Radiant Pulsating Being of Light"

In closing this section of the book, I wish to review in depth for you the actual meaning of this phrase, which I have used throughout the book. The phrase "**Radiant Pulsating Being of Light" (RPBL)** has a very profound and direct meaning. Each word refers to a (W)hole Truth that we are invited to deeply reveal to ourselves, in particular.

Each word also is a (W)hole Truth about who we are in our essence – even when we don't feel it to be so. Each of the parts of the phrase also summarizes an aspect of The (W)hole Point Wisdom WAY model and map and method. Finally, the image implied and invoked by this phrase reaches into every cell of the body and into every element of our beings to honor the (w)hole creator we all are. It invokes the truth that we are (W)hole and (W)holeness right now, despite our (w)holes.

The depth of this phrase can't be fully revealed due to the limited nature and scope of this book; however, it is worth a moment to begin to pull the curtain aside, exposing a hint of the profound invitation that every (w)hole offers each of us: the lived, felt wisdom that we can choose to know ourselves as "Radiant Pulsating Beings of Light" or not. Perhaps this brief explanation will begin to stimulate this wisdom within you to rise up and empower more and more of your life.

As you read this dissection of "Radiant Pulsating Being of Light" phrase, let yourself feel it as well as understand it with your mind. I believe that this is an inspired message which affects very fiber and element of our being, independent of our cognitive agreement or understanding.

- **Radiant** refers to being "conscious of our origin" which is (W)holeness. We are born (W)hole. We are (W)holeness in a body.
- **Pulsating** refers to the vital life force which is in our body (embodied) and is the spirit we are, the ever-expanding Spiral.
- **Being** refers to actively existing (in this form) right now. We are alive as human beings.
- **Of** refers to being "one with" or of the nature of (W)holeness. We are Oneness walking with itself.
- **Light** refers to Oneness or (W)holeness or life essence.

"Radiant Pulsating Being of Light" means to be and live and trust the Wisdom of my (W)hole self. I am conscious of my origin as embodied spirit, actively existing while knowing I am one with All That Is, even when I am in a (w)hole. It means that every (w)hole you trip into is an invitation to reveal yourself to yourself as what you are already – (W)hole. Every (w)hole is an invitation to live your own wisdom WAY. Every (w)hole is a call to wake up and remember who you are. You are a Radiant Pulsating Being of Light.

I extend an invitation for you to walk the Wisdom WAY daily, by saying "Yes" to all you are over and over and over again with each breathe you take. I invite you to begin right now, (w)holes and all. And for the play of it and for the fun of it, I encourage you to say with great glee and a loud voice from inside of you outward, "Yes, I am a Radiant Pulsating Being of Light right now, (w)holes and all. Good for me. Good for me. Good for me."

Chapter 19: Applying the Art of Intentional Spiraling to Other Life Arenas

Once a person has an understanding of the basic anatomy of a (w)hole and the Wisdom WAY map and Intentional Spiraling methods, there are a wide range of applications as well as a great deal of individual depth that may be accessed using what you know. Describing all of this to you is far beyond the range of this book. Over one hundred and fifty hours of direct intensive instruction are offered to simply cover the entire eight levels of The (W)hole Point Wisdom WAY model, and this doesn't include the information in the manuals, which is not directly discussed. However, in the next few sections I will offer to you just a hint of some of what is awaiting you in the world of (w)holes and (W)holeness.

Please understand that these advanced materials are not meant to be inclusive of all the surprises and hidden secrets and mysteries accessed through our (W)hole Life in any of these areas. In fact, I could write an individual book on each of these advanced topics as well as many others. Simply suffice it to say that these advanced notes are merely the hors d'oeuvres for a huge banquet of (W)holeness offered through the Wisdom WAY map, method, and means.

For those interested in learning a bit more about how **Intentional Spiraling is applied to relationships** of all sorts, I have included a brief section on "**PAIRing**." PAIR stands for "*People Activating Intimate Relating.*" In this section, there is a beginning introduction to the wonders of *PAIRing*. In essence, the magic of PAIRing is found in (w)Hole Helping. Being a (w)Hole Helper (HH) is the most important gift given to us by our intimate PAIR Partner. Being a (w)Hole Helper is also the most precious gift we have to give to our PAIR Partner. Whether we are married, in an intimate relationship, dating, or single and looking, this section will offer you a method of maximizing your interchanges to deepen your own (W)holeness and honor the (W)holeness of the other.

For those who are interested in how **our (w)holes directly inform our spirituality,** there is a brief exploration into how our psychology intersects with our spirituality in every life (w)hole. This section may or may not be for you. I would ask that you honor yourself as the expert of your own WAY. When you reach this section, pause after reading the introductory paragraphs, and then decide if now is the time for you to explore this dimension of your (w)holes. In essence, this aspect of Intentional Spiraling reveals the hidden "religions" of our childhood, which are imbedded in our (w)holes. Intentional (w)hole exploration also uncovers your particular Spiral path to (W)hole Life Spirituality, your WAY. This is not about another religion. This is an invitation to come into your own sacred (W)hole Life, consciously and in alignment. It is about revealing your own vital spirituality.

For those interested in learning a bit more about how The (W)hole Point Wisdom WAY model may be applied in management situations and the business environment, there is a brief section covering this topic.

Additionally, you can choose to stop reading here for a time and just apply what you know to your precious life. It takes a bit of practice to digest the essential Wisdom WAY process. Just like anything we learn for the first time, it takes time, patience, and practice.

It is still my contention that live (w)hole instruction which occurs at the live (W)hole Shop Intensives is the most direct and effective means of revealing the (W)hole Wisdom landscape. During these intensives, participants are not only taught the deeper dimensions of The (W)hole Point Wisdom WAY model but are also immediately invited to apply, with support and mentoring, what they have learned to their own lives.

During these intensives, initiatory experiences occur which are beyond the scope of words alone. Ranging from the relief of self-validation to the high vibration of self-embrace, students attending these intensives continue to empower themselves beyond their wildest hopes. I know this because they call to tell me about how their lives have changed and how their hearts have opened. They call wanting Mo-R-e of themselves. It is for this reason that the advanced levels of the Wisdom WAY came to be developed. I invite you to attend a live (W)hole Shop to experience this for yourself.

For those interested in learning even more about the Wisdom WAY map and its multifaceted elements and applications, contact us through our web site at **www.wholepoint.us.**

Chapter 20:
PAIR
"People Activating Intimate Relating"
Waking Up in the Middle of a PAIR

Often I have students and clients who wish to utilize the simplicity of (w)hole play in the context of their relationships. This is a marvelous and powerful application. First, let me say something briefly about this term "PAIRs." By this anachronism, I am referring to anyone who is choosing to activate, to wake up to, and to live purposefully the ongoing process of relating intimately to another person.

PAIRing is a choice to engage in (w)hole play with another – knowing full well that this other person is your greatest (w)Hole Helper (HH) and your best Curb tripper and your most precious Wisdom WAY teacher. PAIRing is a powerful and direct way to discover and access your most precious (w)holes. Intimate relating is essentially a commitment to (w)hole play in depth. Despite all the wonderful and exciting things that go with falling in love or falling into friendship or falling into partnership or parentship or falling into business-ship, it is also all about (w)holes.

This section is an advanced segment in this book and presumes that you are already well-versed in the basic model. Whether you have read the "Spirituality section" or not is irrelevant for the information about PAIRing, although it is my firm belief that relating intimately is one of the greatest doorways to our spirituality. The PAIR information stands firmly upon the basic (W)hole Point Wisdom WAY model, map and method. This element of the (W)hole Point Wisdom WAY model is applicable to husbands and wives, girlfriends and boyfriends, same sex partnerships, employee–employer relationships, co-parenting – almost any relationship you can imagine. Intimate relating happens in all sorts of contexts and environments.

"People Activating Intimate Relating" is a term that points to the effects of bumping up against each other in our daily lives. Each time we interact with another person, we are potentially invited into the possibility of discovering another (w)hole of our own. Each time another person interacts with us, they are potentially inviting a (w)hole discovery of their own. Each time we interact with another person, we are creating the possibility of being a (w)Hole Helper for ourselves or another. Yes, I would firmly stand upon the (W)hole Truth that intimate relating guarantees (w)hole discoveries and (w)hole tumbles.

In preparation:

For ease of comprehension, if you wish, get a blank piece of paper and fold it lengthwise down the center of the page. Open the paper so that you have the crease running down the middle of your paper. On the left side of the crease draw the basic (w)hole diagram. Include all the elements you know, using the same shapes and initials (i.e., HT in the box, etc.) as we have previously described. Do not include the elements from the section on Spirituality. Do not label the two smaller circles we call the "Me" and the "Not Me." Simply leave these blank for now. On the right side of the crease, draw the same basic (w)hole diagram. Again, label everything except for the "Me" and "Not Me" circles. Draw them in, but do not label them. Now what you have is an image of the beginning of an intimate relating moment. The space where the fold is, in between the two diagrams, is what I call the **Sacred Relating Space**. This is the space between two people, or a "PAIR" as I call them.

The Beginning

When we begin activating a relationship, each person shows up with (w)holes. Whether they are aware of this or not and whether you are aware of this or not, every relationship rests on a foundation full of (w)holes. If you look at your paper, this is a shorthand way of exploring the PAIRing space.

Label the left side of your paper "Alex's (w)hole," and label the right side of your paper "Barney's (w)hole." Now before you is an image of the beginning of Alex and Barney coming into intimate relating. As you read through this description, fill in each of their (w)holes on their respective sides of the paper as best as you can.

Initially, Alex and Barney both present to the other their best and most "buffed up" expressions – just like we all do. These are going to be all their "Me" parts. When we are first getting to know someone, whether it is a boss or a friend or a peer, we will lead with our best foot, or our "best parts," so to speak. We have spent ages of time practicing our "Me" parts; however, they will be somewhat distorted, as you know, since they are only one portion of the (W)hole of who we are. All the same, they are the parts that have been allowed to be expressed. Usually, these parts "play well with others."

Additionally, when we are first getting to know someone, there haven't been any Curbs to trip over yet, so often we are not experiencing ourselves in a (w)hole. Consequently, our primary experience in an initial PAIRing is positive and smooth. Each person is actively seeking to move into a greater harmonious intimacy, even if it is just being a good employee or manager.

For example, let us say that Alex was always very quiet, cooperative, and neat, something that had been very prized in Alex's earlier life. Upon meeting Barney, Alex makes extra efforts to pick up and keep a clean household, cooperating with all of Barney's ideas and suggestions for activities and meekly going along. Alex is making sure to be the "Me." Barney is full of life and has great ideas for activities and is very warm and affectionate. Barney is also making sure to be the "Me." Things seem to be progressing nicely. Then stuff happens.

Over time as Alex and Barney get to know each other, they spend more and more time at Alex's apartment. Barney begins to leave stuff around the apartment. The kitchen counters are more cluttered, and the coats are sometimes not hung up. Despite Alex's best efforts, the place isn't as clean as before. This is beginning to bother Alex a bit. However, Alex has often been thought of as being too "controlling," so the "discomfort" feeling goes into a (w)hole.

In addition, every time they get together, Barney turns the boom-box on loud or wants to jump into the next round of adventures. Alex is beginning to miss times of quiet and stillness. Alex now begins making extra efforts to appreciate all the wonderful things that Barney offers including Barney's fun-loving and light-hearted way of being. Alex is still maintaining the "Me" position, but now it is taking some effort. Then one day Barney says, "Gosh, it sure is messy around here!" Alex is enraged! Right on the spot Alex begins yelling. "How could you say that? I have tolerated your loud noisy music, and I have picked up after you lots of times. You never do anything!" You can see we are now "off to the races," as some of my couples say.

When we have (w)holes, it's inevitable that a Curb will appear. The Curb may be something the other one did, said, didn't say, or didn't do. It may be external to the PAIRing, or it may be a change in the circumstance. Life happens, and therefore, Curbs will occur. Sometimes the Curb affects both people, but most typically, the Curb is a (w)hole event for only one of the two in a PAIR. When this happens in the context of a PAIRing, the one suddenly in the (w)hole begins to show the other member of the PAIR the secret "Not Me" expression. This can be quite surprising and shocking.

Let us look at what has occurred. Alex's "Not Me," the loud, bossy, opinionated part, is suddenly quite present. Barney is shocked. "Who is this?," Barney wonders. Alex, after calming down, is also shocked and feels ashamed. "Who was that who showed up?" Apologizing, Alex promises never to yell like that again. Unbeknownst to Barney and Alex, Alex's mother always yelled like that when Alex was growing up, and Alex had promised never to be like that. Barney is secretly worried, and is now unknowingly teetering on the edge of a (w)hole. Barney had grown up in a family where they were always yelling in mean, critical ways. It had been awful. Yes, they had been wonderfully spontaneous and fun-loving, but their sudden, critical and mean reactions were very painful. Barney had learned quickly to get out of their way by withdrawing or getting quiet or simply leaving.

Alex's reaction is now a Curb for Barney. Having learned in the past that yelling back was dangerous and might elicit a smack across the face, Barney gets very quiet and pulls back emotionally. This is Barney's "Not Me" coming to the forefront – quiet, withdrawn, sullen, and tense. Alex feels the distance and the change in Barney. Alex becomes anxious that Barney has stopped wanting to be in a relationship. Alex begins to be extra nice, and Barney, upon feeling some relief, begins to show up again as "good old Barney" – fun-loving, messy, and action-oriented. The dance between the PAIR is beginning to be established. In essence, we can assume a number of truths in PAIRing:

> Our PAIR will be our most frequent Curb.
> Our PAIR will be our greatest (w)Hole Helper.
> Our PAIR will be a version (if not many) of our Horrible Truth.
> Our PAIR will be our "Not Me" expressed right in front of us.
> Our PAIR will blame us for being their "Not Me" until we each take
>   responsibility for our own (w)holes – both sides of it.
> Our PAIR is our reminder that only we can collapse our own (w)holes. No one
>   can do our Intentional Spiraling for us. It is our choice.

In PAIRing there is no place to hide from our (w)holes or in our (w)holes. Our PAIR brings to us the greatest of all gifts – the invitation to embrace all of ourselves one (w)hole at a time. We will be all of these things for our PAIR as our PAIR will be for us.

If you look at the paper you drew, you can now begin to see that in intimate relating the "Me's" and the "Not Me's" begin to flip back and forth between the PAIR. In effect, Alex is Barney's "Not Me," and Barney is Alex's "Not Me." Was this planned consciously? No. Is it inevitable? Yes. Why?

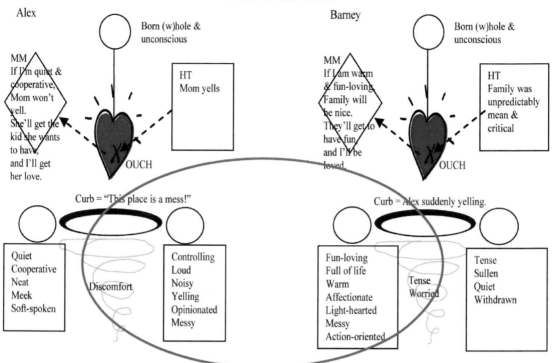

Alex

Born (w)hole & unconscious

MM
If I'm quiet & cooperative, Mom won't yell. She'll get the kid she wants to have, and I'll get her love.

HT
Mom yells

OUCH

Curb = "This place is a mess!"

Quiet	Controlling
Cooperative	Loud
Neat	Noisy
Meek	Yelling
Soft-spoken	Opinionated
	Messy

Discomfort

Barney

Born (w)hole & unconscious

MM
If I am warm & fun-loving, Family will be nice. They'll get to have fun, and I'll be loved.

HT
Family was unpredictably mean & critical

OUCH

Curb = Alex suddenly yelling.

Fun-loving	Tense
Full of life	Sullen
Warm	Quiet
Affectionate	Withdrawn
Light-hearted	
Messy	
Action-oriented	

Tense
Worried

Sacred Relationship Space

When we are walking around in bits and pieces of ourselves, we are secretly questing for our missing parts. At a deep unaware level we sense the presence of our "Not Me" with as much yearning and fearing as we consciously enjoy the presence of the other's "Me." All PAIRings and PAIR moments of tension and of love will take us directly to our (w)holes and the Horrible Truth moments and fears, as well as to our Meaning Making strategies. Activating Intimacy is first of all awakening intimacy with our own inner selves. This means we must become intimate with all of our "parts," our *internal* PAIR. Yes, every "Me" and every "Not Me" are just PAIRs calling for activated intimacy.

PAIRing is first and foremost a decision to awaken to our own (W)holeness. This is what I believe Harville Hendrix, my favorite relationship therapist (who wrote *Getting the Love you want & Receiving the Love you find*) means when he says, "Our relationships are a spiritual path." PAIRing will challenge us to choose to Intentionally Spiral our own (w)holes so we can bring into the Sacred Relationship Space our own (W)holeness. Without that step, the space between the PAIR will become contaminated with the Meaning Making strategies of both parties. Doing our (w)hole play matters to all PAIRings in which we participate. Intentional Spiraling is a profound preparation for a single person getting ready for intimacy, an employee getting ready for a new job, and prospective parents getting ready to welcome home their newborn child.

Contamination of the Sacred Relationship Space

When two people begin to interact, inevitably there will be Curb moments because both participants come into the space with (w)holes. Along with any (w)hole is a Meaning Making strategy which is designed to establish and re-establish the (w)hole to avoid further pain and difficulty. The struggle between two people inevitably rests upon one question: Whose Meaning Making Strategy will predominate over the Relationship Space in any given moment?

Remember, our Meaning Makings saved our lives, and they are now running on automatic pilot beneath our conscious awareness. Often it takes an activation of intimate relating to reveal the MM system that is running underground. Neither PAIR will be comfortable releasing his/her hold of the survival method (MM), for it will invoke within them a sense of risk. Each member of the PAIR created his/her own personal form of "Intimacy Risk Management," which we have known up until now as the Meaning Making Strategy.

Intimate relationship is the context in which every one of us felt our first OUCH from our first Horrible Truth. Our original Intimate Relationship Space is the emotional environment to which we responded by creating (w)holes. Attempting to manage the Free Will responses of the "other" (initially the Big People) so we could "feel better, safer, and loved" is the fundamental motivation of every life (w)hole. Our life (w)holes are our personal efforts to reduce the risk of hurt, pain, shame, and blame within an intimate relationship. In a PAIRing framework, I call our individual Meaning Making systems our **Intimacy Risk Management systems** because we imagine they will prevent the other from hurting us just like we were hurt by our Horrible Truth moments. Unfortunately, our Intimacy Risk Management systems operate to harden our hearts *against* the risk of activating intimate connections.

Upon entering a space of intimate relating with another adult, our original Intimacy Risk Management systems (MM) will be particularly on alert. The closer we get to someone emotionally, the greater the likelihood we will experience hurt caused by that intimate other and the more anxious we become. The reason for this is simple. Our initial relationship with the BIG people of the Horrible Truth was as intimate as we could get. This primary relationship is our FIRST intimacy, our FIRST intimate encounter, and our FIRST experience of feeling "separate from." These are all the same thing. We're left with a quandary – do we move closer, or do we flee?

Once we are exposed to a Horrible Truth, we make an assumption (unconsciously) that *all* others have the potential to be or behave in this same dangerous way. As the intimacy increases in a relationship, so, too, does the fear that this other person will create another Horrible Truth experience. Put simply, the greater the intimacy of a PAIR, the more activated our MM systems become and the more critical it becomes to establish *our* Meaning Maker as "the way" things will be. All we are doing is making an effort to ensure safety, love, and acceptance *our* way. Here is the trouble – the other PAIR is doing the same exact thing!

The Sacred Relationship Space gradually becomes contaminated with a struggle between two Meaning Making or Intimacy Risk Management systems. This is not merely a cognitive tangle. This is an emotional brawl which engages all of our passionate life determinations from which every (w)hole is created. As the skirmishes increase in urgency and frequency, most PAIRs conclude that they are simply not meant for one another and proceed on to another relationship.

The Sacred Relationship Space can be contaminated by three elements:
- The Meaning Making systems of both PAIRs fighting for dominance,
- The lack of Intentional Spiraling skills for collapsing life (w)holes (rather than assigning blame on the other),
- A fundamental terror rises up in each person when confronted by their own internal assumption that the other will recreate the Horrible Truth event. **And** there is also a hidden longing for that Innocent Unity, shattered so long ago. Both of these are opposing PAIRing reactions: "Stay away" and "Get Close"

The excursion into Intimate Relating is made most interesting, potent, and possible by the precious act of Sorting. As we sort through our (w)holes, we invite our PAIR to do the same:
Sorting my (w)holes from your (w)holes
Sorting my Horrible Truths from your free-will choices
Sorting my Meaning Makings from your Meaning Makings
Sorting and owning all my "Me's" and "Not Me's"
Sorting yesterday from today
Sorting me from you and honoring both as equally valid.

Again, we can see that the simple skills of sorting and using curiosity without judgment is at the heart of active expansive Intimate Relating. Each person in a PAIR is invited to engage first in their own (w)hole work. As each person moves into the space of being willing, able, and ready to own both sides of their own life (w)holes rather than push their "Not Me" off onto the other person, the Sacred Relationship Space begins to be cleaner, free of debris. Recognizing a life (w)hole and using the power of Naming to sort and own one's own shattering allows your PAIR to do the same. The Relationship Space begins to be spacious as the clutter of each person's (w)holes is taken back into the sphere of the individual.

Typically, PAIRs initially experience relief that there is someone who is carrying the "other side of their (w)hole" (their "Not Me"), and this is part of the experience of falling into like/love. What a relief it is to be completely free of *that* part which we had so long ago disowned. Now, the PAIR partner can carry this aspect we have decided is not allowed. "Free at last"

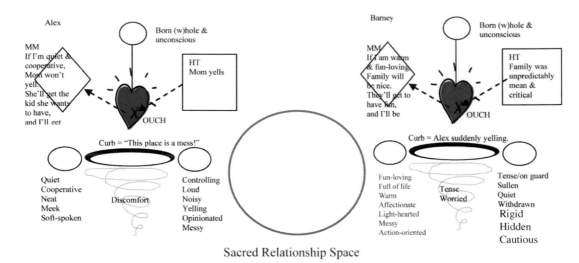

Sacred Relationship Space

is the subtle but potent sensation as the other takes up this task. The difficulty is that no one can be a part of you. You are you, and they are them. Recognizing this "separate from" condition is part of maturing a relationship space. Allowing the experience of separateness is a first step in sorting or Intentional Spiraling within a PAIR context. Ultimately, it is this that allows for the sacredness to enter into the space between the two people. There must be clearly two separate beings before the experience of Intimate Relating feels like oneness. It's a paradox.

For example, Sally's Meaning Making strategy sounds like this: "If I am always carefully thinking everything out ahead of time, be an adult their way, then they (originally her mom and dad) will approve of me and my choices, and they will get a 'mature' daughter, and then I'll get to be loved by them." Her HT was "Mom and Dad judged the kids' immaturity as cause for dismissal." (No room for "childish" behavior). Sally's "Not Me" will be all the wonderful, spontaneous, wild, kid-play qualities and expressions that she had to push away to prevent further shame (OUCH) moments.

Sally's (w)hole comes with her into her relationship when she meets Mike. She is especially drawn to Mike who is "so fun-loving and wildly playful, putting off the hard work until the last minute." How precious it is to meet our "Not Me" face-to-face, literally, and be able to fall into love with ourselves. This is the first experiential moment of Activated Intimate Relating. Our Yuckies and our Meaning Maker will be alerted to the dangerous "Not Me" as the PAIRing becomes more and more intimate. Inevitably, they'll kick into "high gear" through a Curb experience with our PAIR. As we reinforce pushing away our "Not Me" parts, this will also have the intimacy effect of pushing away that expression of our PAIR, of pushing our PAIR away from us. Of course, this same thing is happening inside the other person. Is it any wonder intimacy difficulties are so common?

Sally is feeling the "bliss" of romance until she begins to experience increasing frustrations with what she calls "Mike's irresponsibility," which is Sally's distorted judgment of her "Not Me" kid-ness. She begins to try to "fix" or "correct" his behavior so that she is more comfortable. However, she is actually working to get her "Not Me" back into its correct position – across a space and out of the way. Mike begins to resent Sally's demands and "nagging," which is Mike's distorted judgment of his "Not Me" adult-ness. Even without sorting through their entire (w)hole anatomies, we can already see that they are both operating as (w)Hole Helpers for each other. There is only one question. Will they both do their own individual Intentional Spiraling enough to clean up the contamination of the Relationship Space itself?

Cleaning Up the Contamination

It isn't complicated to clean up the Sacred Relationship Space if each person of the PAIR is willing to engage in their own Intentional Spiraling. We could say that every relationship struggle is an invitation to own our own (w)hole work. When I say "own," I mean to acknowledge that your (w)hole(s) are present and affecting the space, to admit that you are the only one who can sort and collapse them, and to honor your PAIR partner and yourself by getting your focus back upon your own (w)holes and your own (W)holeness.

No one can do your (w)hole work for you because you are the only one who knows the particulars of your (w)hole creations. You cannot do your PAIR's (w)hole play for them. No one can do the work for another, not your PAIR partner, not your therapist, not your friends, not your coach, not your parents. You can always try it, but it will never work because no one else is the expert of you. All of these folks may ask you all sorts of questions that may help you clarify your (w)hole. This type of assistance can be extremely valuable and very helpful with your (w)hole work, and there is lots of this assistance available through your friends, and your coach, your therapist. The key word here is assistance. They can help you, but they cannot do it for you. Only you have the authority and capacity to choose your (W)holeness in the face of the greatest of all risks – loved or not.

Every relationship tangle confronts both people with a Portal Moment. As you know, the challenge of the Portal is to choose to be both parts of you, the (W)hole of you whether the other approves or not. This can feel like an ultimatum – the (W)hole of me OR the relationship. Can you see that this is just another (w)hole (with the key word being "or")? Yes, choosing to be (W)hole can sometimes mean that a PAIR separates because it is just too much to sort out. On the other hand, when two people choose to stay and do their own Intentional Spiraling before speaking to their PAIR, true miracles occur! The relationship becomes truly authentic because the (W)hole of two people are entering into the Sacred Relationship space. Again, it is a question of Free Will choices – your Free Will choice to do your (w)hole work, or not, and their Free Will choice to do the same.

A (w)hole Play Opportunity for You and Your PAIR

Sketch out your (w)hole where your PAIR Partner has been a Curb for you. Invite your PAIR to do the same thing. Then, put the two (w)holes next to each other. Now, invite yourselves to engage in a sharing and an unveiling using these curiosity questions. Remember, the "No Rules" Rules still apply.

How is your PAIR your "Not Me?"

How are you being your PAIR's "Not Me?"

How is your Meaning Making opposite to your PAIR's Meaning Making?

How is your PAIR's Meaning Making opposite to yours?

How has your PAIR embodied your Horrible Truth?

How have you embodied your PAIR's Horrible Truth?

What part of you is your PAIR inviting you to welcome home?

After asking all of these questions, step back, take a deep breath, and let go of blaming your PAIR for a (w)hole you created long before you met them. Our PAIRs are just Curbs and (w)Hole Helpers inviting us to reveal (w)holes we created long ago. How might you receive their gift?

Conditional Regard

Consider this. What led to (w)hole creations to begin with? The **conditional regard** of the Big People. We would be "accepted" as long as we got rid of that part, on the **condition** that we get rid of that part. What is the one risk we are trying to avoid by living within the constructions of our (w)holes? The risk is to experience a repeat of this non-acceptance of who we really are by someone that matters. It's the risk of the Horrible Truth happening again. What is the risk every **PAIR Portal Moment** asks us to take? We risk showing up as we really are – (W)hole. We risk being loved or not by them. It can be a terrifying risk to boldly choose to be our (W)hole selves and find out how they will respond this time (the Unknown AND)!

There are two risks at these **PAIR Portal Moments**. One risk is to find out **how they respond** if we show up as us, with all of our parts. Will they love and/or accept us, even when we have this part? The second and most important risk is an internal one, to find out **how will we respond to us**? Will we love and accept our self, even this part of us, **regardless** of their response? Will we stand by ourselves without shattering again and dare the challenge of receiving a rejected part of ourselves? Each time we collapse a (w)hole inside of us, we are saying "Yes, I accept that I am this too! I accept more of me, even that previously disallowed part."

Each time we collapse a (w)hole, we free ourselves to express "more of Me." When we experience this in a PAIR space where it is allowed and received, the greater (W)holeness is experienced by both PAIRs. This is because when the "Not Me" of one person is received, the "Not Me" of the other person is also involved. Each PAIR is the other's "Not Me. This is the wonderful gift of The (W)hole Point Wisdom WAY model – **(W)holeness invokes more (W)holeness.** And this (W)holeness invites Free Will and freedom into the Relationship Space, which invites greater intimacy and "oneness."

Activating Intimate Relating

PAIRing offers each person in that PAIR repeated and exquisitely accurate invitations to embrace their own (W)holeness. The invitations come in the form of falling into (w)holes. Each person in a PAIR will fall into their own particular (w)holes, with their own distinct MM, HT, OUCHes, feelings, and Portal choices. Each person in a PAIR will operate as the Curb and the (w)Hole Helper for the other in the most surprising and amazing ways. To truly activate relating that is both intimate and (W)hole, **each person** must choose to embrace their own (W)holeness and risk bringing all of themselves to the Sacred Relationship Space.

Our particular life (w)holes are simply how each of us have dodged, skipped out on, and avoided this one very risky choice. Ever since we experienced our first dreadful Horrible Truth because of the dangerousness of the "other," the relationship space itself became a Curb. The choice to engage in intimate relating automatically brings us to this Curb. The Curb and the Horrible Truth in a PAIRing context have the same name: my intimate partner! There are no Horrible Truths, and there are no Curbs without other people!

The only question is whether each participant will choose to take on the joys and pains of collapsing their own (w)holes. The bald, naked truth is that the Relationship Space is sacred and (W)hole to the degree that both members of the PAIR choose to risk all. The "reward" of a truly intimate Relationship Space comes from this willing to risk it all.

Activating Intimate Relating is the choice two people can make through the inescapable experiences of falling into (w)holes in each other's presence and by choosing to "risk it all" – daring to embrace themselves over and over again in the presence of another. The Sacred Space between the two of them has the potential to expand to include "even that and that and that part" **if** each person takes full ownership of their own (w)holes. This "if" is the key to it all. **Both** people in a PAIRing situation are responsible for their own (w)holes and the fact of their impact upon one another. Of course, physical safety of both partners is a pre-requisite to any Intentional Spiraling. In this exploration I am assuming that safety, mutual regard, and respect are the platform upon which a PAIR can fully engage in the wondrous awakening of their own (W)holeness.

Risking It All!

Risking it all means to dare to risk showing up with each new part of you discovered in the darkness of a (w)hole, bringing it into the light, sharing it with your PAIR, and having the guts to find out how they receive even this part of you. Risking it all means to dare to embrace each "new" true part of yourself (the true parts that have dropped the distortions), dropping all self-judgments, and thus, allowing yourself to receive yourself, independent of the other's response. Through this act of mutual risking, the intimacy space is activated between the PAIR. The (W)hole Truth is that (W)holeness is brought alive in and through an activated intimate relationship space.

An Important Notice Before You
Read the Section on Spirituality

In this more advanced Intentional Spiraling expedition, you will be offered an opportunity to look directly at what you have been unconsciously worshipping. Before you read further, please pause and consider if this is an advanced element of (w)holes that you truly wish to explore at this time. Our religious up-bringing and beliefs are very personal. For some they are at the place where curiosity and exploration are not welcomed as it pertains to their religious orientations. For others it is exactly where they want to go. I would ask you to be the expert of YOU. This section on Spirituality with regards to your (w)holes may or may not be something you wish to read at this time. I offer it in this book because it is something many are interested in exploring – that does not mean it is for you!

Please make this determination yourself based on what you know about you. After all, that is the (W)hole Point – to be your own authority over your own life. I am NOT the authority of you.

*In this section we are **not** exploring organized religion, but the belief-systems carved out of and inside your own (w)holes. Many students report being surprised and relieved to be empowered to sort out the difference between their religion, their spirituality, and their family mythology. There is a very big difference between one's religious background, one's spirituality, and one's family mythology. These differences are of great significance when one is in a (w)hole.*

You now know that (w)holes hold our secrets, secrets we keep from ourselves. You know that our (w)holes are places and spaces of distortion.

The Distortion Effect does not stop around the elements of our identity (the "Me" and the "Not Me"). It bleeds into all other aspects of our lives. One of these aspects is the beliefs we hold about "That which is greater than us." Some of us believe that there is nothing beyond this life, and some believe we return many times to this physical experience. What I would like to explore here is the intersection between our psychology (i.e., our (w)holes) and our belief constructions hidden beneath the surface of every (w)hole. Questions about the nature of life will be left to those with far greater knowledge.

Chapter 21: Waking up in the Intersection of Psychology and Spirituality

Our Family Mythology is Our Original Spirituality

When there is a tension between these three elements of belief (religious background, one's family mythology, and one's original spirituality), a person will experience a sense of spiritual dis-ease, which is another effect of (w)holes. How might one come into awareness of how (w)holes reveal distortions in our spirituality? What makes this important?

If we are living our precious lives based upon an automatic and hidden belief structure, while espousing another belief system on a conscious level, we are at odds with our own (W)holeness. This is the essential nature of all (w)holes. There is a tension of opposition between one part of us and another. This interior "push/pull" saps our life force, leaving us in state of low level spiritual fatigue. Now we can say, "It is just a (w)hole" *and* "Oh, it is a (w)hole!" Let's take a look at another way our life (w)holes are invitations to ever-deepening, ever-expanding expressions of our true (W)holeness.

In this advanced section, we delve more deeply into the wonders revealed and hidden in our (w)holes. I would encourage you to first do a number of your own (w)hole studies based on the materials you have already read so you can be most prepared for this advanced work. Jumping into the spiritual aspects without a firm grasp of the basics of Intentional Spiraling will not serve you.

Our original "religion" is formulated at a cellular or limbic level as we are creating our (w)holes. This is a radical statement! Yes, I am suggesting that a type of religion or worship is just beneath the surface of every (w)hole. Of course, we are unaware of this at the time we are creating our (w)holes. Every (w)hole is rooted in our first set of beliefs that we have to pro-scribe for ourselves to keep us safe. Some of these beliefs are "told" to us, and some are our own creations; however, only the beliefs that we choose, albeit unwittingly, form the basis for our particular original religious orientation. At the time I first originated the Wisdom WAY map, I was oblivious to this dimension of the material. It was only later, after many of my own (w)hole studies and those of my students, did I come to perceive this veiled aspect of our life (w)holes.

Consider this: Primitive religions in which children were sacrificed to please the "gods" or appease the "god's wrath" were based on the same premise as every life (w)hole. Our personal primitive original religion or orientation of "worship" is, in fact, our original spirituality, and it is forged from within our particular family mythologies or context. We all do this **inde-pendent of the religious instructions we may be given**. Our personal primitive belief system is created from a child's perspective and within the secret spaces of perceptions, often hidden for years if not our entire lifetime. Let us begin where we began before, with the Horrible Truth.

The Horrible Truth is not only the events or experiences we felt were "horrible;" they are also a part of our family's mythology. We experience this mythology as children, as if it were fact, foundational givens in our lives. As you look at what is revealed about your unconscious spirituality using the Wisdom WAY map with some additional overlays, you may be quite startled. This is an advanced application of the basics of Intentional Spiraling. This section does presume you are well versed in the basics. Now, let us begin to go deeper into the amaz-ing worlds of our (w)holes.

Your personal, ancient, old-time religion begins to sprout in the ground of your being in the very first moments of your life, weaving and twining its way through all the crevasses of your daily life. It will remain active as it is unless you choose otherwise. To choose differently, you must be able to see what you already have in place. What is amazing about revealing your original spirituality, or old-time religion, to yourself is that you give yourself the opportunity to recognize the depth of impact that your (w)holes and Meaning Making have had upon your life's spirituality, religious orientation, and the flow of your life force from childhood all the way into adulthood. Each of your (w)holes offers you an opportunity to examine how you have been at worship, where you worship, and who your "gods" have really been.

We begin with the same map or universal framework with which you are now familiar.

The Horrible Truth "Temple" and the Horrible Truth "gods"

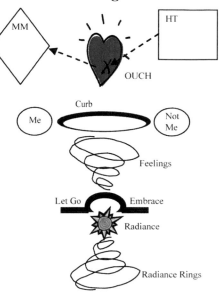

You were born (W)hole and unconscious. All was One in your Innocence Unity. Then you began to experience the horrifying fact of the other. These were the "big" people in your life. They are, in effect, the "gods" of every child's life. What they say goes regardless of the felt experience of the small person. Consider for a moment some of your earlier memories. I am sure there isn't one of us who doesn't have recollections of how they made us "do this" or "stop being that" simply because they were Big and we were Little. They had the power, and we didn't. They got to say how things would go.

What I am about to say is very potent. Let me make a few things very clear first. This is **not** about the value of religious beliefs. This exploration is **not** about any one particular tradition or religion. Everything I am about to reveal to you is about the spiritual elements inside of every life (w)hole. The intersection of the psychological and spiritual dimensions of our being is where (w)holes are formed and where they collapse. Understanding the original belief constructions and how they formed inside our (w)holes is particularly helpful for those on the self-development path. This leaning towards awakening our (W)hole selves requires us to look deeply into the foundations of our life, and it is for this reason that many of us have a great pull towards spiritual studies. Make no mistake, (w)holes have a direct impact on the depth and authenticity of our spiritual awakening.

The "gods" of our lives were there right from the beginning of our physical experience. They were bigger, stronger, and more powerful, and essentially they directed what would or would not occur. You can't get more "god-like." The dictionary defines "god" as "the Supreme Being, the ruler of the universe, that which presides over worldly affairs, any deified person or object" (Random House College Dictionary). Consider what you just read. Feel it. Who were your first "gods?"

Isn't this exactly what our caretakers are? They were the "gods" of our life from the moment we were born. They had a say over what happened in every moment of our lives. They cared for us, or not. They fed us, or not. They responded to our cries, or not. Those big people in our lives were very, very BIG. They were as big as "god!" This is a simple, yet very profound feeling experience and fact of being born a human being.

What makes this part of the Horrible Truth? The HT is all about "them" and is not about "us." Therefore, not only would we put a description of a horrible behavior of theirs in the Horrible Truth box, we would also put their entire way of relating to us in this same box. Perhaps, your "original gods" were kind. Perhaps they were abusive. Perhaps they were something in between. In any event, they *were* the "gods" of your small life. How they responded to you, how they treated you, how they loved or didn't love you mattered deeply! It mattered more than anything else, for your world and your life depended upon the "gods."

If we can face this secret Horrible Truth that they were our first "gods," we are already well on our way to revealing our original religious persuasion. This is a big "if." This dimension of the Wisdom WAY perspective on (w)holes invites us into a deeper level of Compassion Expansion. Can we look at and admit the truth of the "gods" while at the same time love them for doing their best, despite their own (w)holes?

One student of mine said, "I feel as if I have been run over by a steam roller," when she recognized how her original belief system had affected and distorted even her formal religious training. This one (W)hole Truth is a big eye-opener. The first "gods" of our life are those who were the supreme rulers of every moment of every day. We might have called them mom and dad; we might have called them gram or poppy, or maybe they were our foster care parents. Whoever they were, all of us had those big people who cared for us at least enough to keep us alive. These "gods" and their manner of tending to us registers in the most profound depth of our being. In fact, it is how our "gods" responded to us that begins the (w)hole journey of creating (w)holes to save our lives from pain, hurt, risk, and judgments.

How they treat us and how they love us and their behavior towards us has the clout and authority of "GOD." Doesn't this make sense? Our very existence depended upon them. Regardless of whether our primary caretakers were kind or abusive, present or absent, rich or poor, married or single, parents or grandparents, they are "god" right from the moment we are born. The prime directive of our life becomes to either **appease** their wrath when they are displeased and/or to **please and idolize** their awesome powers when they are happy with us. We do all this without any conscious awareness for one purpose: Keep them alive and as happy as possible so we get to live!

I could say it another way: Keeping the "gods" of our lives happy, ideally, and, at minimum, keeping them from reigning their potentially lethal wrath down upon us is all that matters. Now, when they are happy, we are happy. When they are displeased, we feel our fear of "god's" displeasure, and we respond in whatever way we imagine will appease them. Essentially, we have only those two choices: appease or please. Our expressions of pleasing and appeasing are as unique as we are. The relationship between the "god" and the "little one" is determined by the interface point between the two. So, for example, we know that children raised in the same family each experience the family uniquely for the simple reason that different people interact differently. If we look closely at the "god" to "little one" relationship, it becomes clear that it is a "worshipping position." As kids, didn't we all look up to the BIG big kids, the BIG big people? As kids, didn't we all look up to someone? Occasionally we hear, "Oh, he has a crush on his teacher" or " She just follows her dad around like a puppy dog." These are examples of the "little one-BIG one" relationship. These are examples of our original unconscious worship.

The position of the worshipper is based on the attitude of "I'll appease them or please them – whatever it takes!" As the "little one," we are at the mercy of the "gods." As the "little one," we will do all we can think of to live, to be safe, and to be loved even a little bit!

The image I often refer to is that of the primitive religions in which the children were sacrificed at the top of the stepped pyramid to appease and please the "gods." Essentially the position of those at worship was one of powerlessness before the "All Powerful Beings." Obviously, this is a vulnerable and tenuous position. Rain was needed for crops to grow, and lightning-sparked fires were a threat to their homes. Nature, the unpredictable "god," could wreak havoc in an instant. No wonder the people were willing to give up even their precious children to appease this "god." The BIG people were trying to appease the even BIGGER "gods" in an effort to establish their safety – even at the cost of their own children.

This is exactly what we do with some notable differences. Yes, there are sacrifices. Yes, there are officials of ceremony. Yes, there are altars upon which our tributes are laid. Yes, there are the fires. The difference is that **we** are all these different elements! We are the sacrifice, the presiding officials, and the tributes, as well as the fires that all were thrown into! Let's look at this more closely.

We are the sacrifice, and at the same time, we are officiating at the ceremony. What is sacrificed or, we could say, offered in tribute to the "gods," are the parts of us that have been deemed unacceptable. What we lay upon the altar are our inner children that we call the "Not Me's." These interior primal religious ceremonies occur over and over again with the effect that less and less of us gets to live. If we use the analogy of primitive religions, more and more pieces of us are cut off from our (W)holeness, placed on the altar of the gods for the purpose of appeasing or pleasing. The worshiper (you and me as children) is engaged in this entire process without conscious awareness, which allows it to run automatically. Finally, at some level we believe that these interior ceremonies will affect the "gods" in the way we are intending. This is our original religion. The particulars of our form of worship and the nature of our offerings are unique to us.

Let me say this same thing in (w)hole language now. Big people behave in a way that feels horrible and threatening to us (HT). We want to appease or please them to prevent a recurrence, so we make a Meaning Making bargain (MM) with religious fervor and zeal. We figure out that if we lay a piece of ourselves on the altar of the "gods," then they will accept the tribute and become a benevolent caretaker. **We worship by making (w)holes!** This is our original religion or belief structure.

You can begin to see that the name of our Horrible Truth "god" is whatever horribleness we are seeking to prevent. For example, my father chose to die by his own hand. This is a fact. A Truth only. Abandonment was the horror for me. I would do nearly anything to appease the "god-threat" of abandonment. Cutting off parts of myself seemed a small price to pay to avoid the wrath of that "god" and the repeat occurrence of that horrible thing. Now, the original actor in this particular story was my father, but my interior religion generalized over time so that anyone I loved who threatened to "abandon" me would strike terror in the heart of my child self. When this occurred, the interior ceremonial sacrifices would begin. What did this look like? I would diligently seek out the cause **in me** of the potential threat (the Power Point Shift). I am sure you can see it coming now. I would then implement a Meaning Making plan and create another (w)hole to appease/please the "god," stay safe from it's wrath, and live to see another day.

Our Meaning Making strategies of hope are also our unique forms of "worship." Our ancient religion of childhood includes our form of prayer and homage. It includes our form of making offerings of tribute. Creating (w)holes and naming parts of ourselves as the disallowed ("Not Me's") is how the actual interior tribute to the "gods" is made. Making (w)holes is our original form of "prayer" to the "gods" of our world. Our "prayers" are heart-felt and truly offered. It is for this reason, among many, that our (w)holes are so persistent. They are our greatest and youngest "prayers." They are our most primal "religion." They are keeping the "gods" appeased/pleased so we can live!

The Horrible Truth temple or shrine is found in the Horrible Truth box. **What the HT "gods" did**, in particular, is what we were so hurt by. How the "gods" acted, what their behaviors towards us were, how they responded to us as the "little ones" become boiled down to elemental, visceral images. Perhaps it was their sudden yelling or their silence or their absence or their abrupt changes or just that they were bigger. Whatever it was that they did, said, didn't do, or didn't say that felt horrible becomes what we place our focus upon. This becomes the "god" we must appease or prevent. The "gods" of our childhood paradoxically aren't really the people who did those things. The "gods" are their **reactions** to us! As a "little one at worship" our eyes are on them. Isn't this what most any religions ask us to do? "Keep your eyes on the God," was one statement I remember hearing as a child at church. Without any awareness on my part, I was doing just that, except my eyes were on a different "god" than they meant. My eyes were focused on the "God of abandonment."

In summary, the Horrible Truth is that which we, ourselves, named as horrible and which required preventative measures to guard against its reoccurrence. It morphs into that which we always have our eyes on. Whether we are guarding against or longing for it, either way we are in a state of worship, a deep religious fervent worship. When anyone is in worship, they are venerating, paying homage to, revering, or focusing upon that object of worship. This may be in fear, or it may be in love, but it is all encompassing.

Do you now see that the Horrible Truths and the associated OUCHes have been focus points of our worship? We have our eyes on them all the time. Our (w)holes captivate our energy, our attention, and our lives. This is what every (w)hole sets up: a "worship" for the purpose of appeasing/pleasing and controlling the potentiality of another HT occurrence.

When we fall into a (w)hole, we move into a kind of **religious fervor** driven by the desire to appease or please our "gods." We do this by following our MM plan, which tells us the specific tribute we are to offer the "gods." The tribute is the piece of us that has been named "bad" or disallowed. Our Tribute or Offering is our "Not Me." We take the "Not Me" and offer it in tribute with the hope that this will prevent further wrath, danger, or horrors from occurring. This religious response is part of what contributes to the urgency of a (w)hole.

It might sound like this, "I must do whatever it takes to ward off the danger or to earn the blessing of the 'gods' right now, or I am in lethal trouble." To recognize this additional aspect to our (w)holes and to move into a heart-felt space of admitting to ourselves what we have been up to is a potent transformational step of Intentional Spiraling. This is a courageous spiritual **act of maturing** our (W)holeness and ripening our authentic spirituality.

Let me remind you that the Wisdom WAY is **not** about blame or shame! It is all about motion in the direction of (W)holeness.

The temple or shrine of the HT "gods" is visually represented in the Wisdom WAY map in the Horrible Truth square in the upper right corner of the diagram.

A (w)hole Play Opportunity for You

Take a blank piece of paper and draw the HT box in the upper right corner. Now add a small rectangle beneath the HT box and attach it to the box. This is where the "god" of a (w)hole is named.

Now write in that box a guess of the name for something that the big people in your life did that was especially threatening or dangerous or hurtful or "scary." For example, in one of my (w)hole studies, I wrote "Father killed himself" as my HT and "Leaving" was my HT "god." Don't spend too much time on this. This is just a first draft.

Pause for a moment and consider how amazingly creative and loyal a follower you have been to this HT "god." You have spent much of your life engaged in a primal religious effort to manage this "god" of your existence. With determination, persistence, and total dedication, you have lopped off parts of yourself in service of this mission. And you have done this without any conscious awareness of your dedication. Now, as a worshipping NUB, you can begin to appreciate the intensity and depth of your faith. It required the greatest of all offerings – pieces of you!

There is a hidden premise in this "NUB worship" posture. The hope, the magical idea buried here is that a particular piece of you would appease or please the "gods" in a way that would preserve your life and ensure your greatest pleasure. This is true for all of us (w)hole creators. This is true of every (w)hole we have ever created! It's no wonder that so many of us feel confused about our personal spiritual orientation! There are conflicting time zones and conflicting belief structures combined with our profound urgency to be "successful" worshippers.

We have done all of this without any conscious awareness. We did this without consultation with anyone. We figured all of this out, often before we had words. Yes, we are amazing. Not only have we created (w)holes without instruction, we have established our own "religion" and forms of "worship," "prayer," and "offerings" all tailored to the particular "gods" of our little lives. We have been the most fervent of all believers – loyal and steady to our "faith" so we get to live!

Revealing More of Your "Old-time" Religion

Now, on a second blank paper, draw the basic diagram. Take up the whole page so that each shape is big enough to write in. (See the diagram below so you can be sure to include every aspect.)

Begin by picking a life (w)hole of yours that feels alive to you right now. Begin by filling in all the various shapes with the essence of each wisdom element. It doesn't have to be a huge (w)hole, just one of those places in your life where you get tripped up and fall into. It is helpful to have the most recent Curb clear in your mind. Tip: the fewer the words, the better; the more kid-like, the better, and the more "ouchie," the better.

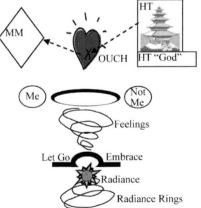

I have found that if you generally follow the order listed on the next page you will move right along; however, if you want to start some other place, do so. You are the expert of you, and there's still no way to fail.

A CURIOSITY LIST FOR INTENTIONAL SPIRALING:

What do you feel when you are in this (w)hole? Write these feelings in the Spiral area.

What was the Curb, the today event, that pushed you into this (w)hole?

What would you name this (w)hole?

What does this (w)hole remind you of from your past, the youngest times you remember? Write this in the HT box in a news bulletin format.

How did that HT feel back then to you? Write this on the OUCH, the "X" on the big heart.

Using the MM formula, fill in the "if-then" solution you created for yourself back then. Put this in the diamond shape. Remember, it is a kid-logic, not the adult-logic you know now.

If I _____(change/ limit me this way)

Then they will (be)_____(the way I want them to be)

They get_____(what I imagine they want)

And I get_____(what I want from them)

Now follow the MM strategy by writing the qualities you got to keep, the "Me's," under the left circle. Write the qualities you pushed away as disallowed, the "Not Me's," under the right circle. Name each list of qualities, making sure that you feel these names and the distortion.

All of this should sound very familiar to you by this time. Notice your increasing comfort with the process of revealing yourself to yourself!

Stop. Now we are going to overlay what you have just learned onto the original Wisdom map. I suggest you use a different colored pen so that you can clearly see what you are now revealing.

Start at the Horrible Truth box. Ask yourself this question, "What was it that they did or did not do that felt so horrible?" This behavior, this expression, this absence of an expression is your **Horrible Truth "god"** by virtue of the fact that when you are in this (w)hole, you are keeping your eyes steadily fixed upon it, on guard for a recurrence. Write the name of your "god" in the rectangle that you will now attach to the bottom of the HT box. This is your "god." It is whatever **the "god"** did or didn't do that hurt so much that you chose to make a (w)hole. The key is to identify the behavior or lack of a particular behavior which is the heart of the "horror." This is not about blaming a person. This is about being curious without judgment so that you can identify the **behaviors** that were so painful. Behaviors include words, actions, responses, and the lack of these same three things.

Now, move to your MM strategy. Read it again to make sure you are satisfied. Here are some questions to insure your best level of clarity: Can you see the magical idea? Is it as simple as you can possibly make it? Does it tell you what part of yourself you must keep? Does it say what they get in this bargain? Are you satisfied with what you have written for what you would get? The power here is in the particular. Can you feel the heart-logic as you run your finger from the HT to the OUCH to the MM?

The Spiritual overlay:

In this next step, we are going to overlay the original and primitive belief system of tributes and offerings onto your basic (w)hole. This step reveals the secret "religion" hidden in the Meaning Making strategy.

My Offering: First, on a separate paper write this sentence, "If I offer this _____.("Not Me")" This is your way to prove your loyalty. This action, this effort on your part, is your offering to appease or please the "gods" of your life when you were a "little one."

The Tribute received: Next write this phrase on the same paper and below what you have already written: Then they _____ (name of HT 'god') will be pleased/appeased.

You are honoring their right to whatever they want. You are paying homage to their power over you and your life. You agree that they need and deserve what they get through your sacrifice.

The (W)hole Blessing: Beneath what you have written and on the same paper, write this phrase, "And then I get _____." Fill in the blank with the final phrase of your MM (Line #4). This is what you are bargaining for. This is what you want so much to get that you are willing to lay portions of yourself on the "chopping block," so to speak. In some form or another you are seeking to live, to be loved, and to not be in ill-favor with the "gods."

Now read to yourself what you have written on your paper:

If I offer this _____(Not ME),

Then the "HT god" of _____ will be appeased/pleased

I will be blessed in this way_____

It is the same as the original Meaning Making strategy yet radically different in what it reveals to us. You have now revealed to yourself your own personal original religious belief system within this (w)hole. This same process can be applied to every (w)hole you sketch out. There is your offering, which is the part of you that you are disallowing (the Not Me). There is the tribute, which is apparently what the "gods" would like, and there is the blessing, which is what you are hoping to get by making this offering or (w)hole.

For example: I would write,

If I offer all the parts that make mistakes

Then the HT "god" of Abandonment will be appeased
And then I will be blessed my Father's Presence – reliable connection.

From the "Worshippers" Perspective – How a (w)hole Feels

Offering: "Yes, I am willing to pay this price for the blessing of my 'gods.'"

Tribute: The "gods" will be pleased or appeased.

Blessing: The blessing I will get to is to "safely live" (since the "gods" will not strike me down) and maybe even be loved or wanted in this particular way.

A Summary of the Ancient Religion of Our (w)holes

If I worship my "gods" by getting rid of the offensive part of me and burning it on the altar, then they will change in the way they are responding to me and offer me their blessing in the form of the relationship which I long for.

These are the elements of many world religions. Revealed before you is a portion of your most cherished form of worship: your personal (w)hole "worship" or what I call the **Horrible Truth religion**.

Be gentle with yourself. Be conscious of any value (good, bad) or judgments you may have. As I said, this is quite surprisingly potent.

Finally, transfer onto your (w)hole study the three phrases below and fill in the blanks with your particulars. Put them next to your MM strategy.

My Offering made: _____
The Tribute received: _____
The (w)hole Blessing: _____

The particulars of your way of worshipping in this (w)hole are now before you. The name of the "god" of this (w)hole is now before you. You have revealed to yourself one of your **HT "gods"** and one aspect of your primitive religion. Every (w)hole contains this level of revelation as well as all that you originally showed yourself. Because we have many (w)holes, we actually have a series of HT "gods." At first, this can be a bit daunting. However, after a period of engaging in Intentional Spiraling, there is a clarifying of the essence of your "god" which seems to apply to nearly every (w)hole. Our (w)holes are the doorways to the mysteries of ourselves and the pathway to our living (W)holeness. Every (w)hole is rich with secrets and filled with precious invitations.

The Sacred Invitation

Every (w)hole offers a sacred invitation in the form of a spiritual question. You may choose to accept the invitation by answering this question: **Do you wish to continue to worship this HT "god?"**

You are the only one who can answer this question. It is for you and you alone to determine your "gods" and your form of worship. The Wisdom WAY is a map of Free Will decisions laid out in particular by us and for us on our behalf. It is true that the Wisdom WAY map is universal, and yet, it is meaningless without *your* particular presence, questions and answers. You are the only one who can respond to the Sacred Invitation of conscious (W)hole spirituality.

It is time now to introduce you to **TheySheHe** and the sacred acts of Sacrifice and Surrender into.

TheySheHe

Who is TheySheHe? Put simply, it is the "they" or the "she" or the "he" that you have named, in particular, in your Horrible Truth box. This is the name of the "great supreme ruler" of all of your life until you say differently. Have you noticed that each (w)hole is built on the premise of managing the reactions of your particular TheySheHe? When we create the space between a "Me" and a "Not Me," we have agreed in that moment to engage in worship of the Horrible Truth "god" TheySheHe. If we were to observe the (w)hole creation in slow motion, what we would see is the inner turning toward the authority of TheySheHe and an abdicating of our own authority over our lives.

Worshipping at the altar of our particular TheySheHe is what every life (w)hole involves whether we are in awareness of this or not. This is a (W)hole Truth. Use the model to see this part of you for what it is without judgment. "How interesting" is often a better response than "This is awful." Be gentle with you. All (w)hole creations were your best efforts to save yourself from the "horrors." Curiosity without judgment is essential as you walk ever more deeply into your own (W)hole Life.

We find ourselves in a (w)hole, again:

There we are; we have tripped on a Curb that reminds us in a feeling way of a Horrible Truth. We feel the similar and familiar OUCH. There is an unconscious primal panic: "Who will take care of me? Who will keep me safe? Who will tell me how to be?" "If I can't be all of me, who shall I be?" "Where is the Big person?" In that moment, we turn to the only source we know – TheySheHe, who is our caretaker and is also the one who participated in the original Horrible Truth experience.

When create a (w)hole, there is an interior abdication of our power. It feels like a desperate ultimatum. They *have to be* my "god," or "I am without a god." This is the ancient spiritual viewpoint of a child. Every child needs their "gods." Being without our caretaker is unthinkable, so we turn against ourselves, bowing humbly in homage to TheySheHe. Rushing to either appease or please our personal and particular TheySheHe, we determine what portion of ourselves must be offered up in tribute so we can re-establish ourselves in the good graces of TheySheHe. The HT temple or shrine is the residence of this Supreme Being in our lives, and hence, we are in paradox. As infants and children we are dependent upon TheySheHe, and yet, they are often the actors in the moments of horror. Around and around we go appeasing and pleasing the only "gods" we know at the cost to ourselves of becoming a NUB.

The Believer

Engaged in passionate, frenzied worship while simultaneously being oblivious to the cost of our offerings, which is our (W)holeness, we place on the altar of TheySheHe whatever parts of ourselves we determine (or have been told) are unacceptable. The "**Me" side of every life (w)hole is a "religious fanatic,"** who is fervently chanting its "prayer-plea" at levels of which we are unaware.

In our unconscious religious frame of mind, we willingly give up to this "god" a piece of our voices and feelings and thoughts and essence. We offer up our (W)hole (W)holeness, cutting off what we believe will result in the most pleasing response from the HT "gods." Understand that though this is done without much, if any, awareness, it is still done with great passion. In our worship we do not hold back!

At a vibrational level, this means that we are radiating out pleas with great spiritual energetics attached to them and of which we are unaware. Those who have studied the realm of spirituality know that it is the emotional intensity or vibrational volume that focuses our life force most powerfully. Our life (w)holes are operating as great megaphones, calling forth and re-enforcing our supposed brokenness, even as we are questing for our (W)holeness. Here we can see a spiritual (w)hole inside of the life (w)hole.

The Non-Believer

The "Not Me" is also the **"I know it all agnostic"** – the part of us that doesn't believe! Just as the "Me" side is the fervent believer in TheySheHe, the "Not Me" side is the non-believer. The "Not Me" side is filled with those parts of us that anger or displease the "gods." The "Not Me" is the one being sacrificed on the altar and thus, would have very little faith or conviction of a benevolent being. Inside of every (w)hole we have a **"religious war"** operating underground. There is the "Me" of us behaving as a fervent "worshipper," while the "Not Me" part of us is being laid on the altar offered up to the "gods," screaming, "No. No. Let me live!" Yes, every (w)hole is a religious battle between the believer and the sacrificial lamb! No wonder we have so many outer wars based on religious perspectives – they are a reflection of our own interior religious conflict! In the name of the religion of TheySheHe, we give up bits and pieces of our (W)holeness without a thought or an awareness that this act of worshipping will also reduce us to a NUB.

What Are We Really Praying For?

Each time we create a (w)hole, we take the "Not Me" and place it on the altar of TheySheHe. The particular "god" we are appeasing/pleasing will be named as the behavior we experienced in the Horrible Truth moment. Because we have many (w)holes there are a myriad of deities to whom we fall down in worship. For example, I used to worship the "god" called "Abandonment" by constantly keeping my eyes on signs of this horrible potentiality. It was a form of (w)hole meditation, a silent meditative chant of "Don't leave me. Don't leave me. Please don't leave me."

Another one of my HT "gods" was "They know best about me – they said so!" and so I placed on the altar my capacity to "trust myself." My meditation chant was directed towards looking to them for approval, direction, and validation. Again, this is a form of (w)hole meditation, with my silent chant of "Am I good enough yet?" These acts of mediation or chanting our "**prayer-pleas**" are disguised "religious practices" hidden within our (w)holes.

Our "prayer-pleas" are fervently, passionately chanted over and over again on automatic pilot almost as a subterranean hum. Is it any wonder we find ourselves so many times experiencing the same type of HT events happening? We are accidentally, unconsciously praying for a repeat of the same experience.

We offer to TheySheHe our most passionate attention and "worship." In a more global sense, TheySheHe is also a way to reference the psychological, spiritual, and physical authority that our caregivers have over us as children. However, this idea is rather conceptual until we bring it right down into every (w)hole we trip into and discover the face of TheySheHe staring directly at us, inviting our worshipful sacrifices. In the next sections, we will add even further to the spiritual elements of the Wisdom WAY map. If you are at all unclear regarding the earlier materials, I suggest you stop and review them before proceeding.

The Power of TheySheHe

TheySheHe is that which holds us all in the core mistaken conviction that this "god" is the one who controls our life, not us. In order to believe in the authority of "they" or "she" or "he," we must give up our own authentic power to choose for ourselves, to live as experts of our own selves. Essentially, we are **reducing ourselves to followers** in our lives rather than as leaders of our lives with choice. In some way or another we all find ourselves at worship of our particular supreme HT "god." The unique name TheySheHe takes on will vary in our (w)holes; however, be assured that TheySheHe is present.

When we fall into a (w)hole, we begin to **chant** in a secret chamber in our hearts, "I believe. I believe. I believe. I have given you this piece of my (W)holeness. Let me live. Love me. Do not forsake me," bowing and kneeling in desperate homage. These chants are also parts of our prayer-pleas. The (w)hole is dark pit of terror. Our terror is that the "god" who has always been there with us since the beginning will forsake us to our death. So we adamantly shatter our (W)holeness, giving up bits and pieces of our (W)hole being to ensure the ongoing benevolent presence of TheySheHe, the one who gives us life.

No wonder (w)holes are big deals. No wonder so many of us have spent years working on the "issues" only to have them reappear in some mutated form or worse, in the same old form. We had no idea that we were actually faced with letting go of our primitive, primal, original religious belief system. Without conscious awareness, there is a core refusal to let go of what we "know" has saved our lives over and over again.

Every "issue" that has repeatedly shown up in your life is simply a mutated form of your primitive "religion." These do not just "go away" despite all we may hope for or wish for. No wonder we find ourselves going around and around the same stuff. We didn't know to look towards the hidden dimension of our own ancient "religion." There is a premise at work here that keeps us enthralled with the HT "god" or TheySheHe. It is the firm conviction that **life-giving power resides outside of us**.

The activity of this original spirituality is one of doing and working and using all of our creative efforts to appease or please that which is outside of us. After all, where does TheySheHe reside? Outside of us. Here is the big news. The "they" or the "she" or the "he" you have wanted to change or control has Free Will! Yes, hidden in every (w)hole is the spiritual issue of Free Will. Hidden in every Horrible Truth is the fact of Free Will. Disguised in every Meaning Making are our frantic efforts to eliminate or control the Free Will of the other. Here is the (W)hole Truth: They have Free Will, and we have Free Will, but as children we didn't have access to our Free Will. Each (w)hole invites us to embrace our own Free Will. **All our (w)holes are invitations to acknowledge our Free Will and their Free Will.** By doing so, we are freed to live our (W)hole Life for real.

Every (w)hole invites us to admit this Wisdom Truth: *They* can't actually be controlled. They get to choose what they will or will not do, regardless of our "burnt offerings." This is the secret we kept from ourselves over and over again. We have hidden it in every (w)hole we have ever created. We refused to embrace the Wisdom Truth of their Free Will and the Wisdom Truth of our Free Will.

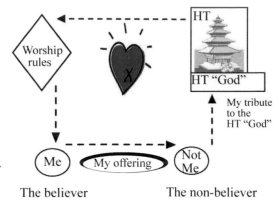

The believer   The non-believer

The central Wisdom Truth found in all (w)holes is **We all have Free Will all of the time**.

Let us Live

This is true no matter how it may feel and no matter how it may look. AND it's no wonder that we took on a religious posture that our freedom is externally controlled and sourced! In the beginning of our lives the BIG people are in charge of our lives, and we depend upon them. Yes, originally, our life sustenance is outside of us!

We were infants, powerless to even walk or talk, so we submitted to their power over us. We were physically little and at their mercy. There was no choice. The difficulty is that we didn't know to stop doing this. The difficulty is we didn't know what our strategies would ultimately cost us. The difficulty is we didn't know or understand about Free Will. Every (w)hole we fall into is an invitation to grow up our spirituality from the inside out and to live from our Free Will authority.

As children we are powerless and very dependent, so we embrace them as our "gods" and often fail to ever engage with our own power of acting and choosing.

Free Will pivots around our attachment to TheySheHe. We have spent many years unconsciously worshipping as a way to manage the scary issue of Free Will. "If" we all act upon our Free Will, what might happen? As long as we are in our (w)holes, we can avoid this essential spiritual question! However, that does not mean that Free Will or its existence disappears. It just means we are hiding out from knowing the impact it has on our particular lives.

Look again at your (w)hole study that you began a little bit ago. Do you see your form of worship? Do you see your version of TheySheHe? Can you feel the depth of your religious fervor? Good for you! If you don't yet, that is OK, too. Just keep being curious, dropping judgment, and doing your (w)hole studies, and you will begin to feel the ripening awaken within you.

Where Our Psychology Intersects Our Spirituality

If a person *only* does psychological work or if a person *only* does spiritual work, there will come a time in which they will notice that they are "stuck" or "ungrounded" or "something isn't enough." Commonly, students will come to me saying, "I have done so much work on myself in therapy, but something is still missing." Or, "I have been studying spirituality for years and have done a great many spiritual practices, but I just keep falling into the same messes!" What makes the Wisdom WAY model so potent is that it accesses the intersection point between our particular psychology and our particular spirituality. The Wisdom of our particular WAY is found at the point where psychology and spirituality intersect inside our personal (w)holes.

A (w)hole Play Opportunity for You

Look again at the basic map of Wisdom, which so deeply reveals our secrets. Notice, we are able to sort and locate ourselves both spiritually and psychologically. Our primitive religious efforts can be sorted and revealed by looking and feeling and sorting all that is above the portal in the diagram. Begin just as you now know to do. First Spiral your (w)hole by sketching out the basics of your (w)hole study. Then apply the spiritual orientation to the (w)hole you have chosen. I suggest you create a clean clear version of your (w)hole study and then add the spiritual wisdom elements. Do this before reading further.

Here are some spiritual questions to ask yourself?

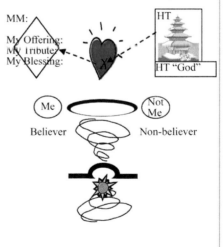

What or who is your Horrible Truth "god?"

Are you pleasing or appeasing the Horrible Truth "god?"

How are you worshipping: What is your tribute?

What part of you are you offering?

What blessing are you hoping for?

Where does your life force and power lie – inside of you or with TheySheHe outside of you?

Are you living from your own Free Will or by their will?

Identifying the Horizontal and Vertical elements of Your (w)hole

The **psychological or "horizontal" line** on the diagram represents our expressions in the world. Notice that the "Me" and the "Not Me" are across from each other in a (w)hole. This is the Horizontal aspect. The **horizontal dimension of (w)holes is that which is related to relationships**: the relationship of me to me and the relationship of me to others. The horizontal is a way to refer to the psychological.

The **vertical dimension of (w)holes refers to that which is "greater than us."** You may call this Spirit, God, Presence, Source, Nature – whatever you choose. What is relevant is to know that the vertical refers to a spiritual dimension which all (w)holes will reveal to us, in particular.

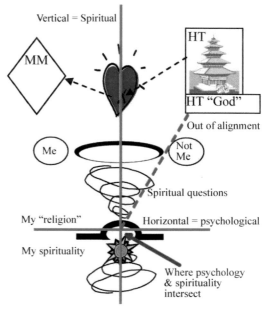

Initially, as I explained the Wisdom WAY model, I primarily spoke of you and the other. This is the way of viewing the model from a horizontal perspective. It is at this level that I always begin introducing folks to (w)holes. In this section I am adding the vertical spiritual dimension, which is what you choose as your "greater-than-ness" framework. Again, I have no attachment or preference for how you choose to refer to "this greater-than-ness." For ease alone, I will use the word "Spirit." Let it mean what you choose. The orientation to that "greater-than-ness" is what matters. I call this the **vertical orientation**.

The spiritual or "vertical" line down the center of the diagram represents where we direct our worship. When we are worshipping TheySheHe, the vertical line will be drawn from the Portal to the HT temple. Notice this is an "out of alignment" or crooked position, and the point of intersection between the Horizontal and Vertical is no longer at "right" (literally "right") angles. When we are conscious of our (W)holeness, we are in alignment: Honoring the Free Will of self and other, Trusting ourselves to live our lives our way (not the way of TheySheHe), and Sourced from inside out rather than outside in. The questions we might ask ourselves are: Who do I say I am? From what internal position do I make decisions? Is my Source inside of me or outside?

A (W)hole Truth: (W)holeness comes alive at the intersection of the vertical and the horizontal when they are in "right" relationship to one another.

Orienting Oneself in a (w)hole

Above the portal we will find our HT "gods," our "religion," our "prayer," our "offerings," and our hoped for "blessings." It is only *below* the Portal, in the Rings of Radiance, where we finally begin to live our own spirituality. I like to call this the "spirituality of the (W)hole Me." Be careful. I do not mean a self-centered life. I am referring to an orientation that is grounded upon solid and conscious psychology and spirituality.

The solidity of our psychology is based essentially on collapsing (w)holes and welcoming home our disallowed parts. The more of Me I am, the more solid my presence is. The level of awakened Spiritually is the degree to which we live from inside out, as opposed to outside in. When we are orienting our lives to TheySheHe, the source is external to our being. When we are living from our own (W)holeness, Radiance, Life Force our own way, the source is internal (where it has always been).

Again, it all comes back to collapsing (w)holes. When we are in a life (w)hole, we are by definition in worship to our personal TheySheHe. When we are empowered (W)holeness, when we are living our (W)hole Life, we are by definition in sacred celebratory play, being ourselves without fear or apology.

Spirituality based in and on (W)holeness is one that can be summarized as "All parts are welcome to the table of Me." Until we allow for the conscious intersection of psychology and spirituality in the particulars of our life, we will not be able to live our (W)holeness. It will remain only a concept.

Let us now move on to the Portal as viewed from the perspective of the spirituality overlay.

The Sacred Spiral Dance of the Portal

Having revealed to yourself your own personal religion of TheySheHe, you offer to yourself an invitation to shift from what I call *doing* "Horrible Truth religion" to the practice of *being* "(W)holly Me spirituality." Put more simply, you now have an opportunity to change your mind.

Up until now we have been operating from a point of blindness, chanting the chants and offering burnt offerings. There are but two steps to the **Spiral Dance**. This dance is what occurs at the Portal. In one way, you have already been introduced to the movement of waking up to your own Wisdom. I shall now deepen your understanding and teach you more of the dance.

The action-choice of Letting Go of the Meaning Maker magic and the action-choice of Embracing the "Unknown AND" has already been discussed. When we overlay the question of spirituality onto the basic map of The Wisdom WAY, we must return once again to the Portal. It is here where the question of our Free Will comes into greatest play. We get to choose. Do we continue to worship TheySheHe, or do we choose the mystery of our (W)holeness? When we choose to go through the Portal, we begin to collapse the (w)hole on the vertical (spiritual) dimension.

The Vertical and Horizontal Dimensions of the Portal

Life (w)holes have both a horizontal (psychological) dimension and a vertical (spiritual) dimension. The horizontal dimension is explored directly by mapping out a (w)hole study for yourself as you have learned earlier in this book. The vertical dimension is addressed as you allow yourself to reveal the actual truth of your worship of TheySheHe. This primitive worship is based on the spiritual (w)hole you created between yourself and your true power. Essentially, we have all handed our true authentic power over to the TheySheHe's of our lives. Since a (w)hole is a space between, it quickly becomes evident that we have (w)holes that are oriented on the vertical dimension as well as the horizontal dimension. This may, at first, seem complex, but remember, "they are just (w)holes," and you know lots about (w)holes.

Choosing our spirituality consciously is something we often believe we have done, when, in fact, at a more primal level, we have been on a "religious automatic pilot." Now it is about expanding our awareness and opening up to a greater vision of ourselves and our spirituality. It is a call to step into the empty unknown void of a living, breathing spirituality of being-ness, of being (W)holly who we are. This is a Mystery until we are being it in that moment. This type of spiritual life is the (W)hole Point, being unknown even unto ourselves until we are known in the experience of ourselves in the moment. To do this we must sacrifice our precious TheySheHe and surrender into the wonders and surprises of who we are.

Discomfort with these choices is different than refusing to use your Free Will to choose again. This Portal, as is any Portal, is awkward and a bit scary. Stepping into the unknown is not a comfortable place. So breathe, be gentle, and drop all judgments while staying deeply curious.

The two actions of the Portal Passage are the same as before (Letting Go of the magic and Embracing the "Unknown AND") and yet, are different. In the Portal, as you can now see, our psychology and our spirituality intersect to reveal our interior belief system, which I call our "HT Religion." To choose a new spirituality requires us to collapse the (w)hole and risk the "Unknown AND" of ourselves as Spirit. This means we need to step into our own Free Will and risk exercising our power to choose on our own behalf and express ourselves by our own authority. This is the only way I know to deeply and authentically change our interior form of worship. This choice to re-create our spirituality, to mature our religious faith, is the invitation offered by every (w)hole we've created because every (w)hole is part of our primitive religion.

Imagine a vertical line and a horizontal line intersecting. The point of intersection is where the Portal forms. The vertical line is a representation of our spirituality, while the horizontal line represents our psychology or Meaning Making and (W)hole Management System.

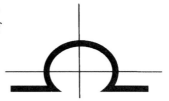

The steps of (w)hole collapsing remain the same. The only difference is the expanded awareness of all that you are letting go of and all that you are offering yourself an opportunity to embrace.

Look at your (w)hole. To collapse any (w)hole, there are two steps. I call these steps the **Spiral Dance of the Portal**: **Letting Go** and **Embracing**. You are already familiar with both of these. When we add the spiritual dimension, these two activities morph into the actions of **Sacrifice** and **Surrender** into. Letting Go becomes the action of Sacrifice. Embracing the "Unknown AND" becomes the action of Surrender into.

First there is the sacrifice, and then there is the surrender into the greater form. This is for the same reason as before. First, we must make room by letting go of that which is no longer serving us so that there will be space for what is new. Only then can we embrace something bigger. What we are always embracing is our expanded awareness of more of who we are. Let us look at each one separately as you apply them to your (w)hole.

Sacrifice: "Letting Go Of"

As we collapse a (w)hole from this expanded viewpoint, we now realize we are not just letting go of the Meaning Maker magic. We are letting go of even more. We are turning away from the religion of our childhood. We are choosing to stand up to the Supreme Being – our HT "god" who has ruled our lives and ensured our existence. Up until this moment there has never been a time when we questioned our "god." TheySheHe ruled, and we obeyed. This action of letting go will feel like a huge risk, a huge sacrifice, and often as a sense of loss.

When we choose such a sacrifice, we are knowingly, consciously, letting go of the deeply held belief that "they" or "she" or "he" knows us better than we do. We now get to choose whether or not we will remain in our primal worship, avoiding the great leap into mature spirituality. No wonder we tremble in fear at those times when we were confronted with the choice of collapsing a (w)hole. Whether we knew it or not, we were standing up to our "god."

Yes, it is appropriate to allow the word "sacrifice" to be applied to this grand release. With each (w)hole that we collapse, we repeatedly challenge ourselves to embrace our power. We are releasing our childish view of the world. We are admitting to ourselves that we are not servants to the outer they's and she's and he's of our bosses, our partners, our parents, and even our circumstances. The option of victimizing ourselves in the name of TheySheHe is sacrificed over and over again as we collapse our (w)holes one after another after another.

An image I find useful is that of watching a huge scaffolding breaking apart and falling down. This is what is happening as we sacrifice our primitive religious convictions. At the heart of each (w)hole is a core spiritual position: TheySheHe is bigger than we are, and we are less than. We have, for reasons already mentioned, believed that TheySheHe can save us from life and all its risks. Our fervent belief has been that by laying a piece of ourselves on the altar of the HT "gods," we will successfully ward off life's dangers, at the least, and at the very best, be blessed by TheySheHe.

When a child is young, they often have a "blankie" or a "binkie" that they carry with them for comfort. Each of us has unwittingly hidden in every (w)hole a spiritual "binkie" of TheySheHe. When we choose to collapse a (w)hole, whatever one it is, we are choosing to sacrifice a long-held cherished comfort. This comfort is the belief that something outside of ourselves can save us, tell us who we are, and live our lives for us. As children it is true that the adults direct our lives. We are adults now. With every (w)hole we fall into, we are giving ourselves an opportunity to grow up spirituality. This process of Intentional Spiraling our (w)holes is a maturation process. It is a decision to step into our (W)hole lives with all of us present and in charge by own authority and Free Will!

What a profound invitation.

So how do we do this? We take a deep breath. We name our HT religion for what it is. You can find it in your Meaning Making magic. And then we sacrifice the wish to be "saved from life" by TheySheHe. We admit to ourselves that our life is in our own hands. We face the fact that as an adult, the HT "god" isn't all that powerful. In a manner of speaking, this "god" is like the wizard behind the curtain. It is time to reveal the (W)hole Truth of TheySheHe. The power of this sacrifice is found in making it particular to you. This is not a conceptual approach but rather a direct encounter with your own true choices.

It is important to know that we are sacrificing this old belief system, and at the same time, we are **not** creating a new one. The (W)hole Point is to melt the frozen places within us – those places which have been frozen in time, those places we call (w)holes. The next step is **not** to make another (w)hole or "fixed" position within us. To do this would defeat the purpose of Intentional Spiraling. In a sense, we are sacrificing the idea that there are any "rules" at all, at least in terms of how they apply to our beingness, our (W)holeness. We are letting go of having a proscribed way of being assigned to us by TheySheHe. We are sacrificing the luxury of hiding from our own Free Will creation of ourselves found in each moment. Our (w)holes are fixed or frozen places in us of a pre-determined way of being or reacting. In a manner of speaking, having a pre-designed "way to be" does take pressure off of us to be present in our lives and in each moment. However, it leaves us puppets to our Meaning Maker dictates. Without our pre-determined "Me's" and our pre-rejected "Not Me's," *who* are we?

Each (w)hole is particular, and therefore, each sacrifice will be and feel slightly different. However, at every Portal, which is at the bottom of every (w)hole and which is the only doorway to our own (W)holeness, stands TheySheHe. We are essentially sacrificing our belief in TheySheHe. This a step of great personal and spiritual courage. The sacrifice at the Portal includes laying aside our particular belief that there is a TheySheHe and that this "outer god" will save us from life happening or save us from us having to live our lives.

Surrendering Into

Embracing the "Unknown AND" is also expanded with the understanding that comes as we sacrifice TheySheHe. Embracing is too small of a word to describe the wonder of the gift we offer to ourselves. What is before us without this buffer of our HT "god?" What is before us is the **empty unknown void** of being ourselves in each moment, naked without directives, choosing and acting from our own authority. What is before us is the unknown self of ourselves without the proscribed identity of "believer in them."

Who are we if we are naked at each moment? How do we make choices without the Meaning Making rules of beingness that we have so consistently turned to? Who are we if we are not following the dictates of our interior religion? The answer of *who we are* will not be made known until we are being it in that moment. This is what we are invited to embrace. This is what we are invited to surrender into. By sacrificing the comfort of our TheySheHe worship, we are also deciding to move into a state of **surrendering into** the "Unknown AND."

We are choosing to surrender into being the (W)hole of ourselves – a surprise in each moment over and over again. We are choosing to admit that we can be nothing but ourselves; everything else is the fantasy of a child. We have not been this being called (W)hole self since we created our first (w)hole eons ago. We are surrendering into – as in falling into the truth – being who we are, not the censored, fixed, and frantic adjusted being of our (w)holes.

Surrendering into the vast unexplored reaches of being (w)holly ourselves is a choice of great magnitude. It can only be a choice of the heart. It is a choice that requires more and more of us with each (w)hole we confront. With each (w)hole collapsed and each "Not Me" embraced, who we are transforms again and again into greater and greater unknowns. The essence of living spirituality is being who you are in each moment freely, without paying homage to TheySheHe. As we do this more and more of our Holy Light radiates from the center of our being, naturally and without effort. Each (w)hole is a call to sacrifice our old-time religion and belief in TheySheHe. Each (w)hole is an invitation to surrender into the "Unknown AND" of more of us: our inner light.

What are the "Hands & Feet" of Surrendering Into? It is to do just as you already know to do. Name this unknowable expression. Since you are this **and** that, who do you say you are? Look at your (w)hole. Say out loud, "I am _____("Me") and I am _____("Not Me"). Since I am both, who do I say I am?" Name yourself. With this you surrender into the greater presence you are. With the name comes the admission that we are both these sides of the (w)hole and we choose to be (W)hole of Me - **loved or not, blessed or not, chosen or not** by TheySheHe.

That is the risk; that is the choice; that is the wonder of the Portal. "Whether I am loved or not by that particular TheySheHe, I choose the (W)hole entirety of me by my own authority and Free Will." This is the act that we have sidestepped, avoided, and danced around since we first began to create our (w)holes. Our Life (w)holes are invitations to move into great revelatory moments of honesty with ourselves about our true beliefs, worships, and "gods" so we can once again choose, but this time with conscious awareness. Our (w)holes are a call to authentic conscious mature spirituality. How very precious every (w)hole you trip into really is – they are the Great Mystery's call to us to awaken into our (W)holeness, to empower ourselves and overthrow the throne of our personal TheySheHe's, and to come once again into our full unity of being.

It really does matter what you do with your (w)holes and your (W)holeness. It matters to the (W)hole world, beginning with your world.

What is a (w)hole? Now Look More Closely.

There is a great deal more to say about the Spiritual aspects of life (w)holes, but let this last bit suffice. As you read the next phrases and thoughts, let them sink deeply into your being, knowing that every cell of your body, every vibrational aspect of your being is resonating to the essential Truths of (W)holeness.

A hole is a space between.

A life (w)hole is a space between parts of ourselves.

A (w)hole is a question.

A (w)hole is an answer.

A (w)hole is an invitation to the Truth of you.

A (w)hole is a call to wake up to who you are.

A (w)hole is a distortion of who you really are, which is A Radiant
  Pulsating Being of Light

A (w)hole is believing in a made-up "Less than-ness"

A (w)hole is a particular form of worship.

In essence, we could summarize what you now know so far by asking two very particular questions:

The (W)hole question is: Who do you say you are?

The (W)hole answer is: Whoever I choose to name myself – (w)hole or (W)holeness.

We could say life is this series of questions coming into our field of awareness over and over again in each moment.

Will I express this "Me" and this "Me" and this "Me?" If your answer is "yes," you are naming yourself more (W)hole with every (w)hole you collapse.

Then there will be another (w)hole, and a question will be asked again. Will I trust this "Me" and this "Me" and this "Me?" If you answer "yes," you are trusting yourself (W)holly.

Then there will be another (w)hole. And a question will be asked again. Will I feel this "Me" and this "Me" and this "Me?" If you answer "yes," you are feeling yourself as (W)holly.

Then there will be another (w)hole. And a question will be asked again. **Will I embrace this "Me" and this "Me" and this "Me?"** If you answer "yes," you are embracing yourself as Holy.

Then there will be another (w)hole. And a question will be asked again. **Will I be who I am?** *And who will you say you are?*

This is the (W)hole Truth about (w)holes. (W)holes are the Universal Story in which each of us participates in our own unique way. We are a piece of handmade crystal, each of us etched with our own patterns called (w)holes. We are also the same, just as all the great wisdom traditions will tell us. We are One.

Regardless of our (w)hole etchings, our path is Universal, and the Spiral Life we walk is the same:

There are Horrible Truths,

There are Meaning Makings,

There are "Me's" selected as acceptable expressions,

There are "Not Me's," the disallowed expressions,

There are the Curbs of today,

There are Portals, created and placed at the bottom of every (w)hole,

There are invitations to let go, to sacrifice our hidey (w)holes,

And finally, there are all the "Unknown ANDs."

It doesn't matter what (w)hole you start with. It doesn't matter if you "get *all* the answers" since you can't fail. It doesn't matter if you fall into the same (w)hole over and over again. It doesn't matter what your stories are. What matters is that you say "yes" to being all of you, one (w)hole at a time.

Yes, Intentional Spiraling is a way to orient yourself when you are head first in a (w)hole, but it isn't the answer either. You are the answer.

I offer you one last bit of wisdom. The (w)hole most folks make at this point is to make a (w)hole about having (w)holes. To say this more directly, you can use the Wisdom WAY as just one more way to judge yourselves – for having (w)holes – which some folks have done until they realized this was just another (w)hole. Instead, you can use it as a bright light that you can turn on in the darkness of a (w)hole so that you can find the doorway at the bottom. You can use the Wisdom WAY to walk awake saying, "Yes, I am the expert of myself." It is truly your choice how your exercise your Free Will.

Chapter 22: Waking Up in the Business Environment

Business environments are essentially conglomerations of people joined together for a purpose of profit or service, with the additional unavoidable effect of many (w)Hole Helping challenges for all involved. These (w)hole challenges may be called "management issues," "employee difficulties," "corporate takeovers," "departmental competition and conflicts," "employee conflicts," and "inadequate management of human resources" – just to name a few. As you know, (W)holeness is about empowering and the implementing clear choices; whether they are made by a human, a team, or a corporation, it matters not at all. When we are operating from a (w)hole, our resources are divided; our energy is squandered, and our focus is split. **(W)holeness makes good business sense.**

In the most simple analysis, any **business challenge** is either the effect of one powerful individual operating from within a (w)hole or the interaction of two or more (w)holes between staff members, departments, intra-company divisions, or corporations. These situations are so widespread that a new profession has emerged called "Executive Coaching." Executive Coaching is designed to help executives sort through their inner and outer complexities without shattering themselves while, ideally, maximizing the effectiveness of their resources. The executives of businesses are expected to manage a tremendous load of details and personnel issues as well as perform their primary tasks while being susceptible to falling into one of their (w)holes.. All of the employees under their direction are also susceptible to falling into their own particular (w)holes, which affect job performance on all levels. Life (w)holes are not left at the door when folks go to work; however, they are often ignored or minimized or aggravated by the responses of their peers and managers and customers. This only serves to reinforce the difficulties and stir up more (w)holes.

With the increasing intricacy of global economics and rapid worldwide communications, no one is free from the inevitable (w)hole falls personally and professionally. Despite the complexity of these situations, the simplicity of (w)hole anatomy and the (w)hole collapse process may still be applied quite effectively. The capacity to assess any situation in bald, naked (W)hole Truth serves not only the executive but all the employees beneath them, as well as the company itself. For example, the capability to empower a Human Resource department to maximize the (W)holeness of all of its resources furthers the betterment of the entire organization. Anytime there are parts of an establishment at odds with other parts, the loss is immediate to that company. Rather than maximizing the over-all effectiveness of the business, vast resources may be squandered because personnel are trapped in various (w)holes.

(W)holeness in a business is demonstrated by profits, satisfied employees, returning customers, creative solutions to difficulties as they arise, and the capacity to recreate the corporation/business anew in response to changing economic environments. Each business owner determines their particular measures of success; however, in essence, **success is (W)holeness in action**, even in business. For example, flexible, expansive, creative problem solving is not possible if the people involved are restricted to accessing only certain parts of themselves, while disallowing aspects that might provide insight and solutions. Steady presence in the face of rapid business changes and sudden demands is nearly impossible without a way to respond to the (w)holes we will inevitably fall into.

Business (w)holes are revealed through identifying conflicts, struggles, and missed opportunities that are affecting success. A comprehensive review of how the Wisdom WAY might be applied in a business setting is a complex topic and perhaps, the subject of separate book. However, we can take a brief look so that you can see what I mean. Let's use the need for a company to "re-make" itself as an example of how the Wisdom WAY map might help to focus the process. Let me start with the premise that all participants would be instructed in the basics of the model and its approach, as well as having had some direct experience of its application to themselves as individuals prior to this process.

Re-Making From Top to Bottom and Inside Out!

The particulars for any one business will be different, but the power of sorting things out will serve, since the outcome is an expanded focus and greater creativity for all concerned. A common structure that is without judgment and still reveals the points of stagnation is necessary for a "re-make" that is actualized, as opposed to a "make-over" that is lip-service level only.

224

We will begin with the primary tool of sorting. Keep in mind the answers I am offering are not the only ones and are just an invitation to explore the application of Wisdom WAY in the business context.

The Wisdom WAY map as applied to a corporation might sound like this:

What is the Horrible Truth? *The competition is taking away customers and profits.*

What is the Curb? *The revenues are down, and the customers aren't satisfied.*

What is the Meaning Making Strategy? Remember, this is the approach that has supported the old way of doing business and will most likely keep the same viewpoints rigidly fixed and in place, thus sealing the fate of the business concern.

> *If we just try harder, with more determination,*
>> *Then they (customers) will see that we have something valuable.*
>> *They will get our solid traditional products.*
> *And we will get to keep our business alive.*

What is the "Me?" The "try harder at doing the same thing" expression of this business. This includes all the methods used for public relations, for management, for product development, for marketing, and for sales. This includes all the assumptions about what makes our "widget" valuable and worthwhile. It also includes all the thoughts and beliefs about staying with the same way (a proven or safe way) rather than trying something new and risky.

What is the "Not Me?" This side of the (w)hole is initially developed using all the opposites of what we have listed on the "Me" side. However, it is also anything that can be dreamed up in a brainstorming manner without restrictions. Included in this are all methods of marketing, organizational adjustments, sales strategies, new product development, and public relations that haven't been considered because of "the old way works" kind of thinking.

If we drew this out on the Wisdom WAY map, it might look like this:

Before proceeding as a group engaged in the "Re-Make" process, there needs to be a shift to the individual "Re-Make" experience. The reason for this is that a company

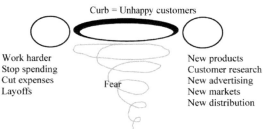

225

"make over" sounds like a great idea until the individuals participating encounter how any "re-make" will affect them in particular. Their (w)hole responses to change will trigger a series of subterranean reactions. It is most useful to deal with this directly.

The individuals participating in a "re-make" of a business will also be challenged individually. Each one of them will experience the challenge of Letting Go of the "old way" of doing things. Whenever we are asked to let go of the familiar, our own (w)holes, fears, and doubts will rise up. At this point in the process, it is encouraged to have each person Intentionally Spiral one of their particular (w)holes using the same Curb. The Curb is "Change in the job environment."

Using this as a Curb, each participant is asked to look directly at what their own reactions might be to the changes that a "re-make" will elicit. There is a well known book called *Who moved my Cheese?* by Dr. Spencer Johnson. The point of this book is that we can't assume the cheese will be in the same place. The mice who didn't shift with the change went hungry. Our (w)holes keep us in a rigid, frozen position of response and perspective because of our Meaning Making strategies.

The (W)hole Truth is that we live stuck and static in our (w)holes until we come alive as (W)holeness. (W)holeness is a dynamic and very fluid experience. Change is one of the greatest Curbs that stimulates the most number of (w)hole reactions. Despite what their words may be, many folks will have interior reactions to the possibility of a shifting work environment. This makes a tremendous amount of sense, especially if we remember that our original shatterings or (w)holes were in response to a horrible change. What occurred back then is that the outer environment became dangerous. Our interior response (MM) was put in place to manage and correct for this change.

What is my point? The point is that an entire "re-make" of a company can be designed and implemented; however, if the particular participants aren't also internally engaged in the "make-over," then there will be subtle and not so subtle sabotage effects. The employees will be falling into their (w)holes frantically – and most likely unconsciously – urgently reinstituting their Meaning Making Strategies while overtly espousing the "re-make." This, too, becomes yet another (w)hole within the entire corporate environment. However, by anticipating this, we can provide a way to support an authentic "make-over." Obviously, there may be those in the company who are unwilling to be open to new learning and growing, then there is that choice too.

Change is associated with many different meanings and previous experiences for everyone. Empowering folks to directly explore their own "Change" (w)holes serves not only them personally but also the company. Remember, exploring (w)holes is all about collapsing (w)holes, not staying stuck in one.

Now let us return to the Global Corporate Re-Make.

Once the Wisdom WAY process of sorting and Intentional Spiraling has brought the group to the Portal, the key elements are now in play. The implementation questions are formed through the two actions of the Portal: **Letting go** and **Stepping into.** For a business to "let go" of the current approaches requires an admission that even if it worked before, it isn't working now. This seems simple and logical, and yet it is where the greatest obstacles rise up. In the act of change, the "let go" action is an act of trust in something that has yet to be tested in the day-to-day environment of the work world.

It may seem easy to convince yourself that childhood magic can be un-done or released, but for the business manager or owner who has created a business strategy as an adult, letting go of the old way can feel like an admission of incompetence, particularly if that is done in a public forum. In truth, this is simply a distortion. Just as we cannot *always* be a certain way, a particular business strategy cannot *always* be the right one for ever and ever. This would only be true if the world stopped changing and if technology stopped evolving. Waking up to the truth of our (w)holes is not only something we do personally, but also professionally. It takes courage to apply Intentional Spiraling, no matter what part of our lives we are exploring.

Just as in individual Intentional Spiraling, this process does require authentic participation AND the full support of the highest level managers. Without this support I suggest the business will settle for sitting in a (w)hole a while longer. Companies are often a reflection of the CEO, and, without his/her full commitment and support, the process will flounder. The ideal scenario is when the CEO and the management team participate fully in the process, including doing their own individual (w)hole work.

For the process of a corporate Re-Make to be successful, the participants are challenged to tolerate the unknown, and release their traditional Meaning Making strategic responses and engage in the risk of empowering a larger vision of the company. This is essentially a corporate (w)hole collapse. No wonder so many businesses end up going only so far! The entire business gets stuck in a (w)hole, and simultaneously its individual departments and individual members are also tripping into their own (w)hole creations.

"Letting Go" and "Stepping into" are the essential challenges for any corporation and for all its participants. Collapsing a (w)hole within this context requires a tiered approach. Each department, each person, and the entire corporation must engage in and participate in Re-Making the business.

Using the WAY for Advancing Employee Health and Wellbeing

No one would challenge the premise that improving employee's psychological and spiritual empowerment leads to business success and endurance. When Human Resource departments offer the Wisdom WAY training to employees, everyone is empowered to perform their jobs better because their (w)holes are not standing in their way. In the case of those who do not choose to move into (W)holeness, their posture is revealed without force by the very framework of the Wisdom WAY model. Because the foundational premise is one of **curiosity without judgment**, any HR department will quickly find that employees will tend to their own (w)hole creations from an open and empowered position. In addition, the HR staff will have the training and the tools available to offer valuable assistance to employees who are engaged in their own (w)hole work. Once people recognize and sort out their own (w)holes, conflicts between people can simply become PAIRing situations, which frequently respond quite well to joint (w)hole studies.

Teams of folks would be able to participate more effectively together and individually because of the PAIRing understandings. Morale would improve because there would be an increased awareness of "Not Me's," and compassion expansion for one's self. The compassion expansion then transfers into compassion and greater understanding of others and their (w)holes.

This is just a hint at some ways this approach might be applied in numerous corporate environments, and it will remain conceptual until it is taken into a particular setting.

It all boils down to this: you, are on one side of a (w)hole and where you imagine you want to go is on the other side of the (w)hole. However, sustainable abundance, for individuals and corporations, is only found on the other side of the Portal.

Chapter 23: Worldwide Radiance
One (w)hole at a Time

Global Free Will

What I am about to say has been said in every great wisdom tradition around the world. In different words and in different languages, we are told the same thing: Free Will is the foundational premise of all of existence. It is a law of the universe. Our Life (w)holes, PAIR (w)holes, corporate (w)holes, and yes, even global (w)holes between countries, are all about Free Will!

We are unconsciously exercising our Free Will from the very first (w)hole we create to the moment we begin to Intentionally Spiral and step through the Portal. The Horrible Truth is a demonstration of Free Will – theirs! It feels "horrible" when we are in the "little" position as a nation, as an employee, as a loved one, or as a stranger. Whatever and however we were received, treated, loved, or abused, the primary actors in that drama were acting of their own Free Will. Now, I know that folks will quickly raise objections – "But they couldn't help it…" "They didn't know any better…" "They should have thought first…" "They could have …." "But I know they loved me even as they…." STOP!

Remember, I am not blaming anyone! I am saying that they had and have Free Will. We **can't** control them. We can threaten someone, but still they choose what they choose. It is this very fact that resulted in our experience of something that we felt was horrible. We didn't choose it! Our reactions are ours. We, too, have free will, and this is the great blessing. We can choose again! Their actions, their words, their absence were their choice, not ours. It is as simple as that.

We can choose to live in our (w)holes or collapse them. We can choose to continue to be "less than," or we can choose to honor the wonder of our own truths. We can choose to continue to flee from the big terrors of revealing our (W)holeness to ourselves, or we can choose to turn and go toe-to-toe with them. We can continue to react from our (w)holes, or we can consciously choose how we want our lives to be. We can continue to be asleep and dream of being all we can be, or we can choose to say, "Yes, I will walk through my days awake being all of me." We can choose to stay stuck in our (w)holes, or we can wake up and live our (W)hole Life. We *have* Free Will.

Free will is the Horrible Truth.

Free will is the Greatest Blessing.

Life is the invitation to walk The Wisdom WAY between the horrors and the blessings.

Yes, this is another (w)hole. Yes, (W)holeness, whatever the context, is you walking awake knowing the WAY.

Will you make a choice to make a (w)hole or collapse one if you discovered it? Will you stop and get curious about your Meaning Making, your "magical beliefs," your truths and distortions? Will you dare to say, "Yes, I am that feeling, too?" Our (w)holes are all about exploring, sorting out, and discovering our Free Will. Our (w)holes are about admitting that it really is all up to us!

(W)holeness is living this admission every day, and when we fall into a (w)hole, choosing to Intentionally Spiral and step up again to the next surprising moment.

Every (w)hole we fall into, get pushed into, or stumble into is an invitation to embrace a greater expression of our Free Will. Folks sometimes ask, "Are you saying it is OK to hurt people?" Absolutely not! That is not what I am saying. The Wisdom WAY model is **not** an excuse to sidestep our own accountabilities or responsibilities or recognition of the impact our actions have upon anyone else. In fact, the Wisdom WAY model is all about being accountable and responsible. Free Will isn't about a free-for-all! Free Will is our natural condition. We have just been hiding in our (w)holes blaming the Horrible Truth or calling out to someone else to take up the responsibility for our life.

Free Will is a spiritual and psychological fact. We all get to choose, even when it doesn't seem like we do. I am not suggesting a "nicey nice" image of life. That would be a distortion of how life really is. Life will continue to happen. Folks will hurt each other. Folks will support each other. People will experience themselves and each other in zillions of ways around the world. That's what makes life so interesting. It's not static and stagnant. It changes in uncountable ways and patterns. However, there is now a difference in our life. We have a map that takes us directly to our choices. Then we get to chose.

Make no mistake; I still fall into (w)holes. I still discover new ones I never was aware of before, and I don't always smile about it! What is different is that I have a path to follow that inevitably takes me to my Free Will choice hidden inside that (w)hole. Then it is up to me!

This book began all because of all the (w)holes I have fallen into, been pushed into, and been dragged into. It came into being because of all the clients and students who shared with me their frustrations and their (w)holes. They shared their confusions about all the ideas of how to tend to this part or that but nothing that brought the (W)hole of it together. This book came about because I chose to sit down and be alone to put words to paper.

I sure am glad that I did because I am now able to offer to you a great, big, shiny light to make your life path easier, to show how your (w)holes are the great blessing that they are, and to reveal to you the (W)hole point! **YOU!**

Our Radiance One (w)hole at a Time

The Wisdom WAY is "All parts welcome to the table of Us."

Over and over again we have explored the wonder, the gifts, the pains, and the truths of a (w)hole. Each time we collapse a (w)hole and re-embrace more of our (W)hole self, we are participating in the awakening of our Radiance. We are participating in the awakening of (W)holeness – globally.

Radiance is a lot like a lost note of our song. Each of us was born with a song to sing, and each one of us has lost some of our notes along the way. Inside each (w)hole that we fall into is a lost note or two of our song. As you now understand, it takes courage, and it takes persistence to re-acquaint ourselves with our missing notes and to sing our own song. And yet, it is quite simple.

The Essential (w)hole

Inevitably, you will discover, if you continue to Spiral, that there is a point where all your (w)holes seem to be the same one. This was not something I initially anticipated when I first began to Intentionally Spiral with my students and in my own life. However, it is so consistent that I now mention this. Treat the (w)hole you return to over and over again as you would any other (w)hole. I call it the **Essential (W)hole**. It does not mean you haven't been collapsing your (w)holes. Your inevitable return to the Essential (W)hole is actually proof of your progressive awakening.

We were born (W)hole. Life happened. We shattered. This, as you know, is the beginning of the Universal Story. When we shattered, we created a (w)hole in which to preserve all of us until such time as we could move into an increased awareness of our (W)holeness. Each time we shattered, we were breaking apart more of the "Me" that was acceptable and thrusting more of what was deemed unacceptable to the far side of a new (w)hole.

That first (w)hole is the one in which all the others are contained. This is the reason it truly does not matter which (w)hole we may fall into or which (w)hole we are Spiraling today. When we are creating motion in any (w)hole, we are automatically creating motion in all of our (w)holes! This is very good news. It takes all the pressure off us to "pick the right one." All we have to do is just Intentionally Spiral whatever (w)hole we notice or fall into.

The Cascade into (W)holeness – the Global Hope

There is a shift of balance or emphasis as folks continue to Spiral with the intent to say "yes" to one more "Unknown AND." After a time, there is more and more of the self that has been welcomed back home. The "Not Me" orphans begin to stream home in a mass of eager and joyous celebration. It is as if the "Not Me's" are now knocking on the door saying, "Let me in now!" "Can I come home?" "Will you say yes even to me?"

Sometimes it seems like there are (w)holes everywhere, and we can feel overwhelmed. The good news is that we know what to do! Breathe, pick one (w)hole, and move into the action of Spiraling. The rest of the (w)holes and all their elements will also begin to move and shift and collapse because they are all connected. It is actually to our advantage to focus on one (w)hole, since sorting out a small pile is easier than an entire mountain of stuff.

Do not make a (w)hole about having "so many (w)holes." We are all full of (w)holes. No one is more (w)holey than anyone else, and no one is more Holy than anyone else. We're all One, playing at being bits and pieces and parts. Having begun to Spiral your (w)holes, you will begin to notice a cascade of "bits and pieces" of yourself waiting to be embraced. The question is, "Will you?" This question is a question that applies across the borders to the our global community. Will we embrace our neighbors as part of the One? Will we embrace the peoples across the ocean as part of the One? Will we embrace the nations on the other side of the planet as part of the One?

Each time you do, stop, and give yourself some credit. It is a signal that you are waking up to who you really are and participating in the global cascade into (W)holeness.

The Table of Righteousness

A long time ago, I stumbled upon an Aramaic definition of the word "righteousness" (Neil Douglas-Kotz). It opened up an entirely new way of being and has contributed significantly to the "Hands & Feet" of (W)holeness. Righteousness, I learned, meant something like "All parts welcome to the table." I had never understood the word righteousness to be anything other than "morally correct" or "upright in behavior" or "virtuous." Whenever I had heard it, I associated it with a sense of judgment. Here was a totally new viewpoint, and I could feel the truth of it. I could feel my own hunger for this to be how I lived my life – **all parts welcome to the table**.

Closing Experience

Welcome to the Table of Plenty where (w)holes & (W)holeness are HOLY

Imagine a huge table in the center of your heart. It goes on for forever and is beautiful in its design. It has a feast of unimaginable richness upon it. At each place there is a chair. You notice that each chair is unique in its design. Some are easy-chairs, each one of a different hue and textured fabric. There are stools of various heights, chairs made of carved wood, each one a piece of art. Some chairs have wide backs, and some are small wooden antique rockers. Each place setting is also unique. Some have exquisite lace placemats. Some have a piece of bark for the placemat. Some settings have beautiful crystal goblets, while others have fanciful plastic cups. Some settings have uniquely crafted silver utensils, while others have large wooden spoons. This table is your (W)holeness waiting for you to say, "Yes, all of me is welcome." You can say this any time you want – YOU sit at the head of the table! You are in charge.

This table is alive; it is pulsating. It expands and contracts depending upon the invitation of the moment. When we fall into a (w)hole, we are saying "No, you are not invited to my table." The seat remains empty although the feast remains. Those elements of yourself that you have deemed acceptable stay seated.

There is no judgment. You have Free Will, and it is honored without evaluation. Yet, there is a "waiting," as if all present know that there is more to come. As the gathering expands with every "yes" you utter and with every "Unknown AND" you embrace, the energy and light around the table grows. It begins to ripple outwards extending a gentle musical call:

"All-me, All-yea, In Come Free," and we fall into another (w)hole so we can meet and greet the newest family member.

Yes, all these guests seated at your heart's table are your (W)hole family. They are you! They are you and me and them and those! Every person you encounter in whatever context you meet them is a "Not Me" or a "Me" inviting you to collapse even that space between until we are truly One in our awareness. This is a radical call to (W)holeness, to Global (W)holeness. Every life (w)hole you trip into is really a call to be the response of (W)holeness as you.

Some of these "not alloweds" are the powerful "Not Me's," the creative "Not Me's," the bold and daring "Not Me's," the "Not Me's" you never, ever thought you could be. Some of them are the most broken parts of us, the "bits and pieces" of our self that only know to resist life every step of the way or want to flee even from living. Some are the angry and ashamed parts that have been hidden in the back corners of our (w)holes.

Many are the elements that aren't so terrible and aren't so great. They're the masses of ignored or taken for granted or held with minimal regard "Not Me's." These are just as precious as the greatest and the most broken. The table fills, and the light ripples out more broadly, all because you began to say, "Yes. I will explore this (w)hole and this one and then that one." All parts must be welcomed for our (W)holly self to come even more alive.

All parts are welcome to the table when you say, not before and not until you say, "Yes, you, too, are welcome at this table of Me."

The greatest secret of all is that there is no end to the ever-expanding Radiant Being you are. There is no destination, no completion, no final "(W)hole Me." Rather it is simply a WAY of being. That WAY of being is saying, "Yes, I am that, too" over and over and over again as you walk through your moments, fall into (w)holes, and feel life being whatever it is. Allowing yourself to Spiral outwardly in ever-expanding rings of radiant light is you being you.

Your wisdom, life force, and compassion for others is found here in this sentence: "Yes, I am this and this and this." The (W)hole Truth is that Spirit already is All-That-Is. We are the ones, the "pieces" of Spirit that are awakening now to this wisdom. We are each a "part of" the One Spirit of life. Every (w)hole collapsed is the awakening and empowerment of the planet. Understand that wisdom is actually "the knowledge of what is true." Your wisdom is the knowledge of the (W)hole Truth of yourself. The (W)hole Truth is unique and universal. It is a paradox. Let it be so.

This table and this gathering is as **you** choose it to be. Most of us have spent much of our lives with very exclusive guests at this table, without any awareness that there were masses of our starving, orphaned "Not Me's" just outside our sight. We were also unaware of the masses of powerful "Not Me's" calmly waiting for our invitation to come in and take their seat at the table. Collapsing (w)holes is not limited to what we might call our "issues" or dysfunctions. On the other side of the spaces are all the "Not Me's" we have disallowed. This includes all the greatest dreamed selves you have dared to admit to and those you have hidden even from yourself.

Expand your vision beyond all boundaries, and consider what (w)holes you have that are disguising or hiding your grandest expressions and your most broken "bits and pieces." Dare to say, "Yes, all of you are welcome at this table of Me!" Then wait and see all of what you truly are, moment by moment by moment.

Watch your light radiate from you, pulsing out the call "All-y, All-y In Come Free, Come Home to BE" around the globe, and the world wakes up with you as the (W)hole Truth: We are ONE (not two).

Yes, it really does matter what you do with your (w)holes, it matters to the (W)hole world!

Yes, it really does matter what you do with your (W)holeness, it matters to us all.

Yes, it really does matter that you wake up to your (W)hole Life – for NOW is the time!

Thank you for YOUR presence – (w)holes and all!

A Surprise Initiatory Invocation

Let me BE this message of LIFE…of HOPE to all people, including myself.
My Hands holding precious all the many beautiful things we have made for ourselves.
My Ears awake to hearing your voices in all voices and sounds.
My Feet, walking as you, upon the Earth's floor…footprints across time to now.
My Eyes beholding the red and purple wholeness of sunrise and sunset and that which IS between…

All made upon our own behalf.

Prepare yourself by breathing deeply and slowly. Soften your body.

When you are quiet within, turn to the Invocation below. Read out loud quietly, as if you were (since you are) in a Sanctuary of the Sacred.

Then…close your eyes for a moment. Feel your physical sensations and your emotional awarenesses.

Now, return again to the Invocation, and read out loud only the ALL capitalized words. Let the message of (W)holeness sink deeply into your being, your cells, and your heart of hearts.

Then once again read the Invocation, this time do it in silence. Let the (W)hole Truth descend upon you as a cloak of "Wisdom-Grace."

Place your hands upon your heart and allow your own (W)hole Holiness to reveal itself to you, one (w)hole at a time, until you feel the cascade of your (W)hole Being into awakened

(W)holeness, as YOU being you.

An Invocation

O Great Shimmering Golden Presence,

whose voices sing to me/us in the winds and call to us/me from the stones.

HERE I AM…Beloved ONE…(W)holeness awakening as itself – now.

I open to ALL-THAT-I-AM: a response in a moment again and again.

Embracing each living minute : all awarenesses concealed now revealed as myself :

I AM WISDOM-GRACE PRESENCE,

Stepping into my greatest expression: BEING ME.

Thank you, Golden Ones, for your witness of my receipt of myself, over and over, again and again,

Softly awaiting me to STEP FORTH from my hidey holes.

Then from every Breath and Step I take,

From every Leaf and Rock I hear…the (W)hole Point…I AM this I am:

Every part of me PRECIOUS—(W)holeness embracing itself.

Thank you for our LIVING-love-SONG—calling me to my own Self.

So your Presence becomes ME, Mirrored IN my eyes, as ONE BEING.

Stepping out of hiding, without shame or fear….

In playful, laughing, dancing celebration…A CHANTING PRESENCE:

Here I AM! Hear, I AM! Here I AM! Hear, I AM!

Revealed again as ME…Wholeness playing at being bits and pieces and parts for the fun of it…

NOW for the Joy and Pleasure of it, I awaken & remember!

There is no such thing as bits, pieces and parts…ONLY (W)holeness…The (W)HOLY Truth of ME

HERE I AM! HEAR, I AM! HERE I AM!

Remember to celebrate your (w)hole opportunities for what they are: Invitations to be Mo-R-e of you!

There will come a time when people will come to you wanting for you to give them what you have found. Don't give them anything at all. Be as normal as you can be – (w)holes and all. Convince them that you are no different than they are. Then, when you are nowhere to be found, the light will come streaming through, and you will touch the other one in a way that words can never explain. By surrendering, all things can be done through you.

Twyman*

A (w)hole, (w)Holy Mystery About the Wisdom WAY Map

I will now admit to something that many of you may have noticed or perhaps not. This is something that those learning the map have reported back to me. This is not something I have done or caused.

The Wisdom WAY map itself seems to be infused with an energetic imprint of sorts, which is laid beneath the written words. Do not be surprised when you find yourself experiencing on-going transformations, realizations, or activation moments out of the blue. As I have experienced this imprint, it is a reflection or mirror of your own Soul Self looking back at you through the map. Additionally, your own Soul's call – **"All-y, All-y In Come Free, Come Home to BE ME"** – is a vibrational resonance or song which seems to be woven as a thread throughout the text and images. You need not concern yourself with this, for all effects are determined by you and your Soul Self. My joy and promise is to open the door to the wonder of (w)holes and the (W)hole Point of them. I share this with you only because my greatest teachers, my students, have repeatedly pointed this out to me. The rest is between you and your Soul Self.

You could do further reading OR you could collapse some (w)holes
&
Change the (W)hole World!

Wake up to your (W)hole Life.
Now is the time!!!

Appendix

Appendix I
Feeling Words

SAD
Dejected

Sorry
Unhappy
Sorrowful
Discouraged
Empty
Choked-up
Despairing
Hopeless
Lonely
Heartbroken

ANGRY
Mad
Jealous
Resentful
Furious
Irritated
Bitter
Defiant
Enraged
Fuming
Critical
Tense
Hateful
Disgusted
Annoyed
envious

HAPPY
Glad
Calm
Content
Satisfied
Peaceful
Pleased
Cheerful
Playful
Blissful
Encouraged
Grateful

Thankful
Confident

Secure
Safe
Elated

LOVE
Welcome
Affectionate
Sexy
Flirtatious
Playful
Connected
Touched
Excited
Warm
Close
Sympathetic
Empathetic
Loved
Caring
Cared for
Supported
Safe
Assured

FEAR
Afraid
Guarded
Scared
Anxious
Terrified
Panicky
Apprehensive
Horrified
Worried
Alarmed
Threatened
Nervous
Cautious
Hesitant
Skeptical

Overwhelmed

HURT
Offended
Crushed
Heartbroken
Embarrassed
Judged
Abused
Frustrated
Victimized
Cold
Insensitive
Shamed
Guilted
Rejected

STRONG
Fearless
Brave
Courageous
Bold
Daring
Determined
Open
Sharing
Firm
Confident
Certain
Proud

REJECTED
Ignored
Unseen
Invisible
Alienated
Humiliated
Shamed
Guilted
Judged
Lectured
Controlled

Distanced
Avoided

OTHER
Jealous
Powerless
Tired
Concerned
Curious
Reassured
Protective
Doubtful
Untrusting
Fascinated
Surprised
Tolerant
Inquisitive
Uncertain
Validated
Inspired
Confused
Withdrawn

Appendix II
(w)hole Signs & Signals

This is not an inclusive list, but a running start to revealing your own signals of being in a (w)hole.

PHYSICAL SIGNS

I say automatic words (i.e. "OK," "You know…" etc.)

I make physical movements I am unaware of doing (i.e., sway back and forth, slapping my leg, clearing my throat, etc.)

I confuse myself in my thinking, in my feelings

I can't think – "Like a deer in headlights"

GENERAL SIGNS

I back up emotionally

I run away – physically and emotionally

I disconnect emotionally

I go blank

I am distant or aloof

I have thoughts in my head

I have screams in my head

I leave the entire situation

I react automatically

SPECIFIC SIGNS

I long for someone to notice me

I create great drama

I focus on the trauma and dive into the extreme feelings of struggle

I wish for someone to "choose me"

I seek validation or approval or judgments or blame

I blame others (i.e., for bringing me down, for doing it wrong, for not being how I want them to be, etc.)

These are some of the ways one notices that they are in a (w)hole. This list was birthed by the "faculty" of teachers at The (W)hole Point Institute in response to the question "How do you know you are in a (w)hole?" Much gratitude to Rochelle, Jean, Anne, Marianne, Lisa, Steven, Steve B., Lizzy, and Alaya—pioneers of embodied (W)holeness! (Alaya is responsible for all adjustments to the listed items)

Appendix III
(w)hole Studies

(w)hole Study #1

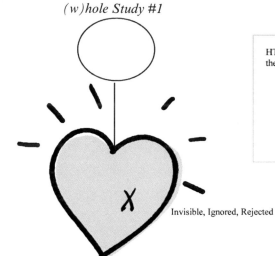

If I do and be what they
value, then they'll see me.
They get a child worthy of
their attention, and
I'll be valuable/ loved.

HT = Parents focused all
their attention on sister.

Invisible, Ignored, Rejected

Ignored by husband

Cookie Factory

Make your own damn cookies

- Make everyone happy
- Anticipate their needs
- Be good at everything
- Flexible/adaptable
- Strong

Exhausting
Empty
Resentful
Rage

- My happiness first
- Fulfill my needs
- Mess up/mistakes
- Rigid/inflexible
- Weak

Let go of belief that by being their
way, they will see me.

Embrace being who I am, whether
they see me or not.

Have my cookie and eat it too.

(w)hole Study #2

If I agree to be her servant, she'll be able to get her work done.

She'll be a successful business woman, and I'll be loved.

HT = Mom used child as "free labor" for her business.

Used, lonely

Asking for a raise.

Cinderella

Wicked Queen

- Do what they want
- Helpful
- Good worker
- Subservient
- Take orders
- Practical
- Controlled

Angry
Unimportant
Degraded
Stuck

- Do what I want
- Selfish
- Bossy
- Demanding
- Give orders
- Dreamer
- Wild

Snow Princess

If I'm independent and thrifty, they'll feel less burdened.

They'll get more for themselves, and I'll be loved and appreciated.

HT = Family was poor

Embarrassed, shame

Buying something frivolous

Amazon Woman

Wimpy Girl

- Independent
- Thrifty
- Efficient
- Intellectual
- Ambitious
- Stylish
- Fit in
- Respected by others

Embarrassed
Small
Powerless
Shy
Angry
Invisible
Silent

- Dependent
- Careless
- Wasteful
- Emotional
- Lazy
- Frumpy
- Shut out
- Ridiculed by others

Let go of belief that money/things can make others love/appreciate me.

Embrace my worth and importance on who I am, not what I have.

Diana the Huntress

(w)hole Study #4

If I'm good enough, she'll come back.

She'll have a reason to stay, and I'll have my mom.

HT = Mom left

Shame, guilt, left alone for no reason

Doing something risky

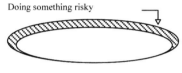

Altar Boy

Rogue

Fear
Self-loathing

- Best behavior
- Quiet
- Do well in school
- Listener
- Striving
- Earn my keep
- Cautious

- Misbehave
- Loud
- Goof off
- Motor mouth
- Easy going
- Lazy
- Risk taker

Let go of belief that I was the reason she left.

Embrace who I am, whether they leave or stay.

Free Spirited Man

Appendix IV

How some theories & practices may relate to The Wisdom WAY

Neuro programming – NLP
Logo Therapy
Constructivism
Schema Theory
Hypnotism
Personality Theories
Freudian Theory
Cognitive Theories
Jungian Theory

Wholeness
Religions of the world
New Age viewpoints
The Beginning
Wisdom Traditions
Creation Theories

Genogram Theory
Sociology – Anthropology
Theories of dysfunction
Family Systems Theories
Biology – Genealogy
Psychological genetics
Object Relationship Theories

Inner child work
Gestalt Therapies
Co-depence work
Journaling – Artist's Way
Suffering

Imago Relationship Therapy
Psychotherapy – Psychoanalysis
Ontology – Buber – The Space Between
Curiosity – Inquiry Theories – Rogerian Theory
Satir – Gestalt Theory – Stone Center Research
Presence Practices
Communication Theories
Carl Jung – Jungian based theories
EMDR – TFT
Shamanic Soul Retrieval – Journeying
Internal Family Systems
Integration of multiple Family System Theories
Parts Theories – Inner Child Explorations

Mindfulness Practices
Alternative Healing Modalities – Reiki – Ennersense
Wicca Practices – Eco Psychology – Ritual Practices
Alchemical Healing Processes & Practices
Embodiment Practices – Experiential Seminars – Yogas
Spirituality Studies – Granting Significance – Mastery Apprenticeships
Still Point Energetic Trainings – Options Theories
Choice Practices – Integration Practices
Tel Shai Ya Training – Oneness Wisdom Traditions
Inquiry Practices – Meditation – Interior Reflection Processes
Stillness Practices – Awareness Practices – Mindfulness
Diamond Heart

Lar Short – Klas
Spirituality – Transpersonal Therapies
Carl Jung – The Book of Job
Holistic Therapies – body & mind & soul
Visionary & other Cranial Sacral Therapies
Holistic Theories
Theologies – World Religions
Unitarian Philosophies – Quantum Physics
Unity – The Mystery of All That is – Paradox
Living a (W)hole Life Consciously
Oneness

Appendix V
(w)Hole Helpers and (w)Hole Spiralers and Spinners

(w)Hole Helper (HH): the person who "pushes" someone into a (w)hole. Most of the time this is done accidentally and inadvertently. Often the HH is unaware of their impact on the Spiraler *until* the Spiraler finds a way to tell the HH. When this occurs, there is an opportunity for great healing for all.

(w)Hole Spiraler (HS): the person who finds themselves head first in the (w)hole, apparently due to the HH. The (w)hole was already there, and the HH simply presented themselves in a way that tripped the Spiraler into the (w)hole.

When you are the (w)Hole Spiraler: As soon as you recognize you are in a (w)hole, begin to apply all your (w)hole wisdom to *your* process. Blaming the HH is merely a distraction from your own (w)hole exploration. Begin to Intentionally Spiral. Sometimes we can only do a "Good for Me," the (w)hole is so painful. Sometimes we can sketch the (w)hole immediately. Sometimes we know we will require a Spinner to come to our aid. Regardless of your particular (w)hole experience – keep in motion, keep pulsating, stay curious, do a silly, and take action while staying in touch with your feelings.

When you are the (w)Hole Helper: This is a precious invitation to deepen in your own work. Being a HH is not just about the person who tripped into their (w)hole; it is also about the HH themselves. Most often the HH has acted unknowingly. "What did I do?" is often a HH's initial response to learning they have tripped someone into a hole. Any indifference to what the spiraler is experiencing when in a (w)hole is a way for the HH to avoid an opportunity to do their own Intentional Spiraling. Below are inquiries you might ask as a HH when diagramming your own (w)hole. This assumes that the HH has been given the gift of information about the HS's experience directly or indirectly. Note: this is not always the case!

What am I revealing to myself about myself?
How is their (w)hole a reflection of my own (w)hole? How are they "Me," "Not Me?"
What impact have I had on them?
What does it feel like to be them (as I imagine it)?
How is their pain mine?
How does their reaction to me make sense? Can I validate their reaction to me, the HH?
How am I their "Not Me?" How am I their "Me?"
What hidden vulnerability of mine have I revealed in being their HH?
What am I feeling as their HH? What have I hidden from as them?
What risk am I asking myself to take as a HH to them?
How am I the HT I haven't wanted to be?
What secret have I hidden from myself that is now revealed by my being a HH to them?

What gift am I offering myself as I am being their HH?
How might I tend to their heart, while I am simultaneously being a HH?

How might I explore my heart and thus an invitation to reveal more of myself to myself?
How are they my HH? HT? Dreaded "Not Me?"
What risk am I avoiding, ignoring, covering up by not looking at my own (w)hole?
When else have I caused similar reactions in different people?
How can I be more sensitive (open-hearted) if this situation were to present itself again?

Shame is an indication of a (w)hole. The opposite of Shame is **blame**. Either feeling indicates a (w)hole is present. Shame or Blame are common ways of avoiding what is being revealed regarding our own (W)holeness, presence, and tender-heartedness to self and other.

The key is: All Parts welcome to the Table – there are NO unacceptable parts, expressions, or feelings!

(w)hole Spinners: the person who is asking the (w)Hole Spiraler questions. One can become certified as a "Radiance Master-Healer" through the (W)hole Point Institute. A Spinner is skilled at curiosity without judgments and in the particular questions helpful to invite a (w)Hole Spiraler to answer for themselves. Spinners do not need to be psychotherapists. Intentional Spiraling is based on curiosity without judgment, the Wisdom WAY map and the conviction that the (w)hole creator is their own expert.

Appendix VI
Sorting and Sifting - (w)hole Play Step by Step

Identify - in any order your prefer

> **Feeling**
> **Curb**
> **Horrible Truth**

Identify - the First Shattering or OUCH

Identify - the Meaning Making (MM) using the "stem outline" of:

> If I _____
> Then They will do/be/say_____.
> They will get _____
> Then I will get/ be_____

Identify - The "Me" (indicated by the first line of the Meaning Maker) and list qualities and behaviors. Note: "I am always this."

Identify - The "Not Me" (indicated by the opposite of the "Me") and list qualities and behaviors. Note: " I am never this."

Name the "Me" (be sure the names are **not** real people's names or descriptions).

Name the "Not Me."

Identify the **Truth and the Distortions** of each side in a *feeling* way. Notice and feel the exaggeration.

Identify the Magical beliefs in the MM – look closely. Once you see it and feel it, the magic created by the genius child – the creator of your (W)hole – will become obvious.

Identify what you would Embrace and the risk (even if they ____) if you chose to collapse this (w)hole.

Appendix VII
Some How-To's for (w)hole Collapsing

Get yourself to the Portal when **YOU** are ready. Then and only then begin to apply any of the following approaches to collapsing the (w)hole itself. All of them work sometimes. Be gentle with yourself.

Lean into Terms of Endearment and the "No Rule" Rules. Remember, everything happens at the perfect time, so don't push, force, or effort to "make" a (w)hole collapse.

Notice, **Name**, and then **Let Go** of the **Magical beliefs** from the Meaning Making and **Embrace** the thing you have always wanted (fourth line of the MM) even if the HT happens again and in the face of the risk of "their" reaction. Ask, *"How has this MM helped me?" How is it hurting me now?"*

Let go of the "**OR**" and embrace the "**AND**" between the "Me" and the "Not Me."

Name the "Me." **Name** the "Not Me." Then ask yourself, *"If I am this AND that, then who do I name me to be?"* Then **Name** your **(W)hole Me**. (3rd thing)

Name the "Me." **Name** the "Not Me," then spend a day watching yourself be the "Me." Next, spend a day watching yourself be the "Not Me" (even in little doses). Alternate days until one day you decide to name the third thing. Consider writing down how you feel when you are the "Me" and when you see yourself as the "Not Me."

Map another (w)hole up to the point you are able to. Then map another (w)hole! Trust that as you create motion, all your (w)holes will begin to spiral themselves until there is a cascade into (W)holeness.

Stay in the middle of the (w)hole being curious without judgment for as long as you like. *Hurrying is a (w)hole.* Don't push yourself, but don't get passive either. Keep pulsating – the key is curious without judgment. No one can do your (w)hole spiraling for you.

Feel, Feel, Feel all the parts of the (W)hole. When in doubt, pause, feel, do Good for Me, feel some more.

Name the risk of collapsing this (w)hole and bringing the parts together. Find the risk by looking at the HT and/or considering the courage it will take to be **both** parts whether they will like/love you or not! This is a huge act of heroic heart action.

Ask yourself, *"How am I helping myself by NOT being that "Not Me?"* *"How am I keeping myself away from truly living by not allowing that part home?"* There is always a very "good" reason for our (w)holes.

Pause and appreciate who you are! Remember, you saved your life by creating your (w)holes, so drop all judgment about any of them and any judgments about you! Celebrate your genius, and then go back to Intentional Spiraling.

Appendix VIII
A Glossary of (w)hole Point Wisdom WAY Terms

Blessing

That which we will receive from the Horrible Truth "gods" once our Offering has been made.

Cascade

A motion that once begun, continues without further efforts.

Collapse a (w)hole

The activity of bringing what is on either side of a space, or gap, together in such a manner as to allow a return to the natural condition of wholeness.

Compassion Expansion

Extending or making more spacious the capacity to appreciate, accept, and hold in regard that which has been revealed.

Conditional Regard

Conditions or standards that must be met before respect is offered.

Curb

A recent event that initiates an inner reaction out of proportion to the event; the raised edge of a pit or hole, which trips someone into falling.

Distortion Effect

The result of having only a portion of an element. Over time the missing portion becomes filled with a distorted reflection of the element so that it may be seen as complete in itself.

Embrace

To engage in the action of admitting, "Yes, this expression is part of me also;" the action of receiving oneself consciously.

Feelings

Emotions such as sad, happy, glad, mad, hurt, etc.; the interior felt experience of life touching us (different than physical sensations).

Free Will
: The condition of being able to choose how one wishes to act; the condition of being able to act consciously without inner restraint; a state of being in which all choices are available (though not necessarily only preferred choices).

Fusion Effect
: A perceptual condition in which one person merges with another person; a conviction of "what I do dictates the condition of the other."

Global Free Will
: The acceptance that each person makes his/her own choices independently.

Heart Logic
: A rational or strategic premise that results from a deeply felt experience. In the Wisdom WAY model, it is denoted as a line moving from the "Horrible Truth" to the OUCH on the heart and through to the "Meaning Maker."

Horizontal Elements of Life
: Those elements which are of the psyche or psychology of a person; those elements associated with relating to other people or to our inner self.

Horrible Truth "god"
: Past conditions, qualities, events, facts, behaviors, beliefs, and/or other people which currently have an influence on the present day adult behavior, mind set, and (w)holes.

Horrible Truth™ (HT)
: An event or behavior of another person that we experience as so dreadful as to warrant the activity of "avoiding any future occurrence of this event at all costs."

Innocent Unity
: A state of being or an orientation of being unaware of anything other than Oneness with all that is around or within one's being.

Intentional Spiraling Toolbox
: The skills and tools of the (W)hole Point Wisdom WAY, such as "curiosity without judgment," naming, sorting, Good for Me's, and the practice of being particular; a set of skills which can be applied to a point of difficulty in life when one wishes to respond from a state of wholeness.

Intentional Spiraling™

The action or activity of moving with purpose and direction through the elements of a (w)hole towards Radiance; the activity of collasping a (w)hole; the skill of applying the tools of naming and curiosity without judgment and following the sorting/shifting procedures.

Intersection of Psychology & Spirituality

Human beings are made up of interior mental and emotional states or psychological patterns. Human beings also are animated by a life force beyond mere chemical components of the physical body - this is often called spirit. How any one person understands this element of human existence is their spirituality. In each person is an intersection point where these two sets of elements come together and influence one another.

Intimate Relating

Personal interactions between two or more people in which there is an exchange of honesty, trust, and feeling experiences.

Letting go of

To release or cease to cling to; in the Wisdom WAY model this is an action which occurs at the Portal where we cease to cling to the magical belief created by a child's mind.

Me ("Allowed to be Me")

The expressions and behaviors of our self that we determined to be acceptable and allowed; In the Wisdom WAY map this is drawn on the left side of the space, called a (w)hole and defines what is left of our self when the disallowed expressions are rejected.

Meaning Maker™

A characterization of an internal strategy or Meaning Making.

Meaning Making™ (MM)

A strategy designed to prevent a reoccurrence of the pain we felt as a result of the actions of others.

Memory Lane

The felt internal link or emotional pathway between a recent (Curb) and the historical event (Horrible Truth) which created the need for a (w)hole.

Mystic Moment | The physical and emotional experience which occurs the instant we release resistance to an aspect of our wholeness.

Naming | The activity of declaring ownership by applying a designation or label to a list of qualities or characteristics.

Not Me ("Not allowed to be Me") | The expressions and behaviors of our self that we determined to be "Not Allowed;" In the Wisdom WAY map, the "Not Me" is drawn on the right side of the space or (w)hole.

NUB | The condition of feeling unworthy, small, "like a nothing," etc.; direct meaning is "Not enough of yoU to Be"; the result of creating many (w)holes; the condition most of us spend our lives living.

Offering | That which we give up to the "gods of the Horrible Truth" as a way to appease or please them.

Old Time Religion | The set of beliefs that we unwittingly subscribe to based on the viewpoint of the child whose caretakers were the "gods" in his/her life; the belief structures and premises of our child's heart.

OUCH | The deep pain we feel when an event happened that was deeply hurtful (HT); the core felt experience of a person deeply wounded by an experience or event or behavior of another.

PAIR Play | The activity of a PAIR (a partnership of two people engaged in intimate relating) in which the skills of Intentional Spiraling are applied to their interaction.

PAIR™ | An acronym for "People Activating Intimate Relating"; A state of being in a close partnership or an intimate relationship with another person (not limited to marriage, but rather any form of partnering).

Portal | The doorway at the bottom of every life (w)hole; the point of integration of the "Me" and the "Not Me"; the choice point of saying "AND."

Portal Passage	The pathway and the felt experience of walking through a doorway into wholeness.
Power Point Location Shift™	The shift from a position of powerlessness in the face of the another person's actions to the made-up position of having "power over it all"; an internal belief movement in which the child claims ownership over elements of their world.
Radiance	The wholeness of one's entire life force; that which is emitted from the core of a person when there are no barriers to their full life expression; the condition of wholeness resulting from the embracing of those dis-allowed elements.
Radiant Pulsating Being of Light™ (RPBL)	The state of being conscious of our origin, as embodied spirits, existing actively, as One with All-That-Is.
Religion	A set of beliefs about one's life, the universe, and how the world works; a core orientation and belief structure about how one "ought" to orient one's self in daily life and includes codes of conduct and ritual observations designed to appease or please the "gods" of that body of beliefs.
Sacred Relationship Space	The expanse between two people which is created by their decision to move into intimate exchanges. This space becomes sacred only when it is invoked or created by two people risking to be boldly truthful and who are open to giving and receiving this truth.
Sacred Spiral Dance of the Portal	The movement towards, around, and through the Portal in the felt shape of a spiral.
Sacrifice	the action of "letting go of" a belief which is embedded in our Meaning Making Strategy of Hope; composed of the first and last line of the MM formula.
Shattering	The heart-felt feeling that occurs when life hurts too much to bear and we disown aspects of our own selves in an attempt to prevent further pain; the heart action of breaking our wholeness into bits and pieces and parts.

Sorting — The action of separating one type of element from another; to arrange according to common elements; an essential activity of Intentional Spiraling.

Spiral Pathway (Spiral) — The road or pathway from the top of the (w)hole to the bottom of a (w)hole, which is compressed until curiosity without judgment is applied; the hidden map particular to every (w)hole which is revealed when one begins to sort and shift through the elements of their concerns.

Spiraling — The action of moving deeper into the space between two elements (the "Me" and the "Not Me"); the the action of collapsing a (w)hole by continuously decreasing the space between the "Me" and the "Not Me" elements so that both sides are embraced before the Portal, which is located at the smallest point of the spiral.

Spirituality — One's orientation to soul, life force, or spirit.

Surrender — The action of embracing our (W)holeness by conscious choice and acknowledging it is the "Unknown AND"; the action of embracing ourselves as more than we were the moment before; to welcome ourselves home.

Table of Plenty — An analogy for wholeness in our hearts; an image of a table at which all expressions of being are welcomed.

Table of Righteousness — An analogy for wholeness in our hearts; an image of a table at which all expressions of being are welcomed; "Righteousness" means "all parts welcome to the table;" the table is the place of inner gathering; a heart of inner welcome.

TheySheHe™ — A phrase which refers to the "They" or the "She" or the "He" who dictates our lives and to whom we defer.

Thoughts — Mental constructs; ideas and conclusions; premises or "givens."

Tribute	That which we determine the Horrible Truth "gods" want.
Universal Story	The repeated sequence of events which we all pass through in a lifetime - born whole and unconscious with a big heart; stuff happens; and we shatter. The remainder of the event is our response to the essential framework.
Unknown "AND"	That which is not within range of awareness or felt-knowledge; that which we have not yet experienced; the unification of a "Me" and a "Not Me," the union of which is not within our felt comprehension because they were separated long before we had an awareness of them as distinct and separate.
Vertical Elements of Life	The aspects of belief about the "gods" in our lives or that which is considered greater than us.
WAY™	An acronym for "Walking Awake saying YES!"
(w)hole™	A space or gap or void or pit; a space between the "Allowed-to-be Me" and the "Not-allowed-to-be Me"; a felt-place in our hearts that hurts; a life-hole; a collapsed spiral.
(W)hole™	Conscious wholeness.
(w)Hole Helpers™ (HH)	Events, people, words, interactions, thoughts, etc. which "push" us headfirst into a (w)hole in our hearts; every element of life can be a (w)Hole Helper; that which occurs in today and directs our attention to a gap in our own wholeness; a gift and guide to our (W)holeness; that which reveals the presence of a (w)hole or issue.
(w)hole Play	The action of engaging, with curiosity, in the activity of exploring of the elements of a (w)hole.
(w)hole Play Opportunity	An activity moment in this book designed to invite the reader to engage in the process of Intentional Spiraling.

(W)hole Point Wisdom WAY Model™	The map and method to explore one's life patterns.
(w)hole Spinner™ (Spinner)	A person who is skilled in the art of Intentional Spiraling and is able to apply "curiosity without judgment" to The Wisdom WAY map on behalf of the person in the (w)hole.
(W)hole Spiraler™ (Spiraler)	A person who is actively engaged in exploring their own (w)hole using the tools of Intentional Spiraling.
Wisdom WAY™	A reference to "The (W)hole Point Wisdom WAY model of empowerment, transformation, and healing."
Yuckie	An inner voice and position of judgment against the disowned aspects of oneself; an "employee" of the Meaning Maker hired to maintain the Meaning Maker strategy.

Appendix IX
Suggested Reading

Alter, Robert M. and Jane Alter. *How Long till my Soul Gets it Right: 100 Doorways on the Journey to Happiness.* Harper One, May, 2001.

Barnett, Libby, and Maggie Chambers and Susan Davidson. *Reiki Energy Medicine: Bringing Healing Touch into Home, Hospital, and Hospice.* Healing Arts Press, May, 1996.

Braden, Gregg. *The Spontaneous Healing of Belief: Shattering the Paradigm of False Limits.* Hay House, April, 2008.

Braden, Gregg. *Secrets of the Lost Mode of Prayer: The Hidden Power of Beauty, Blessings, Wisdom, and Hurt.* Hay House, January, 2006.

Covitz, Joel D. *Emotional Child Abuse: The Family Curze.* Sigo Pr, June, 1986.

Douglas, Lloyd C. *Magnificent Obsession.* Mariner Books, April, 1999.

Ford, Debbie. *The Dark Side of the Light Chasers.* Riverhead Trade, June, 1999.

Goleman, Daniel. *Emotional Intelligence.* Bantam Books 10th Anniversary Ed., September, 2005.

Hendrix, Ph.D., Harville, and Helen Hunt, Ph.D. *Getting the Love you want: A Guide for Couples.* Henry Holt & Co, June, 1988. 20th Anniversary Ed, Hold Paperbacks, Dec. 2007.

Hendrix, Ph.D., Harville, and Helen Hunt, Ph.D. *Giving the love that Heals: A Guide for Parents.* Atria, August, 1998.

Hendrix, Ph.D., Harville, and Helen Hunt, Ph.D. *Receiving Love: Transform Your Relationship by Letting Yourself be loved.* Atria, October, 2005.

Johnson, Spencer, MD. *Who Moved my Cheese?* G.P. Putnam's Sons, 11th Ed., 2002.

Michaels, Lesley. *Just Roll Over and Float: The Path to Living Boldly.* Be Life Publications, February, 2008.

Redfield, James. *The Celestine Prophecy.* Grand Central Publishing, September, 1995.

Ruiz, Don Miguel. *The Four Agreements: A Practical Guide to Personal Freedom, A Toltec Wisdom Book.* Amber-Allen Publishing, January, 2001.

Tolle, Eckhart. *A New Earth: Awakening to Your Life's Purpose.* Penguin, January, 2008.

Tolle, Eckhart. *The Power of Now: A Guide to Spiritual Enlightenment.* New World Library, September, 2004.

Young-Sowers, Meredith and Caroline Myss. *Wisdom Bowls: Overcoming Fear and coming Home to Your Authentic Self.* New World Library, July, 2006.

Young-Sowers, Meredith. *Spiritual Crisis: What's Really Behind Loss, Disease, and Life's Major Hurts.* Stillpoint Publishing, January, 1993.

Credit Appreciations:

Chapter 21, sub-heading, page 197. Thank you to Al Turtle, of the Imago community, for this inspirational insight. All changes made by Alaya.

Page 239*. An inspired learning from James Twyman's Daily Spiritual Lessons. All changes made by Alaya.

Photography on the back cover by Tim Byrne.
www.timbyrnephoto.com Photo ©2007 Tim Byrne

A special thank you to Sue Moss and Anne Suddy, who have read this manuscript repeatedly with love and care. Thank you once again.

Photograph by John R. Chadwick – "Sanctuary" – Radiance Pond

~

There is no way to offer a bibliography of one's life journey. Suffice it to say that these books will start you off, if you wish to read further. OR you could choose to do a (w)hole study, Intentionally Spiraling your own (w)holes, and change the (W)hole World!

Appendix X
About The (W)hole Point Institute, LLC

You have all you need to know right now to begin actively collapsing every (w)hole in sight, and there is much, much more to this simple, yet profound model called The (W)hole Point Wisdom WAY.

Below is an overview of the expansive terrain, only some of which can I point to in this book. If you want to experience all the richness of the Wisdom WAY, go to The (W)hole Point Institute's web site. There you will find more information on all of the (W)hole Shops offered as well as a list of the Certified Master Teachers of Radiance (CMTR). These are the folks who will come to your area to teach live (W)hole Shops, and they are the only folks who are certified by The (W)hole Point Institute to teach the Wisdom WAY. Our web site is **www.wholepoint.us**. (W)hole Shops are sequential experiences which are practical and above all fun. In these two-day intensive seminars, the students are introduced to the various levels of the Wisdom WAY.

Level One is the introduction to the basics.

Level Two focuses on where and how spirituality and psychology intersect in (w)holes.

Level Three examines the Portal in depth – its terrors, and its surprises.

Level Four focuses on Radiance and Transparency.

Level Five expands the map from a two-dimensional drawing and understanding to three dimensions.

Level Six turns the model upside down and the surprise introduction to YOUR Soul Self

Level Seven focuses on Oneness lived.

Level Eight focuses on the Return to the Market Place – walking your (W)hole Self into the world.

All of the (W)hole Shops are founded upon and rooted in the basic Wisdom WAY map, and throughout the (W)hole Shops the student remains the expert of themselves. The emphasis is practical and particular to each person, while expanding in surprising ways upon the basic skeleton of the Wisdom WAY. The method of teaching is designed to include the mind, the feelings, the body, and the spirit of the student. It is also created to touch the brilliant inner child who created so many of our precious (w)holes and the breadcrumb path to (W)holeness.

As individuals move through the (W)hole Shop series, there are many initiatory and alchemical changes that occur. The Wisdom WAY is about profound and deep transformation. It is not just another cognitive theory or process. Students often return again and again only to discover that the wisdom embedded in the model has carried them to even greater aliveness.

For more information, go to www.wholepoint.us

About Alaya

Alaya obtained a master's degree in divinity from Yale University and a master's degree in social work from the University of Connecticut. She has lived on a Kibbutz, studied in Switzerland, traveled across the country, participated in Outward Bound™, sailed in the Caribbean, among many other life altering adventures. Life has now led her to this latest adventure: writing this book.

Prior to entering the healing professions, Alaya held positions in corporate sales and administration. After returning to school for her master's degrees, she spent the next twenty-seven years practicing in the field of traditional and alternative healing. During this period, she developed The Wisdom WAY™, a powerful and a sustainable process of self-awakening.

Already working on her next book, *Alaya's Fables*, a book of original stories for heart and soul, she continues to invite herself and others to embrace themselves in wonder and to boldly come alive.

Alaya is a practicing Teaching Reiki Master as well as a Certified Imago Therapist, and an ordained minister. Her private consultation practice of (W)hole Life Coaching focuses on empowering individuals, relationships and organizations by creating positive change.

Currently serving as the founder / director of The (W)hole Point Institute LLC, as well as being a co-director with her husband, John, of "Sanctuary," a sixty-five-acre healing location in New Hampshire, Alaya is living her dream of offering folks direct access to practical "hands and feet" approaches for empowered awakening.

Alaya's classes, apprenticeships, and consultations continue to touch people around the globe. For more information about The (W)hole Point Institute,LLC visit our website: www.wholepoint.us

About Lisa

Lisa Scally is a certified teacher of The (W)hole Point Wisdom WAY. She is also a Reiki Master. Before becoming a teacher, Lisa spent over twenty years in the corporate world as a proofreader, copywriter, and international marketing manager. She has a B.S. degree in business, and since leaving the corporate world, she earned an associate's degree in interior design. Her dream is to incorporate her Wisdom WAY and Reiki training with her interior design skills to help people live their radiance inside and out. Lisa's husband, Steven, is also a certified teacher, and they incorporate their teaching in the raising of their two children.

"We learn by revelation, not by acquisition." *Martha Harrell*